SACRED COMPLEX OF BUDHI SANTANI

ut the Author

ta Kumar Acharya got his M.Sc. degree in 1979 and Ph.D. in 1994. He started er as Lecturer in Anthropology in 1981 and rendered his service in different of the State Government of Orissa till July 1998. Thereafter, he joined na Choudhury Centre for Development Studies (ICSSR Centre), Bhubaneswar, Reader in Social Anthropology.

thor has a number of research contributions. He has submitted reports on 13 nities of Orissa to the prestigious "People of India" project conducted by ogical Survey of India. Apart from publishing several research papers in oks, he has produced reports on projects, namely "Comparative Study on n Orissa and Tamil Nadu", funded by the Planning Commission of India; Welfare Schemes for the Scheduled Castes and Scheduled Tribes in by the Committee of Governors of India and many other research state, national and international level agencies.

SACRED COMPLEX OF BUDHI SANTANI

Anthropological Approach to Study Hindu Civilization

PRASANTA KUMAR ACHARYA
Reader in Social Anthropology
NKC Centre for Development Studies
Bhubaneswar, Orissa

CONCEPT PUBLISHING COMPANY, NEW DELHI-110059

ISBN 81-8069-049-0

First Published 2003

Published and Printed by
Ashok Kumar Mittal
Concept Publishing Company
A/15-16, Commercial Block, Mohan Garden
NEW DELHI-110059 (India)

Phones: 25351460, 25351794
Fax: 091-11-25357103
Email: publishing@conceptpub.com

PREFACE

For a pretty long time anthropologists concentrated only on the study of primitive societies. Anthropological researches on civilization came into force in 1950s with initiatives taken by Robert Redfield. Inspired by Redfieldian approach to civilizational study, L.P. Vidyarthi developed the sacred complex model, which helped in analysis of the characteristic features of Hindu civilization as reflected in places of pilgrimage. Vidyarthi's trichotomic concept of sacred complex attracted several Indian scholars to carry forward similar studies at different places of pilgrimage. The present book reveals novelty in application of the sacred complex model. Apart from sacred geography, sacred performances and sacred specialists—the three components of sacred complex defined by Vidyarthi—the author has thrown light on other integrated components of sacred complex such as sacred sacrificers, sacred symbols and sacred beliefs. Thus a broader structural dimension of sacred complex has been discussed. The book has presented a portray of combination and compromise of great and little traditions, functional integration of different sects and castes and structural synthesis of the presiding deity, goddess Budhi Santani, whose body-parts are worshipped at distantly located places. In addition, the book has highlighted that the nature of organization of sacred performances reflects the local pattern of Hindu social organization. This book will be useful to the research-scholars, academicians and general readers who are interested to know about the integrational as well as dynamic aspects of Hindu civilization. In spite of best efforts, errors and omissions might have been committed and the author will be grateful if these are pointed out and suggested for improvement of this book.

N.K.C. Centre for Development Studies
Bhubaneswar, Orissa

P.K. ACHARYA

ACKNOWLEDGEMENTS

In order to complete my doctoral thesis on "The Sacred Complex of the Budhi Santani of Berhampur (Orissa): Anthropological Approach to Study Hindu Civilization", I have taken the assistance, suggestions and inspiration from a number of scholars, informants, institutions, students, friends, teachers and sacred intellectuals. Although it is not possible to extend my thanks and gratitude to each of them individually, I acknowledge my indebtedness to some of them whose active co-operation and encouragement practically helped me to end up this work.

In fact, after going through the contributory work of Prof. L.P. Vidyarthi in the field of Hindu civilization by introducing the sacred complex model, I became enlightened and encouraged to undertake the present study in which I have adopted his concepts and methods, of course, with little modification and addition depending on the field situation, to analyse and interpret the empirical data. As such, his work on the *Sacred Complex of Hindu Gaya* gave me the initial stimulation and inspiration to go ahead with the present work. I feel proud to take this opportunity to express my deep sense of gratitude to him.

After completing the first phase of my fieldwork on the present study, I met Prof. M. Jha, University Professor of the Centre of Advanced Study in Anthropology, Ranchi University, who ungrudgingly accepted me as his scholar after a brief initial discussion on my work. Since then, he has consistently guided me giving critical remarks and valuable suggestions. Moreover, at the time of discussion, he placed before me his personal experiences and works at different places of Hindu pilgrimage, which enabled me to make a comparative assessment of my own work. I personally remain indebted to him for whose constant supervision and regular encouragement I could pursue this study fruitfully.

While doing fieldwork, I had come across many doubts at the contextual level. However, these doubts were patiently clarified to me by a number of sacred intellectuals among whom I am particularly grateful to Surya Narayan Behera, T. Kedarswamy and J. Mukholingam, who had unhesitantly spared their valuable time to sit for a discussion as and when required by me.

The organisation of the Thakurani Yatra being tradition-bound, many rituals related to it were not permitted for the observance of the outsiders. But the Organizing Committee of the Thakurani Yatra and the Thakurani Mandira Kalyan Samiti specially allowed me to observe at close distance to all the rituals. They also permitted me, for the first time in the history of the Thakurani Yatra, to take photographs of certain exclusive rituals. In this connection, I acknowledge my indebtedness specially to P. Basavraju Desabehera and T. Kedaraswamy of the Organizing Committee of the Thakurani Yatra and S.N. Behera, K. Gantayat and B. Mohapatra of the Thakurani Mandira Kalyan Samiti. I am also thankful to my students Hari, Arup and Saroj for their assistance during the fieldwork. My thanks are also due to my informants, namely Kaira Patra, Rama Krushna Gantayat, K. Ramamoorty Kuvera Senapati, Simadri Ghadei, Tuna Patra, Biswambar Raula, G.C. Patra and M. Satyam who had extended unstincted co-operation to me at the time of data collection. I do acknowledge my gratitude to the authorities of the National Library and the Anthropological Survey of India at Kolkata for providing me the necessary library facilities. I also owe a deep sense of gratitude to Prof. Deka and Prof. P.K. Das of the Department of Anthropology, Utkal University and Dr. P.K. Mishra (B) of the Department of Anthropology, Government College, Phulbani for providing me the journals and books related to the present study. My debts are unlimited to all the authors, mentioned in the bibliography, whose valuable articles were utilised by me to make this thesis presentable.

I cannot forget the assistance provided by the authority of the Office of the Inspector of Endowments, Berhampur who kindly placed before me the official records, which were required for the present study. I am also extremely thankful to Prof. R.K. Das, and Miss Rasmi Rekha Patnaik, who ungrudgingly made necessary literal corrections of the thesis.

I shall always remember the exemplary patience and forbearance of my wife, Suchitra, for whose active co-operation and encouragement the completion of this work could be made possible. At the end, I express my special thanks to N. Biswal for typing the thesis competently and expeditiously.

PRASANTA KUMAR ACHARYA

CONTENTS

LIST OF TABLES

LIST OF MAPS

LIST OF PLATES

LIST OF FIGURES

INTRODUCTION

Works Done So Far

Anthropological studies in India took a turn, both conceptually and methodologically, with the beginning of the second half of the twentieth century. A group of Chicago-bred anthropologists initiated a series of empirical works to study the diversities and unitary characters within the Indian civilization. The scope of Indian social anthropology, limited as it was to the isolated folk societies, extended gradually to the study of peasant societies and also to their interaction with larger societies or civilization of which they were parts. The nature of Indian civilization was analysed, both from theoretical and methodological points of view, giving rise to the emergence of a number of concepts like rural cosmopolitanism (Lewis, 1955), processes of universalization and parochialization (Marriott, 1955a), great and little traditions, cultural specialists, style of life (Redfield, 1955a, 1956), cultural performances and cultural media (Singer, 1955; Redfield and Singer, 1956).

Under the influence of and stimulation received from the American scholars, some Indian social anthropologists, in replacement of the traditional 'fact finding mission' (Jha, 1983), carried out analytical studies of different communities having motivation towards formulation of terms, concepts, theories and methods so as to Indianize the critical understanding of Indian civilization. Vidyarthi along with Sinha professed that 'Indianizing' the social anthropological approach will help in better understanding of the cultural process and civilizational history of India as reflected in the teachings and ideals of numerous social thinkers and in ancient scriptures and, therefore, coined the term 'sacred complex' as a model for studying Hindu places of pilgrimage. Although it was a proposition in the light of the conceptual and theoretical frameworks of Redfield (1955, 56, 57) and Singer (1955, 58), sacred complex was a terminological modification in adaptation to the field situation at Gaya in 1961. Under the generic term of sacred complex, a number of analytical concepts such as sacred centre, sacred cluster, sacred performances, sacred specialists, etc. were incorporated, which are now in vogue in the study of Indian civilization.

In addition to a typological development for a description of the pattern of a sacred complex, the study is based on trichotomic interrelated phenomena such as sacred centre, sacred performance and sacred specialist. Viewed on such a paradigm, this novel field of investigation provided a scope for academic as well as applied manifestation. While on academic ground, it helped in the formulation and development of several concepts, methodology and hypotheses in order to focus fresh light on the nature and process of compromise and co-operation among various faiths, sects and traditions of Hindu civilization as reflected at a Hindu place of pilgrimage, on the applied ground, it explores the traditional channels of civilizational integration among people of diverse cultural heritage, which may be made use of in understanding and tackling the problems related to Hindu civilization.

Fascinated by the new methodological dimension, a band of young Indian anthropologists made further experimental studies on Vidyarthi's findings at different sacred centres in detail (Jha, 1971; Narayan, 1972; Vidyarthi, Saraswati and Jha, 1978) alongwith many article-oriented publications. Characteristically, minor studies were limited to focus either on the geographical as well as organizational set-up of sacred centres (Saraswati, 1962b, 1967; Upadhyaya, 1974; Mohapatra, 1974; Jha, 1980) or on pilgrims and structure of Hindu pilgrimage (Saraswati, 1962a; Chakravarti, 1974; Jha, 1978) whereas exhaustive studies were carried on sacred complex as a whole.

Saraswati in an article "Holy Circuit of Nimasar" (1962a, 1965) reflects the nature of relationship among the pilgrims, the ritual specialists and the peasant villages located on a *Parikrama* route. In his work on *Temple Organisation in Goa* (1962b) while he describes about the organisational role of the sacred institution as a whole, in another article "Cultivation of Excellence in Religious Organisation" (1967), which was an analysis based on census figures, he speaks of the vitality of a more complex organisation that is the organisation of the ascetics of Kashi. Based on an anthropological method of fieldwork, Chakrabarti (1974) has made an humble attempt in his article, "Some Observations on the Pilgrims and their Pilgrimage: A Case Study of Tarakeswar" to present the societal composition of a particular section of pilgrims—the Jal-Jatris belonging to the Tarakeswar Sacred Complex, along with their mode of behaviour and purpose of pilgrimage. In this paper, the author deliberately delimits his anthropological observation on the study of pilgrims for the reason that enough attention has not been focused on this area of research by the anthropologists. However, the study fails to speak about other aspects of the sacred complex and makes no examination of the hypotheses so far utilised in the study of sacred complex.

Upadhyaya (1974), in his attempt to study the Sacred Complex of Dwaraka, has described sacred geography in detail along with introductory remarks on sacred specialists and sacred performances. However, his deliberation is restricted only to the Dwarakadhisha temple. In the same manner Mohapatra (1981) has made a study only with reference to the "Traditional Structure and Change in an Orissan Temple." In this study he has highlighted the changes in the traditional structure and organisation of the temple whereas the trichotomic relationship among the three elements of the Sacred Complex of Lingaraj temple has been overlooked.

From a nomenclature study of the following few articles, viz., "Social Structure of a Pilgrim Town Tarakeswar (West Bengal): An Exploratory Study"; "Puri Pilgrim Study: Area of Origin and Some Socio-economic Characteristics of the Pilgrims"; "Symbols in Communication to the Supernatural in Hindu Religion—The Case of Siva"; "The Sacred Centres of Kathmandu: History and Typology"; "The Badu—A Service Caste at Lingaraj Temple at Bhubaneswar"; "Studying Specialists in Traditional Learning: The Pandits of Kashi"; "Sacred Geography of Rameswaram and Tirupati"; and "Structure of Hindu Pilgrimage: An Anthropological Appraisal", one thing comes out clearly that these article-oriented studies throw light on one or the other aspect of a sacred complex touching without its entirety.

Anthropological researches on different aspects of sacred complex while made some progress, some scholars carried out a totalistic examination of the findings at Gaya (1961) in different civilizational centres with universal or regional level of importance. The first of its kind was made by Jha (1971) in the study of "The Sacred Complex of Janakpur" in Nepal. In this methodological study he brought to light the fact that the civilization has a greater historic depth as well as territorial extension and the extension of the Hindu civilization is beyond the political boundary of India. After his doctoral work on the Sacred Complex of Janakpur, Jha took up a novel attempt to study an ancient Hindu kingdom, namely Ratanpur in Central India, as a dimension of Hindu civilization. The Sacred Complex of Ratanpur reflects a contextual level of synthesis and systematization of various Indian religions, faiths and beliefs at one place because of a consistent royal patronage from the first quarter of the eleventh century to the mid-fifties of the nineteenth century.

Huble and Vetschera (1976) in their work on the "Sacred Complex of Madhi" focused a new light on the pattern of unitary characters among several semi-nomadic tribes, who assemble every year in the month of March in Madhi, a village in Ahmednagar District (Gujarat), to take part in the fair of saint Kanifnath. They have vividly discussed the historical background, based on oral tradition, of the temple of Kanifnath where the saint is venerated by the Muslim as well as Hindu. Both the Muslim and the Hindu officiate as the priest in this temple, being known as '*Mujawar*' and '*Poojari*' respectively. However, in this article, integrational features that is discussed with regard to the pilgrims as well as the temple priests have not been reflected at the level of sacred geography and, furthermore, the scope for an analysis of various sacred centres within the Sacred Complex of Madhi has also not been explored.

Narayan, instead, was more explicit in analysing the sacred complex as a uniting agent among different classes and castes. His doctoral work on the "*Sacred Complex of Baidyanathdham*" located in the tribal belt of Santal Pargana has been a splendid analysis of the sacred complex as a balancing force between traditional and modern cultures.

While anthropological studies were predominantly carried on the sacred complexes having a Saivite or a Vaishnavite shrine as the dominant sacred centre, Morab and Goswami, with an intention of making up a series of study on temples and involvement by castes, initiated their work with reference to the Chamundeswari, a Shakti temple with regional level of importance in Mysore. As its main findings, this study justifies that a temple is a civilizational centre to the extent of interaction between different cultural traditions. Evidently, the holistic studies of sacred complexes thrusted upon experimenting the findings at Gaya (1961) as far as possible. However, one thing came out prominently that some of the phenomena observed at Gaya were found in other sacred centres also, although certain regional variations in the sacred performances as well as in the organization of the sacred specialists have also been noticed (Jha, 1978). These variations in certain elements of sacred complex called for a re-examination of the concept of sacred complex not only in the form of cross-regional situations but also in the nature of the things that have been perpetuated both in respect of textual categories and contextual transformation. Consequently, Vidyarthi, Saraswati and Jha selected Kashi for an all-round re-testing of the concept of sacred complex because of its comparatively more complexity so far as the continuity, co-existence and varieties of sacred traditions are concerned. Viewed as the 'Microcosm' of Indian civilization, the study of the "*Sacred Complex of Kashi*" while reveals, on one hand, the wider applicability of the trichotomic elements of sacred complex in the analysis of Hindu sacred centres towards interpretation of the core of Hindu civilization, on the other hand, it provides facts to conclude that there is a textual and contextual continuity in the *tirthas* of India. Moreover, the study of Kashi stands as an eye-opener in conceptualizing and classifying the various aspects of sacred complex in certain sanskritic terms, viz., broad categorization of sacred performances into 'Shastric' and 'Laukik', which combine among them various elements of socio-religious importance, 'tantrik', 'folk' as well as 'pauranik'. Anthropological, investigations in Kashi have revealed that the boundary and sacred scriptural description of Kashi Kshetra is a changing phenomenon. The complexity of the varied sacred centres can be elaborated and classified in the context of sectarian relevance, physical nature of the shrines and temple architecture (B.N. Sahay, 1974). The heterogeneous composition of the pilgrims can be analysed with reference to caste, class, linguistic regions and educational, political as well as social background (Narayan, 1974). The sacred performances as practised in various sacred centres can be grouped into different categories on the basis of the component elements of the rituals, the objectives of observing the rituals, the contexts of sacred performances, sectarian diversity, types of vow and also according to time (M.N. Jha, 1974) whereas a classificatory interpretation on the sacred specialists can be made with reference to the varieties of rituals, castes and linguistic groups (A.K. Sinha, 1974).

During 1980s two World Conferences on 'Pilgrimage' drew the attention of many anthropologists towards the study on the pilgrims and pilgrimage aspects of the Hindu civilisational centres. Consequently, a number of analytical as well as historical papers were presented to these two conferences. Thus, to the World Conference on 'Pilgrimage', held at the University of Pittsburgh, U.S.A. in 1981, Jha, the only Indian delegate, presented his paper on "Structure and Function of Hindu Pilgrimage" (in press). In the next World Conference on 'Pilgrimage', organised in 1983 at Vancouver, Canada under the Chairmanship of M. Jha, papers like 'Origin, Type, Spread and Nature of Hindu Pilgrimage' (Jha), 'Hindu Pilgrimage and Patronage: A Study in the History of Politicalisation of Hindu Tirtha—Jagannath Puri' (Jha), 'Pilgrims and

Pilgrimage: A Case Study of Tirumala—Tirupati Devasthanams' (Naidu), 'The Concept of Pilgrimage in Folk Tradition: A Case of the Chamundeswari Ritual Complex' (Morab), 'Ujjain: A Centre of Pilgrimage in Central India' (Samanta), 'A Rural Temple and the Devotees: A Study on Continuation and Change' (Choudhury), 'The End of an Endless Journey' (Saraswati), 'Jagannath of Puri and his Pilgrimage' (Behura), 'An Appraisal of the Traditions of Hindu Pilgrimage in the Garhwal—Himalaya' (Singh) and 'Myths and History of the Regional Places of Pilgrimage' (Choudhury and Choudhury) were discussed. Later on, in 1985, all these papers were published in the form of a book, *Dimensions of Pilgrimage* edited by M. Jha.

Although during 1980s, anthropological interest on Hindu civilization tilted towards the study of its pilgrimage aspect through short articles, the original interest on the holistic study of Hindu sacred complexes was maintained by scholars like Sahu, Kumar and Rajaure in their doctoral researches. Sahu (1987) studied on 'The Sacred Complex of Rajarappa' where the presiding deity is Chhinnamastika, one of the ten great incarnations (Dasa Mahavidyas) of the Mother Goddess. In his exhaustive analysis, he presented a critical appraisal of the Sacred Complex of Rajarappa from various angles like sacred geography, sacred specialists, pilgrimage, temple structure, myths, legends, fairs and festivals and pointed out that Rajarappa, as a centre of religious activities, binds together the people of different tribes, castes and sects and further strengthens the socio-religious solidarity. Kumar specifically highlighted the impact of high altitude ecological set-up on different aspects of sacred complex in his study (1987) named as 'The Sacred Complex of Badrinath: An Approach to Study the Himalayan Pilgrimage as Dimension of Indian Civilization'. Rajaure's work (1988) on 'The Sacred Complex of Swayambhunath in Kathmandu: A Study in Buddhism-Hinduism Continuum' was an empirical effort towards understanding the nature and characteristics of the functioning of the two great religious traditions of Nepal which yielded facts about the real process of Buddhism-Hinduism continuum in Nepal.

Perspective

The body of existing knowledge in this line demands further interpretation and analysis of the crux of the problem and necessitates the emergence of the present study. Keeping in view the findings of earlier studies regarding the nature of and process within the Hindu civilisation as unravelled through an analysis of features of sacred complex of a city, considered to be a compact sacred geography with various dominant shrines, the present study attempts to apply and test these findings in the sacred complex of a single dominant deity, Budhi Santani, whose body-parts are worshipped at three physiographically distinct sacred segments, which are distantly separated. Confining the concept of sacred complex to a single dominant deity instead of a particular sacred city, a methodological modification has been made on the basis of the following considerations relating to field situation:

(a) That the anthropomorphic body of the deity, Budhi Santani, is dividedly worshipped at three places in the undivided Ganjam district of Orissa. The head of the deity is worshipped as her symbolic representation at Berhampur, an orthogenetic city of the district, whereas her trunk is worshipped at Pitala, an indigenously developed village approximately 30 kms. distant from Berhampur and her feet are worshipped at Boirani, a small town about 45 kms. away from Berhampur and 20 kms. distant from Pitala.

(b) In addition to the orthogenetic features of all the three sacred places, certain common and integral characters are also found in the sphere of sacred symbol, rituals and ritual organization, sacred beliefs and the sacred specialists.

(c) Besides the daily ritual worship and seasonal festivals at the temple, a sacred fair named as 'Thakurani Yatra' that takes place at each sacred segment attracts a large number of pilgrims, which will be within two to three lakhs. Moreover, unlike the normal occasion, the *yatra* expands the scope of sacred sacrifices with diverse forms. The rapid popularity of the *yatra* tends to elevate the sacred complex of the deity from a local level to a regional level of importance.

(d) A compromising character among people of different sects, castes and linguistic groups of Hindu civilization is reflected in various aspects of the Sacred Complex of Budhi Santani, which needs examination and justification.

(e) On one hand while Budhi Santani, as the single dominant shrine, can be understood as a nexus of ritual activities, which radiate outward and interlink with other shrines through a series of myths and rites, on the other hand, as a religious institution, it provides a scope for economic and social ties among the sacred specialists, especially the priests of different sacred centres, maintaining durability and fluidity within the system.

The present study on the *Sacred Complex of Budhi Santani* with its regional level of importance provides an area of research to test not only the applicability of hypotheses put forward in the study of the *Sacred Complex of Gaya* (Vidyarthi, 1961) but also to test the regional variations in sacred performances and sacred organisation as an adjustment to the local pattern of social organisation.

Sacred complex of a civilizational centre has so far been analysed as a conflux of three elements, namely sacred geography, sacred performances and sacred specialists. However, this trichotomic explanation does not elucidate the symbolic factors that motivate both the sacred specialists and the devotees to develop a strong sense of belief in the sacredness of the whole complex. In the present study a subtle attempt has, therefore, been made to explore the level of continuity, compromise and combination between great and little traditions as reflected in various elements of sacred complex such as sacred geography, sacred performances, sacred specialists, sacred sacrificers, sacred sacrifices, sacred symbols and sacred beliefs. Moreover, in contradiction to the non-Hindu pattern of life as exhibited in the Muslim, Christian, Bouddha and Jaina sacred complexes, the present study keeps interest only in the Hindu pattern of life. It considers Hinduism as a set of religious doctrines governing the Hindu social life. Further, it assumes Hinduism as an amalgamation of three major cults, Saivic, Vaishnavic and Shakti and, therefore, it attempts to find out a compromise and combination among them.

Hypotheses

Having made the specifications of the present study, following hypotheses have been formulated for an empirical verification:

1. That the sacred complex of a Hindu deity reflects a level of integration and continuity among various elements, namely sacred centres, sacred performances, sacred specialists, sacred sacrificers, sacred sacrifices, sacred symbols and sacred beliefs.
2. That the sacred complex of a Hindu deity reflects a level of compromise and combination between great and little traditions and coexistence among Saivic, Vaishnavic and Shakti cults.

3. That the sacred specialists of a Hindu sacred complex develop a common style of life because of their functional involvement in the institution of sacred either by popularising certain texts and myths as the ritual consultants or by officiating as the ritual specialists or by serving as the ritual associates.
4. That the nature of organization of sacred performances reflects the local pattern of Hindu social organization.
5. That the sacred complex, in general, and the sacred specialists, in particular, have been in the process of modification and transformation as a result of a general development in the larger universe of Hindu civilization of which they are a part.

Area of Study and the People

As per the requirement of the present study, fieldwork was done at three places, Berhampur, Pitala and Boirani of Ganjam district. However, Berhampur was chosen to be the major area of study among the three places since at Berhampur, unlike the other two places, the Thakurani Yatra was a regular biennial fair and, hence, provided a scope for empirical study.

Berhampur is a city in Ganjam district, which lies between 18°12′45″ and 20°25′40″ North latitudes and East longitudes, 83°33′20″ and 85°15′ of Orissa, a State in the east coast of India. The Ganjam district, which is bounded on the north by the Cuttack and Puri districts, east by the Bay of Bengal, south by the Vizagapatam district and west by the Phulbani and Koraput districts, is divided physiographically into plains and hilly tracts. Berhampur city, with a population explosion from 23,599 to 1,62,407 during the period from 1881 to 1981, is situated in latitude 19°20′ North and longitude 84°50′ East. It is distant from Chennai 1,046 kilometres, from Kolkata 520 kilometres and from the State capital Bhubaneswar 179 kilometres. The city stands on a rocky ledge of 78 feet above the mean level of the sea. It is surrounded by an extensively cultivated plain and in a direct line, it is 11 kilometres distant from the sea. On the east and south, this plain is open and slopes towards the sea but on the north and west it is bounded by the Mohuri hills, some 2,500 feet high and distant about 13 kilometres from the city. The city is not flooded with any river but numerous tanks and irrigation channels swell during the monsoon rains to make certain areas dampy and filthy.

Ethnically Berhampur city is composed of Hindus, Muslims and Christians. Populationwise Hindus excel the other two communities. Of the Hindus, the Dera, the Bhandari, the Brahmin, the Khadura and the

Kumuti constitute the vast majority. In certain localities the Dhoba, the Medri, the Raula, the Dalua, the Reddika, the Madhuvaishya, and the Bania are scattered in patches. Lower castes such as the Hadi, the Dandasi and the Jagili are distributed in the localities, which were earlier in the outskirt but now come well within the Municipality area. Among all these castes, the Dera and the Kumuti are most organized under the control of their traditional caste councils. On the other hand, the Khadura, the Raula, the Medri, the Dhoba, the Dalua, the Madhuvaishya, the Hadi and the Bhandari are rejuvenating the caste-level integration by restructuring their caste councils in a democratic set-up. The caste communities of Berhampur may be classified into two linguistic categories—Telugu and Oriya. The Deras, Kumutis and Reddikas speak Telugu whereas the Raulas, Bhandaris, Daluas, Odia Medris and Khaduras use Oriya as their script as well as spoken language.

Methods Adopted for Fieldwork

While working as a Lecturer in the Department of Anthropology at Khallikote College, Berhampur, during 1981 to 1986, I had undertaken ethnographic studies on certain communities who had migrated and settled at Berhampur for more than hundred years. It was during these studies when I came to know that Budhi Santani is reverred by them as the presiding deity of Berhampur, and the Thakurani Yatra, which is celebrated in reverence of her, has a regional level of importance. Subsequently, I met Shri Surya Narayan Behera, a senior priest of Budhi Santani temple, and Shri Tuti Kedaraswamy, a septa-generian associated for the last five decades with the organization of Thakurani Yatra. Both of them briefly narrated me the sacred performances performed by different sacred specialists at the temple as well as during the *yatra*. This created an interest in me to undertake a full-length study on Budhi Santani and her *yatra*. I initiated my work with a search for the scriptural references on it but unfortunately found it to be scanty and non-systematic since no scientific study had so far been made on it by either any anthropologist or scholar from other disciplines. Hence, I carried on my study with a synchronic approach. However, relevant diachronic data, obtained from textual references, folk beliefs and life history analysis, were also taken into consideration to support the empirical facts.

After the initial phase of my fieldwork, which began from November 1984 and continued at a stretch up to May 1985, I had an opportunity of discussing my empirical findings with Professor L.P. Vidyarthi and Professor Makhan Jha. Keeping in view the peculiar field situation in case of Budhi Santani and her *yatra*, we arrived at a conclusion to explore and analyse the data in the framework of the sacred complex model but confining the concept to a single dominant deity, instead of a particular sacred city.

Before undertaking the second phase of my fieldwork I made a literary survey of the earlier studies done in the field of sacred complex. Some of the hypotheses formulated in those studies were selected for further test. In addition to this, on the basis of the first phase of fieldwork two more hypotheses were also formulated for empirical verification.

In order to test these hypotheses at the contextual level, data were collected with the help of schedules as well as questionnaires. Schedules (see Appendix-I) were specifically designed to collect data regarding the life history as well as the sacred beliefs of the sacred specialists and the social life of their castes. These schedules were also framed to get data with respect to the changes undergone in the style of life of the sacred specialists due to the impact of the overall transformation of Hindu civilization. In addition to this, these schedules were utilised to find out the level of reflection of the local pattern of Hindu social organization in the organization of the sacred performance. The informants for this purpose were selected by purposive method.

For interviewing the sacred sacrificers to note down the level of integration and compromise as against various differences and diversities among them, I had formulated an oral questionnaire (see Appendix-I). The questionnaire was used to interview a sample of five hundred sacred sacrificers who were sampled by purposive method.

Apart from this, I had made use of the case study method essentially to collect data on the pattern of making certain sacred sacrifices. At the same time, I had also used this method to know the nature of relationship emerged and established between the sacred sacrificers and the sacred specialists due to various types of sacred sacrifices.

In order to test the integration and unity among various elements of the sacred complex and the combination as well as compromise between the great and little traditions, I had taken help of the interview method, both at individual and group levels.

Before utilizing the data on a particular topic for the analysis of the hypotheses, I had cross-checked those by interviewing persons separately and also in group. These data were further verified by observation methods of both participant and non-participant type.

For a fruitful fieldwork I had taken all precautionary measures to establish perfect rapport with my informants. For this purpose, I had put on a gentleman's dress and controlled my behaviour while interacting with informants of various categories. In order to please them I had also taken their photographs while they were engaged in different sacred performances. Since for the first time in the history of the Thakurani Yatra I was permitted to take such photographs, my informants were very much interested to get a copy of their photos. In fact, the photos greatly helped me in establishing rapport.

Chapterization

After cross-checking the data, I organized and classified them under such heads as sacred geography, sacred performances, sacred specialists, sacred sacrificers, sacred sacrifices, sacred symbols and sacred beliefs. These data were then analysed and presented in seven chapters.

In the first chapter, which focuses on the sacred geography of the Sacred Complex of Budhi Santani, the sacred centres have been analysed and classified as per their locational distribution and organisational linkage. Moreover, while discussing the organisational linkage among various sacred centres, the combination and coexistence among the deities of different sects has been described. In addition to this, a structural continuity among the sacred segments has been brought out.

An elaborate description of the sacred performances has been made in the next two chapters. In the second chapter, the sacred performances, which are observed at the Thakurani temple, have been discussed. The presentation of these sacred performances has essentially been done as per their typological variation. Since the sacred performances find their maximum elaboration during the Thakurani Yatra, a separate chapter, therefore, has been dealt. In both of these chapters, an account of the continuity and integration between little and great traditions as expressed in the sacred performances has been presented. Apart from this, these two chapters also focus on the nature of the organization of sacred performances, which reflects the local pattern of Hindu social organization.

Chapters 4 and 5 are essentially concerned with the sacred specialists who are functionally associated with different sacred performances. While Chapter 4 is devoted to a typological analysis of the sacred specialists and, hence, to discuss the functional variation among them, Chapter 5 describes their style of life and justifies that against all differences in terms of caste, sect, occupation and sacred performances, there exists a common cultural consciousness, which is identified here as the 'Sevaka Culture', among them. In Chapter 5, there is also a discussion on the level of continuity and change of traditions, as expressed in their style of life, under the impact of the general development of the Hindu social life.

Chapter 6 examines the level of unity and integrity brought about by the sacred sacrificers in the entire system of the Sacred Complex of Budhi Santani due to different sacred sacrifices. It also discusses the way the sacred complex, in turn, develops integration among the sacred sacrificers against various cultural differences.

In Chapter 7, there is a brief narration about the sacred symbols and the sacred beliefs, which are part and parcel of the Sacred Complex of Budhi Santani. It expresses not only the symbolic manifestations of the sacred centres and the sacred performances but also examines their association with different sacred beliefs. This chapter also narrates how the sacred symbols and sacred beliefs act as catalysts in integrating various elements of the Sacred Complex of Budhi Santani. But the primary aim of this chapter is to discuss the combination and compromise of little and great traditions of Hindu civilization as reflected in the context of sacred symbols and sacred beliefs of the Sacred Complex of Budhi Santani. At the end, I have summarized the findings of all the previous chapters and then, verified the hypotheses with the available facts in Chapter 8.

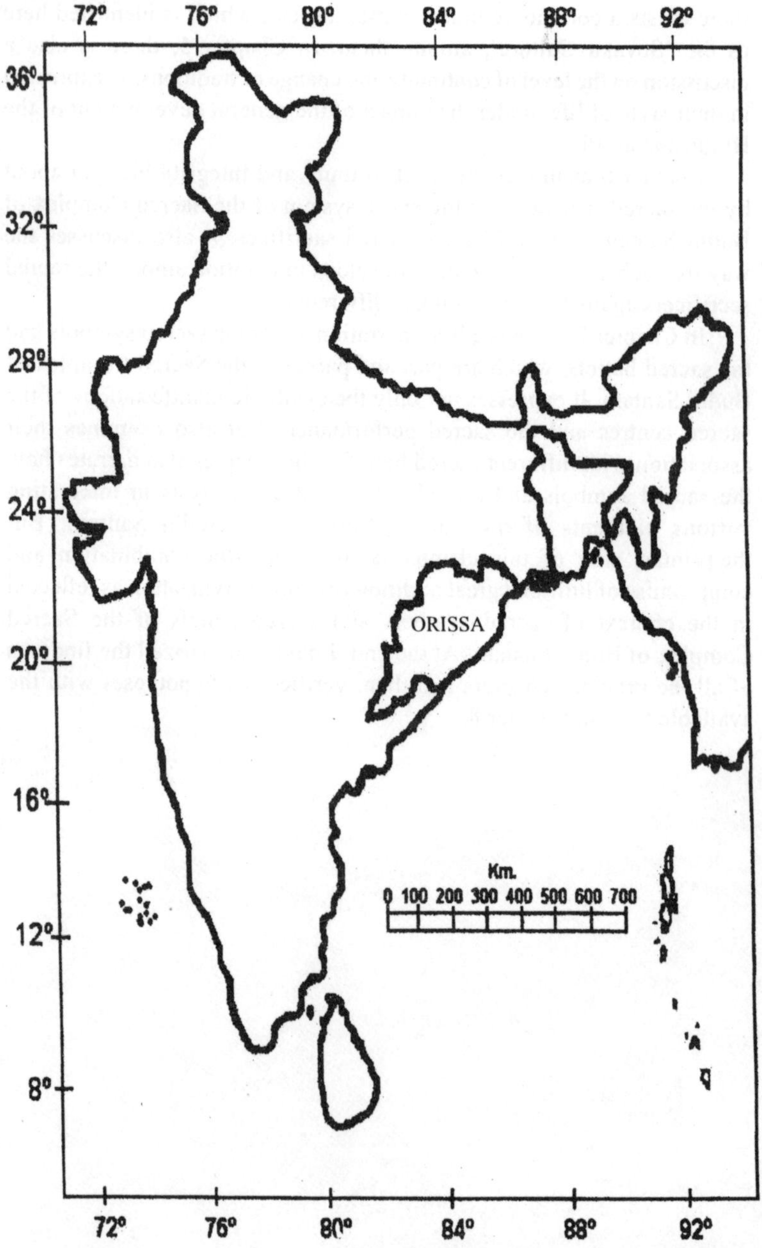

MAP 1: Place of Orissa State in India

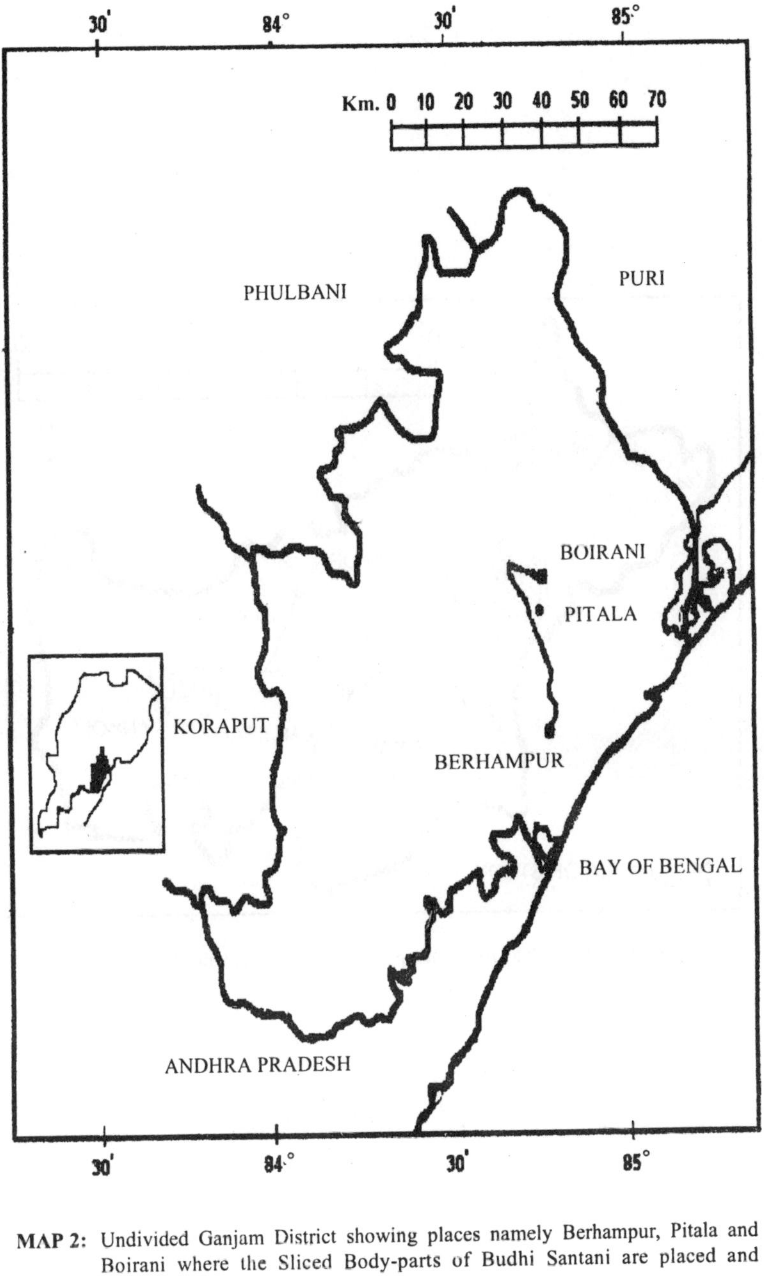

MAP 2: Undivided Ganjam District showing places namely Berhampur, Pitala and Boirani where the Sliced Body-parts of Budhi Santani are placed and worshipped

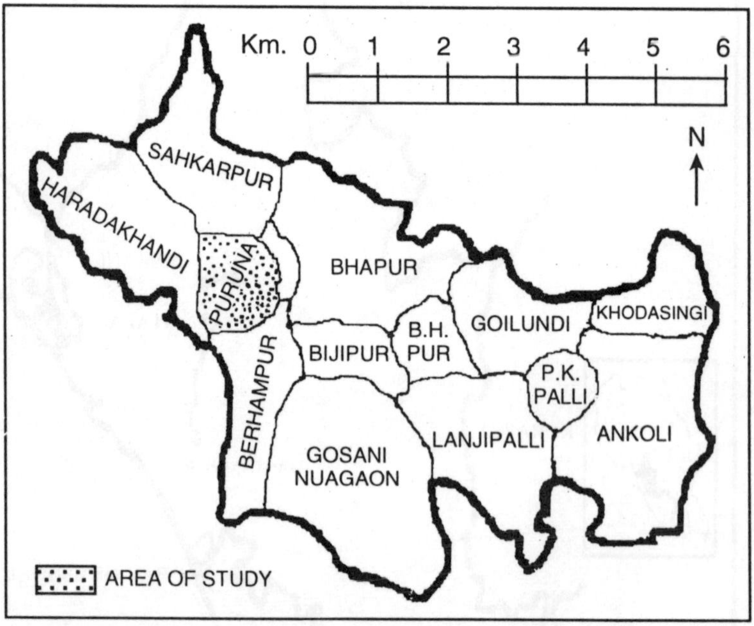

MAP 3: Master Plan of Berhampur Municipality showing Area of Study

1

SACRED GEOGRAPHY

In this Chapter, I have discussed about different sacred centres, which exhibit an organizational linkage or a structural integration among them so as to form the Sacred Complex of Budhi Santani. The Thakurani is believed by the local Hindus as the Budhi Santani form of the *Adi-Mata*. The deity had an anthropomorphic body with not more than two hands. But later on, she is believed to have been sliced into three pieces at Boirani by one of her devotees and subsequently, the head and trunk were thrown by the devotee to fall at Berhampur and Pitala respectively whereas her pair of feet remained at Boirani. In course of time, each spot carrying a body-part of the goddess was considered to be a sacred centre having the *shakti* of the goddess. With subsequent royal patronization the sacred area of each sacred centre was elaborated along with accretion of the sacred centres of other deities. Moreover, in order to popularize the Thakurani, various seasonal festivals and a *yatra* were organized. For the purpose of the *yatra*, a number of temporary sacred centres were installed. On the organizational level, these sacred centres express a compromise among different Hindu sectarian deities whereas on the locational and spatial levels, these provide a scope for a classification using the concepts like single sacred centre, multiple sacred centre, sacred cluster and sacred segment as framed in the study of Kashi (1974).

Classification of Sacred Centres at Locational and Spatial Levels

A single sacred centre is considered here to be a single spot, which is construed as an abode of a deity, where sacred performances are performed for propitiation of the deity and where the spot has a sacred area that generates or tends to generate sacredness in the mind of the devotee. When more than one sacred structures are built up within the precinct of a shrine dedicated to a specific deity, they are referred by the term multiple sacred centre. The term sacred cluster has been used when more than one multiple sacred centres are located in congregation. The same term has also been used when a number of single sacred centres are located in congregation with one or more multiple sacred centres. When one or more sacred clusters form a continuous segment, there the term sacred segment has been used.

The sacred centres, which are interrelated to form the Sacred Complex of Budhi Santani are of varied nature, ranging from a photograph of a deity hanged on the wall to the image of a deity engraved on the wall, from a mystical object placed under a tree to an anthropomorphic idol installed at the sanctum sanctorum in a temple, from a bamboo pole carrying a flag to an elaborate placement of an anthropomorphic image of a deity on a chariot or a symbolic representation of a deity by a material object like a *ghata,* and from an instantly created sacred spot for the worship of the Thakurani during her *Sahi Parikrama* to an organized construction of an *Utsav Mandira* at the time of the Thakurani Yatra.

Among these sacred centres, the single sacred centres are very limited in number and include the wooden anthropomorphic images of Jwalamukhi, Kali and Narayana, which are exhibited on chariots during the Thakurani Yatra and the inanimate objects like *Dharma Jhanda* and *manasika ghatas* of Budhi Santani, which are also installed during the Thakurani Yatra. On the other hand, most of the sacred centres form multiple sacred centres. For instance, the temple of Budhi Santani Thakurani at each place, Berhampur, Pitala and Boirani, forms one multiple sacred centre. Here, the anthropomorphic symbol of Budhi Santani placed at the sanctum sanctorum is treated as the principal sacred centre. Apart from the symbolic structure of Budhi Santani in this multiple sacred centre, sacred structures of Naba-Grahas, Dasa-Mahavidyas, Siva, Krishna, Vishnu, Laxmi, Saraswati, Jwalamukhi, Durga, Shitala, Parvati and Brundavati in the form of mythical idol, anthropomorphic images, photos, wall paintings and trees are also included. The *Utsav Mandira* during the Thakurani Yatra forms another multiple sacred centre, where the earthen *ghata* of Budhi Santani is the principal sacred centre and other sacred structures include the earthen *ghatas* of Kali, Bankeswari, Charchikai, Birajai, Phulasundari, Samalai, Hingulai and Mangala, the wooden anthropomorphic heads of Baidhara and Kali and the Subhakhunti of Budhi Santani.

At each place Berhampur, Pitala and Boirani, the multiple sacred centres and the single sacred centres combinedly form a sacred segment.

Thus, in total, the Sacred Complex of Budhi Santani is composed of three sacred segments and these exhibit a structural integration among themselves through the different body-parts of Budhi Santani, which are worshipped at her temples in Berhampur, Pitala and Boirani.

Classification of Sacred Centres at Sectarian Level

At the contextual level, the deities affiliated to various sacred centres broadly fall under the three sectarian categories, Shakta, Vaishnava and Saiva. However, most of these deities belong to the Shakta category. For instance, at the Thakurani temple, the principal sacred centre belongs to Budhi Santani but apart from it, goddesses like Shitala, Kali, Tara, Durga, Sadosi, Matangi, Chhinnamasta, Bhubaneswari, Bhairavi, Kamalatmika, Dhumavati and Bagalamukhi also have their sacred structures installed and worshipped. Similarly, at the *Utsav Mandira*, all the sacred structures belong to the Shakta deities such as Budhi Santani, Phulasundari, Bankeswari, Charchikai, Birajai, Mangala, Samalai, Hingulai and Kali. In addition to this, sacred structures of Jwalamukhi and Kali are also installed on *rathas* during the Thakurani Yatra.

Although very limited in number, the sacred structures of the deities of Vaishnava and Saiva sectarian categories are also installed in the Thakurani temple as well as during the Thakurani Yatra. For instance, on the inner wall of the *garbha-griha* of the Thakurani temple, photos of Siva, Narayana and Krishna are hanged along with those of Durga, Parvati, and Laxmi. Similarly, during the Thakurani Yatra, a huge image of Narayana is installed and worshipped by the people. Thus, in the context of the Sacred Complex of Budhi Santani, there exists both a combination and a co-existence of the deities of different sectarian categories.

Classification of Sacred Centres at the Level of Great and Little Traditions

Depending on the extent of popularity the deities of different sacred centres may be classified broadly as little traditional and great traditional types. The deities like Durga, Jwalamukhi, Narayana, Krishna, Parvati, Laxmi and Siva, who have popularity at universal level, may be included in the great traditional category. The deities like Sadosi, Matangi, Kali, Tara, Bhubaneswari, Dhumavati, Kamalatmika, Chhinnamasta, Bagalamukhi and Bhairavi are universally accepted as the *Dasa-Mahavidyas* of Durga and, therefore, these deities may also be kept under great traditional category.

On the other hand, the deities like Phulasundari, Hingulai, Bankeswari, Charchikai, Birajai, Mangala, Samalai and Budhi Santani are all of local origin. Moreover, their importance is limited either to local level or to regional level for which these deities may be included in the little traditional category.

Thus, at the contextual level, I observe a combination and co-existence of deities of both great and little traditional categories. In addition to this, I also observe that there exists a compromise among the deities of these two categories. For instance, Budhi Santani is equated with Durga and, therefore, her *Bije Pratima* is structured like that of Durga and not her. Further, since Budhi Santani, a little traditional deity, is equated with Durga, a great traditional deity, therefore, the *Dasa Mahavidyas* of Durga are also regarded as the *Dasa Mahavidyas* of Budhi Santani.

Apart from this, at the local level, people believe that Kali is the daughter-in-law of Budhi Santani, who is respected as the *Adi-Mata*. This state of compromise, as exibited at kinship level between Budhi Santani, a little traditional deity, and Kali, a great traditional deity, further substantiates the finding that the combination and compromise between little traditions and great traditions is a contextual phenomenon in Hindu civilization.

To sum up, as at Kashi (1974), the sacred centres of the Sacred Complex of Budhi Santani also provide a scope for their classification, on spatial and locational level, into single sacred centres, multiple sacred centres, sacred clusters and sacred segments. Moreover, at the level of multiple sacred centre, sacred cluster and sacred segment, a coexistence and combination of different Hindu sectarian deities, Saiva, Vaishnava and Shakta, has been established. Apart from this, there also exists a combination and compromise of great traditional as well as little traditional Hindu deities. This speaks that the sacred complex model designed at Gaya (1961) can also be applicable to interpret the core of Hindu civilization by the analysis of Hindu sacred centres having a regional level of importance. After the analysis of the sacred centres, a number of questions emerged. For instance, can we make a similar interpretation on the core of Hindu civilization by analysis of the sacred performances performed at different sacred centres? Does the nature of organization of the sacred performances reflect the local pattern of Hindu social organization? All these questions are dealt in the second as well as third chapters where there is a detail discussion on the sacred performances.

2

SACRED PERFORMANCES AT THAKURANI TEMPLE

In the previous chapter, I have mentioned that a sacred centre is a spot where a deity is believed to exist and where rituals are performed in reverence of the deity. These rituals may be of different forms such as offerings, fire rituals, prayers and recitations, observance of some sacraments and festivals, sacred baths, water offerings, artistic and dramatic performances etc. To these rituals, Singer (1955: 26-27) termed as cultural performances but Vidyarthi (1961: 30) preferred to use the concept, sacred performances. In the present study I have used Vidyarthi's concept of 'sacred performances' while interpreting the core of Hindu civilization by analysing the rituals performed at different sacred centres.

In the present analysis, I have classified the sacred performances into two broad categories such as those performed at the temple of Budhi Santani and those performed during the Thakurani Yatra. In this chapter I have discussed only the first category of sacred performances whereas the second category of sacred performances are dealt in the third chapter.

The shrine of Budhi Santani being the principal sacred centre at the Thakurani temple, the sacred performances are customarily framed and traditionally performed primarily to propitiate her. However, while propitiating her, the temple priest also makes ritual worship at other sacred centres of the temple. The sacred performances, which are performed at the Thakurani temple, may be classified into three broad categories, such as those related to the daily ritual worship, those concerned with the seasonal festivals and those associated with the fulfilment of desires by the devotees.

Daily Ritual Worship

The daily ritual worship at the Thakurani temple is patterned so as to propitiate Budhi Santani Thakurani but while doing so, resin incense is also offered to other deities of the temple. The daily ritual worship is performed essentially in an agamic procedure. However, a strict *yogic* way of agamic worship is not practised everyday and besides the days of religious importance, the preliminaries of agamic worship are observed by the priest only as a mere formality. In this agamic form of temple worship, which ranges from the simplest *japa* to the most complicated forms of *saparivara* worship, the deity is treated with a royal honour.

Rituals for daily worship at the temple are performed on four principal occasions, such as (1) *Mangala Arati*, which is initiated with the awakening of the goddess and ends with an auspicious waving of earthen lamp; (2) *Anna Bhoga*, which includes rituals observed during mid-day when the goddess is offered with a lunch; (3) *Sandhya Arati*, which involves rituals performed at the time of decorating the goddess in the evening; and (4) *Pahada Bhoga*, which consists of a set of rituals beginning with the dinner offered to the goddess till she retires to bed.

Mangala Arati

Everyday while propitiating the Thakurani in the morning the temple priest makes an auspicious waving of lamp. This occasion, called as *Mangala Arati,* begins when the temple priest, after taking his bath and putting on a silken *dhoti*, opens the main door of the temple in the *Brahma-muhurta* (usually between 4 a.m. and 4.30 a.m.). Before opening the door he gives a symbolic clapping to awaken the Thakurani and the first ritual that he performs after opening the door is a royal salutation to her. Thereafter, he cleans the *garbha-griha* and *darsana-griha* and keeps Thakurani's bed-stead at a corner.

Before initiating the *Mangala Arati*, the temple priest arranges the ritual materials, such as flowers, a brass pot containing water, sandal paste, incense stick, camphor, a small bell, vermillion, banana, sweets and fried paddy seasoned with sugar. The priest then performs a series of rituals in connection with the purification of *asana, atma* and *upakarana* after which rituals related to *samkalpa, digabandhana, dhupa* and *avahana* of Thakurani are executed. Soon after the Thakurani is invoked, rituals related to *padya, achamana, madhuparka, snana, vastra* and *abharana* are performed and thereafter, the Thakurani is worshipped by *panchopachara* procedure, where five materials, such as sandal, flower, incense, light and food are offered. During this *panchopachara upasana* an *arati* is offered to the Thakurani by burning camphor and/or wicks whereafter it is offered to devotees. At the time of *arati* the priest tinkles a small bell holding it by left hand while the devotees ring other bells, hanged from the roof of *darsana-griha*. The *dhupa* offered to the Thakurani during the rituals of *Mangala Arati* is also given to all other deities residing inside the temple campus.

Anna Bhoga

After the *Mangala Arati*, devotees are allowed to have a *darsana* or offer a *puja* to the Thakurani till the preparation for *Anna Bhoga* that is made in between 1.00 p.m. to 2.00 p.m. Soon after the materials for *Anna Bhoga* are arranged, the entrance door as well as the exit door of *darsana-griha* of the temple are closed. The temple priest cleans the *garbha-griha* and the *darsana-griha* and then performs rituals related to purification of *asana, atma* and *upakarana*. He, then, performs the rituals concerning *samkalpa, digabandhana, dhupa* and *avahana* of the Thakurani. After the *avahana* of the deity, the priest offers her sandal paste, flowers, resin incense, light by burning camphor and the food prepared for lunch following the *panchopachara puja paddhati*. When the Thakurani takes her lunch, the priest remains outside the temple after closing the entrance door to *garbha-griha*. Five minutes later, he enters into *garbha-griha* after clapping twice at the entrance door. A piece of betel leaf and a few betel-nuts are kept at the left side of the Thakurani and to her right a glass full of *pana* is placed for her consumption. This offering is made on the basis of a traditional Hindu belief that drinking *pana* and chewing betel after a meal do help in the process of digestion. After *Anna Bhoga* is offered to the Thakurani, the temple priest, without elaboration of *panchopachara puja paddhati*, offers *dhupa* and *naivedya* to other deities present inside the temple campus. After the completion of *Anna Bhoga* rituals, the doors of *darsana griha* are opened for the devotees.

Sandhya Arati

In between 6 p.m. and 6.30 p.m., *garbha-griha* is again cleaned and the Thakurani is decorated with fresh flowers for the *Sandhya Arati* to be performed by the priest. As a part of the *panchopachara puja paddhati*, incense by burning resin is offered by an assistant priest at each sacred centre inside the temple campus whereas the rest part of *panchopachara* is performed at *garbha-griha* on the eve of *Sandhya Arati*. The *arati*, waved before the deity, consists of five or seven number of wicks and the waving is done considerably for a longer period in comparison to

Mangala Arati. The devotees, amidst the waving of *arati*, tinkling of small bell, ringing of large bells and a smoky atmosphere due to the burning of resin, make a *darsana* to the Thakurani. The devotees await in the *darsana-griha* till the end of *arati*-ritual to have a share of the *arati* when offered by the priest.

Pahada Bhoga

At around 10 p.m. preparations are made for *Pahada Bhoga*, the last ritual of the day. But prior to it, *garbha-griha* as well as *darsana-griha* are cleaned and washed and then following the *panchopachara puja paddhati* the Thakurani is offered with dinner. The food usually consists of boiled rice, boiled pulses, vegetable curry and fried pot-herb. On Tuesday and on the day of *Sankranti*, fish-curry is additionally prepared to satisfy the deity.

Soon after dinner, a ritual related to *Pahada Bhoga* is performed while sweets are offered to the deity. Thereafter, the sleeping cot of the Thakurani is placed north-southwise in the *darsana-griha*. The bed is arranged with pillows kept on its southern end. The image of the deity is not brought but instead a few flowers from her head as her sacred symbols are placed on the bed. And all the doors of the temple are closed till the next morning.

Seasonal Festivals

At the Thakurani temple, certain special rituals are performed during the seasonal festivals like Sankranti, Dasahara and Deepavali. This results in a little deviation in the system of daily ritual worship. However, during the Saraswati Puja, Laxmi Puja, Sivaratri, Ganesh Puja and Ratha Yatra, special rituals are not performed at the Thakurani temple.

During all the Sankranti days, a special ritual named as 'Sankranti Bedha Parikrama' is performed before the *Pahada Bhoga* of the day. The *Sankranti Bedha Parikrama* ritual begins at about 11 p.m. when the Bije Pratima of the Thakurani is kept on a *pidha* in the *darsana-griha*, which is earlier washed and cleaned for this purpose. The priest, then, makes *puja* to the Bije Pratima. After a while, it is carried on hands by the priest and then in a procession, the priest makes *parikrama* of the *Mandira-bedha* for three times. In the procession, the musicians remain at the front, the conch-shell blower and the Kahali-player remain by the two sides of the priest and the devotees remain at the back of the priest. After the completion of *Bedha-Parikrama*, the Bije Pratima is placed in the *garbha-griha*. The priest, then, performs the *arati*-ritual at the *garbha-griha*. Thereafter, *bhoga*, which consists of *ukhuda, bundi* and *chuda-ghasa*, is offered to the devotees. This marks the end of the *Sankranti Bedha Parikrama* ritual.

In the month of *Ashwina*, Dasahara or Nabaratra Puja is also celebrated at the Thakurani temple. It begins from the first day of *Ashwina*, when the ritual worship of a *Kumbha*, symbolically representing the abode of the Thakurani, is performed. *Kumbha-puja* is done for nine days and on the tenth day, its *bisarjana* is done. During these nine days, different types of *bhogas* are offered to the Thakurani in different days. In large number, devotees come to the temple in these days and offer *bela-patras* to the Thakurani.

On the day of Deepavali, the daily ritual worship system is not disturbed only except in the evening, when, after the *Sandhya-Arati*, a *Maha-deepa* is rekindled and placed at the top of the temple.

Sacred Performances related to the Fulfilment of Desires

Apart from the sacred performances associated with the daily ritual worship and the seasonal festivals, certain sacred performances are made at the Thakurani temple occasionally and these are made basically to fulfil the mundane desires, which are broadly of two categories: (1) *Artha* and (2) *Kama*. These mundane desires are considered by the temple-priests to be of three types, such as those concerned with birth related troubles, those concerned with diseases and those concerned with *graha-shanti*. For the fulfilment of these three types of mundane desires, special sacred performances are also performed. Thus, for a trouble-free delivery, the *Khandadhuapani* ritual is performed. In this ritual, first the sword of Budhi Santani Thakurani is washed in clean water and this water is then placed near the Thakurani in the *garbha-griha*. The priest then propitiates the Thakurani by uttering the *Matangini Mantra* and after the *puja*, he brings a *mandara phula* from her head and puts it into this water, which is then consumed by the expectant mother. It is believed that by doing this, the delivery-pain will be reduced.

Khandadhuapani ritual is also performed when anybody suffers from diseases like smallpox and diarrhoea. However, in this case, instead of *Matangini Mantra, Sitala Mantra* is used during the *puja* of the Thakurani. Some amount of the water, after the *puja*, is sprinkled over the patient for whom the ritual is performed and then, the rest is given for consumption. It is believed that the disease has been caused by the Thakurani out of anger and hence, *Sitala Mantra* is used for her pacification.

The Hindus, many a time, take it by faith that misfortunes come due to the *ashanti* of the *grahas*. For instance, when they are unable to pass out in examinations or they have missed their children, they feel such events in life as due to misfortunes and they try to amend these by performing the '*Graha-Shanti*' ritual. Such *Graha-Shanti* ritual is also performed at the Thakurani temple. This ritual involves a *puja* by different *mantras* to pacify the *grahas* as well as all the gods and goddesses. It is believed that the misfortunes can be overcome by performing this ritual.

The *Khandadhuapani* ritual and the *Graha-Shanti* ritual are performed prior to the fulfilment of the mundane desires, but, certain sacred performances are also made at the Thakurani temple after the fulfilment of mundane desires. These sacred performances broadly involve a ritual offering of sacred sacrifices which are vowed by the devotees. These are offered only after the fulfilment of their mundane desires by the Thakurani. While offering these sacred sacrifices, the goddess is worshipped by 'Bana-Durga' or '*Matangini*' *Mantra*.

To sum up, I observed that the sacred performances bring out an interrelationship among the sacred centres, the sacred sacrificers and the sacred specialists. Moreover, when certain sacred performances are performed on the basis of different sacred beliefs, which are associated with the sacred centres represented in the form of sacred symbols, this interrelationship becomes more integrated.

My second observation is that neither the sacred specialists nor the sacred sacrificers consider the deities, which are propitiated at different sacred centres, to be supernatural powers who lead a life unlike that of the human beings. But instead, they have the belief that the deities lead the pattern of life, which is ideal of the highest order in the local Hindu social organization. The daily ritual worship is a kind of reflection on the plain of religious rituals of this ideal pattern of Hindu social life.

The conclusions so derived from this analysis, however, need to be substantiated further by the rituals performed during the Thakurani Yatra, which are discussed in the next chapter.

3

SACRED PERFORMANCES DURING THAKURANI YATRA

Thakurani Yatra is believed to have been observed as a biennial festival since 1698.[1] As per the authorisation of Mohuri Raja, Desabehera, the caste headman of Devanga community, conducts the yatra.[2] In 1935, British Government had also approved Desabehera's authority in organising the yatra.[3]

MYTHICAL BACKGROUND OF THAKURANI YATRA

Long back Desabehera had an encounter with Budhi Santani Thakurani. One day, Desabehera found that a young girl was sitting on the verandah of his house at midnight. He asked politely: "Daughter, it seems you are in trouble. Please say what can I help you?" The girl replied, "Because of night I dare not to proceed to my village and hence, I am in search of a shelter till tomorrow morning." Desabehera suggested: "Look, this old man is like your father. You can take rest in my house without fear." The girl said: "Well, I accept your proposal but I have my baggage at a distance. Please give me company to bring it." Speaking this, the girl proceeded ahead followed by Desabehera. But to the astonishment of Desabehera, the girl vanished after a few yards.

The girl was none other than the "Narirupi Thakurani," which Desabehera failed to recognise. Instead, he thought the whole event as an illusion. Next day in the usual manner Desabehera went to the Thakurani temple to perform the morning ritual worship. As a part of the ritual when he placed flowers on her head, the flowers fell down repeatedly. Being surprised, Desabehera prayed her for an excuse for any mistake he might have committed unknowingly. Thakurani reminded him of last night's happening and said: "Since I have accepted you as my father, I cannot accept a *puja* offering from you." But I am afraid, replied Desabehera: "If this is your desire how can your daily ritual worship be performed?" Thakurani said: "Well, when you will go out of this temple, whoever you meet first, ask him to perform my daily ritual worship from today onwards." With a remorseful tone Desabehera said: "I have nothing to disobey you but I mind that I cannot serve you henceforth." Thakurani said: "Dear father, I feel your sentiment and I swear that I shall visit your house for a couple of days when you will invite me celebrating a *yatra* biennially." Being satisfied with this while Desabehera was coming out of the temple, he first encountered the village barber and conveyed him the wish of the Thakurani. From that day onwards, the barber and his descendants have been worshipping the Thakurani as temple-priests and Desabehera has been conducting a biennial "Thakurani Yatra" inviting the deity to spend a couple of days at his house.

PRELIMINARY ARRANGEMENT OF THAKURANI YATRA

The biennial Thakurani Yatra has been conducted regularly from the beginning and it is observed in the month of *Chaitra* (February-March). Around a fortnight before, following preliminary steps are taken.

Public Meeting

This meeting is called for by Desabehera and for the purpose, a Harijan drum-beater is engaged with remuneration to spread the message to the people of different *sahis* within the Berhampur village boundary. The meeting is held at night so that people can participate after taking their dinner. Under the Presidentship of Desabehera, the meeting is conducted where people of various castes, sects and occupations participate to take decisions on issues like selection of the date regarding the arrival and return of Thakurani and formation of an organizing committee under the headship of Desabehera.

Subha-Khunti Sthapana

It is a ritual concerning the *samarpana* of a pole to the Thakurani and thereafter, its placement at the site where the *Utsav Mandira* of Thakurani for the purpose of *yatra* is to be constructed. It is construed that with its placement the construction work of *Utsav Mandira* will be auspiciously conducted.

Soon after the public meeting a piece of bamboo of six to seven feet height and three to four inches in diameter is arranged. This bamboo pole is washed with turmeric water. At its apex, *sindur* is smeared and a *phulamala* is placed. The pole is then taken in a procession under the leadership of Desabehera to the Thakurani temple. The procession starts with '*Haribola*' and '*Jai Mahamai Ki Jai*' slogans. While at the front drum-beaters and flute-players march on, Kashinath Prusti, a man of Tulabhina caste residing at Aga Sahi, carries the pole at the middle of the procession. The roles of carrying the pole, beating drum and playing flute are hereditarily entrusted to the families of Kashinath, Simadri Nayak, a Harijan residing at Dhanamera Sahi and Kashi, a Raula priest of Balunkesvar temple, respectively.

As the procession reaches the Thakurani temple, only Desabehera and the pole-carrier enter into its *darsana-griha*. The pole is handed over to the temple priest who places it in front of the Thakurani in such a manner that its apical portion faces her. By making a ritual *samarpana* to her the pole is then considered to be auspicious to all following rituals during the *yatra*. The pole, henceforth called as *Subha-Khunti* or 'Auspicious Pole', is handed over to its carrier. As the ritual is over, public outside the *darsana-griha* shout *Jai Mahamai Ki Jai* and the drum-beater as well as the flute-player carry out their action. In a procession the Subha-Khunti is brought back to Desabehera Sahi and placed at a place where the *Utsav Mandira* is to be constructed for the *yatra*. While going to and coming from the temple, the procession travels through a traditionally specified route (see Fig. 3.1). The Subhakhunti is then worshipped by Desabeherani with an offer of *dhupa*

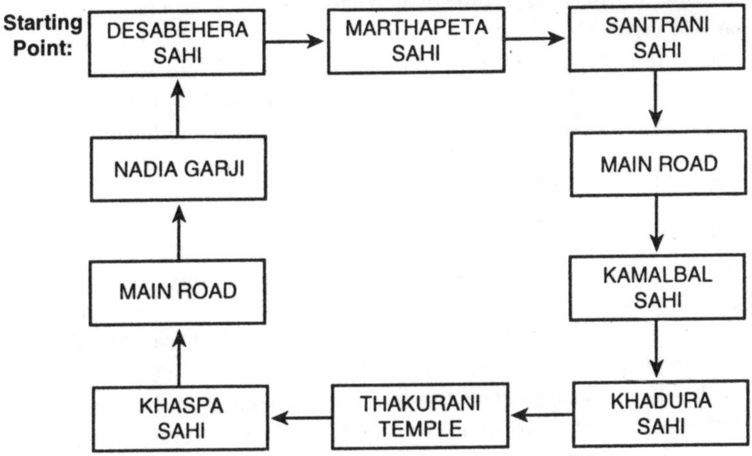

FIG. 3.1: Showing the Route of Subhakhunti Procession.

and *deepa* everyday at the evening till the beginning of *yatra*. However, it is displaced only after the *yatra* is over

Construction of Utsav Mandira

Although for the purpose of *yatra*, Thakurani is brought to Desabehera's home the deity is kept in a thatched house-structure so that devotees can have a *darsana* and offer a *puja*. This structure is constructed on the Sahi road in front of Desabehera's house. Since this is used as an abode of the Thakurani purely for the purpose of *yatra* or *utsav*, it is called as *Utsav Mandira*. The construction work is auctioned and the auctioneer makes a two-chambered house-structure, one is treated as *garbha-griha* or sanctum sanctorum whereas the other as *darsana-griha*. In the *garbha-griha* a '*Pitha*' or an altar is constructed whereupon the Thakurani is placed. The construction work of the *Mandira* is cared much so as to be completed one day before the beginning of *yatra*. This gives time to cleanse the floor of Utsav Mandira with *gobara-pani*. The *Utsav Mandira* is demolished a few days after the end of *yatra*.

DAY OF ARRIVAL

The auspicious time and day for inviting and receiving Thakurani is priorly decided at the public meeting. However, at the time of decision-making, Desabehera takes the help of a Brahmin astrologer. The Thakurani is invited on the first day of *yatra* and for this purpose, Desabehera and others come to the Thakurani temple in a large procession at late night. On this day a number of rituals are performed and all of these are collectively intended to deliver an auspicious reception to the arrival of Thakurani. Certain arrangements are made to receive her with royal ovation. These are discussed under the following headings.

Public Declaration

Since the Thakurani is received with a large procession involving participants of various castes, sects and occupations, to enable their participation, Desabehera spreads the message in the morning regarding the auspicious time of arrival of the Thakurani to Utsav Mandira and invites people to participate in the reception procession being decorated with different masks. The responsibility of spreading the message has been traditionally entrusted to the family of Simadri Nayak of Dhanamera Sahi. A male member of his family, who performs the duty, visits different *sahis* within the village boundary of Berhampur where he draws the attention of public by beating a drum and thereafter reads out loudly the "contents of the message" written on a piece of paper. For the sake of witness, he takes the signature of some important persons of each *sahi* on the paper. A transliteration and then, translation of the contents of the message as declared during the Thakurani Yatra of 1985 is given below.

Transliteration

> "Sri Sri Sri Budhi Santani Thakurani aja dina 14.4.85 tarikha rabibara rati 12 ghanta tharu 2 ghanta madhyare Desabehera Sahi Utsav Mandiraku vijaya hebe. Enu Gramabasimane besa dhari Patarla Basavaraju Desabehera Ghara nikataku rati 10 ghantare asiba pain adesa deichhanti."
>
> *Santaka* *Sahi*

Translation

> "Sri Sri Budhi Santani Thakurani will be coming to Utsav Mandira at Desabehera Sahi in between 12 O'Clock to 2 p.m. at night on today, i.e., Sunday dt. 14.4.85. Hence, the villagers wearing all their dresses are ordered to reach the house of Patarla Basavaraju Desabehera at 10 O'Clock at night."

Barana Puja

Before receiving the Thakurani at his home for the purpose of *yatra*, Desabehera along with his elderly male and female family members, kinsmen and people of other castes visits the Thakurani temple to perform the '*Barana Puja*' or 'invitational ritual'. He comes in the afternoon in a small procession where the drum-beaters and flute-players march on at the front and the Jangam, messenger of Devanga caste-council, carrying the wicker containing ritual offerings for *Barana Puja*, moves by the side of Desabehera. At the time of invitation, Desabehera requests the Thakurani to take her dinner at his house instead of at the temple. However, *Barana Puja* is performed by the temple-priest on behalf of Desabehera.

After the completion of *Barana Puja*, Desabehera along with the procession visits the temple of goddess Kali near the Municipality office. Since Kali is believed to be the daughter-in-law of Budhi Santani Thakurani, Desabehera offers her a *puja* expressing his desire and expecting a positive consent with regard to inviting the Thakurani to his home. Thereafter, Desabehera returns to his home. The invitational procession, while going to and coming from the Thakurani temple, traverses through a traditionally specified route (see Fig. 3.2). During the Thakurani Yatra of 1985, the whole process of *Barana Puja* covered a time-period from 2.10 p.m. to 3.35 p.m.

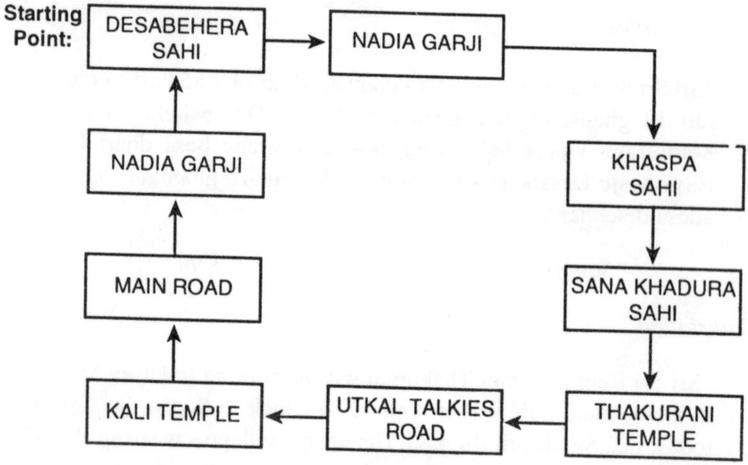

FIG. 3.2: Showing the Route of Barana Puja.

Pitha Pratistha

Within a time period of 2.45 p.m. to 4.15 p.m. during the Thakurani Yatra of 1985, a special ritual was performed to consecrate the *pitha* or sacred place for the Thakurani at Desabehera's home since it was his maiden attempt to invite her to his home. The consecration ritual was performed by a Brahmin in a vedic procedure. It involves a vedic sacrifice for the propitiation of various gods, goddesses, stars, planets and deities presiding over the ten points of the earth.

Changudi Puja

Changudi Puja is a tantric ritual performed by the Utsav Mandira priests who belong to the Damla caste. Priorly a *changudi* having a length and breadth of 18 inches each and a depth of 6 inches is collected traditionally from M. Satyam's family belonging to Medri caste of Medri *sahi*. A *phulamanda* is also collected from Kashi Raula's family of Balunkesvar temple locality. The *phulamanda* is a conical bunch of five garlands made of brick-coloured *itala* flowers. Besides the *changudi* and *phulamanda*, a number of ritual materials (see list of ritual materials, p. 247) are also collected. These ritual materials including the *phulamanda* are kept inside the *changudi*. An *Akhanda Deepa*, which is placed at the middle of *changudi*, is lighted at the time of *changudi puja*. The *puja* is offered for the propitiation of the Thakurani in the evening.

Digabandhana

Digabandhana is the last precautionary ritual observed at least two hours before Desabehera and others go for receiving Thakurani. Since the Damlas are tantric priests of Utsav Mandira, they are entrusted with the responsibility of performing the "*Digabandhana* ritual." At the time of the ritual along with the Damlas only Desabehera and Jangam carrying a plateful of *Khichri* remain present. All of them go to the two-terminal points of Desabehera Sahi where the ritual offering of *Khichri* along with a cock-sacrifice is made in a tantric procedure to satisfy the supernatural spirits and deities, or else they may disturb in the ritual observances during the *yatra*.

Reception Procession

As soon as *Digabandhana* is over, Desabehera and his wife take bath and put on new dresses. During the 1985 *yatra*, auspicious time period of reception was between 12.10 a.m. to 2.00 a.m. and a large number of people, about fifteen to twenty thousand, had gathered near the Utsav Mandira by 12.30 a.m. to participate in the reception procession. At the centre of the procession Desabehera along with his wife, carrying on head the *changudi* containing all the ritual materials, remain surrounded by a few elderly fellow kinsmen and the Damlas. While four fellow castemen hold a canopy on the *changudi*, eight to ten washermen spread cloth over the road on which Desabehera and his wife will pass to the Thakurani temple. This is done to pay royal respect since Desabehera and his wife are considered to be *Kula-raja* and *Kula-rani* respectively of the Devanga caste of Berhampur. Since a large public participate in the procession, policemen make a cordon to protect them from the crowd. The procession moves ahead towards the Thakurani temple and people rejoice the occasion by putting on different masks, which makes the procession colourful. As soon as the procession reaches the temple, the *changudi* is handed over to the priest who allows only Desabehera and his wife into the sanctum sanctorum to sit in front of the Thakurani to receive her. In order to seek the Thakurani's consent of going to her paternal house, the temple priest performs a ritual. In the ritual, the *phulamanda* is first kept upon the head of the Thakurani and then, after making *panchopachar upasana* the priest extols the Thakurani with recitation of *Malasri Mantra* till the *phulamanda* jumps down. The fall of the *phulamanda* is anxiously observed by all, since it symbolizes the Thakurani's willingness. People applaud it by shouting *Jai Mahamai Ki Jai* and *Jai Thakurani Ma Ki Jai*. The *phulamanda* now as a symbolic representation of the Thakurani is kept in the *changudi* and is handed over to Desabehera's wife who brings it, with all royal respect, to the Utsav Mandira along with the reception procession by a specific route (see Fig. 3.3). At the Utsav Mandira the *changudi* is kept on a *pitha* and thereafter, the Damlas perform the *Pana Bhoga* followed by *Anna Bhoga* and *Pahada Bhoga* in a tantric procedure.

On the second day, no significant ritual is performed except the daily ritual worship.

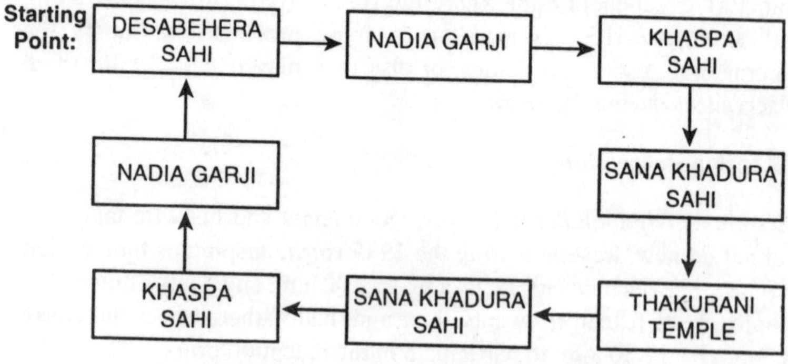

FIG. 3.3: Showing the Route of Reception Procession.

DAY OF GHATA SANSTHAPANA

Third day is the day of *Ghata Sansthapana* and from this day onwards, *Sahi Parikrama* of the Thakurani commences. The ritual activities of the day is discussed under three broad headings, namely preliminary arrangement, *Ghata Sansthapana* and *Sahi Parikrama* of the Thakurani.

Preliminary Arrangement

Ghata Sansthapana takes place at night and in the day time necessary ritual materials are arranged for the purpose. In the morning by 9 a.m. from *Kumbhara Sahi* of Pankilapalli two married females (in 1985 Thakurani Yatra, by R. Laxmi, 50 years old and R. Kanta, 35 years old) of a hereditarily entrusted specific potter family (family of R. Krishna Rao) bring *ghata, deepa, rukha* and *ghodani*, each of nine number, to

Desabehera's house. These materials are, then, painted by Kali Charan Dash, an amateur painter and also a Brahmin priest of the Trinath Jagannath temple of Chandramma Sahi. Soon after the painting is completed by evening, the Damlas take them to *Utsav Mandira* and necessary *puja* materials such as *chaula, gota haladi, harida, kalakunchi, barakoli patra, gota gua, panchamrita* and some coins are arranged. Of the nine *ghatas* one is a bit larger than the rest and is termed as *mukhya ghata* or Thakurani *ghata* since the *phulamanda* is kept in it. In the *mukhya ghata*, from the ritual materials, two palmful of chaula, one *gota haladi*, one *gota harida*, one *kala kunchi*, one *barakoli patra*, three *gota guas*, few drops of *panchamrita*, coins of rupees five and paise twenty-five and the *phulamanda* are kept inside whereas inside the other *ghatas* one palmful of *chaula*, one *gota haladi*, one *gota harida*, one *kalakunchi*, one *barakoli patra*, one *gota gua* and coins of one rupee and thirty paise are placed. In order to purify it ritually the exterior surface of each *ghata* is smeared with paste of *haladi* and *sindur* and a *gota haladi* is tied to its neck by means of a thread. Each *ghata* is covered with its *ghodani* and then sealed by a piece of yellow cloth. Each of the nine *rukhas* is also tied with one *gota haladi* by means of a thread.

Ghata Sansthapana

It is the ritual concerning a customary establishment of *ghatas* in the Utsav Mandira. As such, nine *ghatas* are placed upon the *pitha* and in front of each *ghata* one *deepa* is kept upon a *rukha*. The *deepa* in front of the *mukhya ghata* is called as *Mahadeepa*, which remains burning day and night till the end of *yatra*. Before placing the *ghatas*, the chief Damla priest performs *Pithasthapana ritual* by tantric procedure whereupon *Ghata Sansthapana* ritual is also done in a tantric method. On the left side of the *ghatas* a wooden image of the deity Baidhara's head is placed. To his neck one *gota haladi* is tied by a thread. His forehead is smeared with a paste of *haladi* and *sindur* and after encircling a piece of yellow cloth round his head, few drops of *panchamrita* are offered. A wooden image of goddess Kali's head, placed on the right side of the *ghatas*, is given the same ritual treatment as that of Baidhara. During the process of this ritualistic *sthapana* of *ghatas* as well as the images of Baidhara and Kali, Damala recites *abahana mantra* invoking the power of Thakurani, Kali, Baidhara and Sata Bhaunis, namely Phulasundari, Virajai, Bankesvari, Samalai, Hingulai, Charchikai and Mangala into their corresponding *ghatas* and images. Thereafter, *mukhya ghata* is decorated with flowers and a crown.

Sahi Parikrama of the Thakurani

After *ghata sansthapana*, the *ghatas* and images are believed to have possessed the Shakti of different deities where the presiding Shakti is that of Budhi Santani Thakurani. Various categories of devotees, from places far and near, come over to the Utsav Mandira to have a *darsana* or to offer a *puja* or even to make different sacrifices to the Thakurani. However, the Thakurani wishes to make a *parikrama* to different *sahis* so that people can get a better scope to have a *darsana* or to offer a *puja* or to make sacrifice to her. With this latent idea, the Sahi Parikrama of the Thakurani begins from the third day onwards till the end of the *yatra*.

For the Sahi Parikrama, the Thakurani *ghata* is carried on head by Desabehera's wife whereas other *ghatas* are carried on head by the wives of eight Senapatis of eight Dera *sahis*, namely Pitagundi Sahi, Chandrama Sahi, Bachuari Sahi, Santrani Sahi, Sanibarapeta Sahi, Kamalbal Sahi, Malubera Sahi and Lala Sahi. The images of Baidhara and Kali are carried by two Damla priests. All the carriers maintain the ritual purity and in case of pollution, another married female of the same family becomes the carrier. At the time of carrying the *ghatas* and images, each carrier is besmeared with *sindur-haladi* paste on forehead by the Chief Damla priest who at that time recites *abahana mantra* and sprinkles *haladi-chaula* on them. Thereafter, they go for Sahi Parikrama in a procession led by persons carrying the images of the Thakurani and Kali followed by Harijan drum-beaters, Raula flute-player and musicians of Oriya Medri caste. Along with the procession, the Damlas remain to see the carriers of deities if anyonc is affected by the tantric effect of a tantrika. Besides, the people of different castes and important Dera persons, Bhandari priests of the Thakurani temple and their relatives also move along with the procession. During the Sahi Parikrama the carriers of the Thakurani *ghata* and others stand a while at different places making these places 'instant sacred centres'. Females of nearby households pay homage to the Thakurani by washing the feet of the carrier of Thakurani *ghata* with *haladi pani*. They also offer a *bhoga* of *nadia* and *kadali* for consumption of the deity. Ritualistic offering of *bhoga* of these devotees is performed by the Bhandari priests who, for the purpose, take *dakshina*. Everyday, excepting the day of *Sahi Parikrama* to Bachuari Sahi, the Thakurani before making a *Sahi Parikrama* visits Mohuri Raja's palace at Raja Sahi to enable to Raja for a *darsana* whereas on the day of *Sahi Parikrama* to Bachuari Sahi, the Thakurani visits Raja's palace at the end of the *parikrama*. It is because of Thakurani's special attraction to see the 'Binchana Ratha' of Bachuari Sahi. However, on the first day of *Sahi Parikrama*, the Thakurani, after visiting Raja's palace, covers only the Desabehera Sahi from its eastern to western terminus and then returns to the Utsav Mandira.

RITUALS OBSERVED FROM FOURTH DAY UP TO THE LAST DAY OF THE YATRA

All the ritual activities performed from the fourth day onwards up to the last day of *yatra* can be classified under two headings such as daily *puja* and special rituals.

Daily Puja

Daily *puja* of the Thakurani can be discussed (a) as observed in Utsav Mandira and (b) as performed at the time of *Sahi Parikrama*.

Daily Puja in Utsav Mandira

As in the Thakurani temple, daily *puja* at Utsav Mandira is performed four times, such as (1) *Mangala Arati*, (2) *Anna Bhoga*, (3) *Sandhya Arati*, (4) *Pahada Bhoga*. However, considering the tantric *sansthapana* of the Thakurani and other deities at Utsav Mandira, Damlas, professional tantric priests of Pitala and Ambapua, are entrusted with the daily *puja* instead of the Bhandari priests of the Thakurani temple who are not adept in tantric *puja paddhati*. The Damlas get up early in the morning and after taking a bath and putting on a silk cloth, open the gate of Utsav Mandira and blow conchshells at *Bramhamuhurta*, i.e., 4 a.m. Thereafter, numerous female and male devotees come to Utsav Mandira for a *darsana, puja* or a sacrifice. *Mangala arati* is performed at about 6 a.m. following a tantric *panchopachar paddhati* whereas *anna bhoga* is offered in between 1 p.m. to 2 p.m. The *anna bhoga* is prepared on behalf of Desabehera by married female members of his family. The *bhoga* includes *bhata, dali*, vegetable curry and cake made of powdered *chaula* and *muga*. This *bhoga* is offered in a leaf-plate to each deity.

In the evening the Thakurani and other deities are decorated with flowers and the chief Damla priest performs *sandhya arati*, after which the deities go for *Sahi Parikrama*. Considering the deities to have exhausted, *pana bhoga*, a liquid mixture of *dahi* and *nabata pana*, is offered after the *Sahi Parikrama*. This is followed by an offer of *anna bhoga* to the deities in which the dishes are *bhata, dali* and vegetable curry. Throughout the *yatra*, although *anna bhoga* is offered in a tantric *puja paddhati*, non-vegetarian dishes are never an item of food. Before taking a rest for the night, *Pahada Bhoga*, consisting of dry sweets, is offered to the deities.

Daily Puja During Sahi Parikrama

Everyday after *sandhya arati*, the Thakurani alongwith other deities make a *parikrama* to different *sahis* within the *sarahada* (see Fig. 3.4) of Berhampur village. It may be referred here that today Berhampur is considered to be a city and neither the features of a village life nor a clear-cut geographical boundary of Berhampur as a village is present. Only the ritualistic restriction to *Sahi Parikrama* of the Thakurani during the *yatra* reflects a traditional consideration of a village *sarahada*. People as well as the organisers of the *yatra* believe that a violation to this restriction shall cause harm for all, since Thakurani may be displeased.[4] The *sarahada* is extended to Hanumana Mandira on east, Panigrahi Pentha on north, Balajee Pentha and Khadura Sahi on west and south respectively.

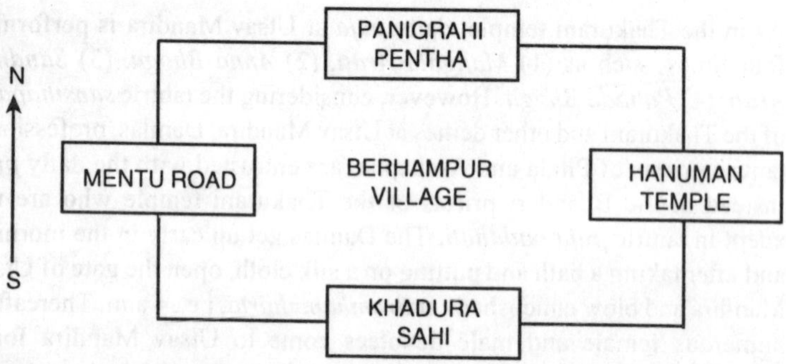

FIG. 3.4: Showing the Sarahada of Berhampur Village.

At the time of *Sahi Parikrama*, a distinct route chart is not priorly maintained because the *parikrama* of *sahi* is done only as per the desire of the Thakurani.[5] However, the investigator has noted down her *parikrama* of different *sahis* during the *yatra* on 1985 and found the ritual restriction with regard to *Sahi Parikrama* within the village *sarahada* to be perfectly maintained. During the *Sahi Parikrama*, the Thakurani stops at places making instant sacred centres so that female devotees of neighbouring households can offer a *bhoga* to her. *Bhoga* mainly constitutes cocoanut and banana but before offering a *bhoga*, every female washes, by pouring turmeric water, the feet of the carrier of *mukhya ghata*, who is respected at that moment as the Thakurani herself. At the time of *Sahi Parikrama*, the Thakurani expresses her desire to the head man of certain *sahi* to make *ratha*-demonstration.

Special Rituals

Besides the daily rituals performed by the priests inside the Utsav Mandira and by the devotees at the time of *Sahi Parikrama*, a number of special rituals are also observed in connection with the Thakurani Yatra, either (a) at the Utsav Mandira or (b) in different *sahis*. Special rituals at the Utsav Mandira involve the *puja* in connection with various sacred sacrifices. Since a detail discussion on sacred sacrifices will be made in Chapter 6, here an account only on *bala bhoga* shall be presented.

Rituals Observed in Utsav Mandira

Bala Bhoga

During the *yatra*, Desabehera, on behalf of his family, offers *bala bhoga* more than once to the Thakurani for a blessing of good health and happiness to his family members. This *bhoga* includes dishes like *dahi bhata*, cocoanut and banana. The *bhoga* is offered in presence of Desabehera and his wife and while offering it, the priest recites *mangala bandana*, Durganama and Nabarat-namalika. *Bhoga* is first offered to the Thakurani and thereafter to other deities.

Rituals Observed in Different Sahis

During the Thakurani Yatra, certain special rituals are observed in different *sahis* in between the fifth day and the penultimate day of the *yatra*. These rituals are broadly of two categories, such as (i) exhibition of *dharma jhanda* and (ii) the exhibition of *ratha*. These rituals, performed at the instance of the Thakurani, provide a multifarious scope of sacred and secular involvement for the people. The organizational aspect of such exhibition reflects a spirit of co-operation and community feeling among the inhabitants of each *sahi* and at the same time it bears witness to the widespread popular Hindu faith and interest in spiritual emulation by exercising devotion in fasting, worship, ablution, and in the practice of austerities and physical hardships. On secular plane, these rituals lend joy, zest and variety to life's monotonous routine in addition to providing a dimension for cultivating artistic excellence.

Exhibition of Dharma Jhanda

Dharma jhanda is a red flag tied to the narrow upper end of a bamboo pole of forty to fifty feet length. During the *yatra* it is placed about fifty feet away in front of Utsav Mandira but before such exhibition, a series of ritual activities are performed.

On the fifth day of *yatra*, the inhabitants of Kamalbal Sahi, collect a red-coloured *bena*, tie it to a long pole made of bamboo and place prostrately the whole thing near a blackberry plant. Married females of the *sahi* make a *puja* to the Thakurani offering a *bhoga* of cocoanut, banana and *pana* and thereafter smear the red flag with *sindur*.

After the necessary rituals are finished, a drum-beater[6] starts beating a drum, and the *dharma jhanda* is then carried on shoulder by a group of people who put on dresses resembling King, Minister, Warrior and even that of Police Inspector as well as Constable. They move in a procession towards Utsav Mandira holding the flag side of the pole to front. While a specific route chart is traditionally followed (see Fig. 3.5), at Chandrama Sahi, a black flag is offered to the Thakurani and tied hereditarily along with the red flag by a male member of Kolla Konta's family. *Dharma jhanda* is first kept prostrately in front of Utsav Mandira, the flags facing Budhi Santani Thakurani and after offering a *puja* to the Thakurani, it is placed erectly on the eastern or front side of the Utsav Mandira keeping a distance of about fifty feet. During the *yatra*, many female devotees, before offering a *puja* to the Thakurani, smear the base portion of pole with *sindur* and turmeric paste and pour turmeric water to it.

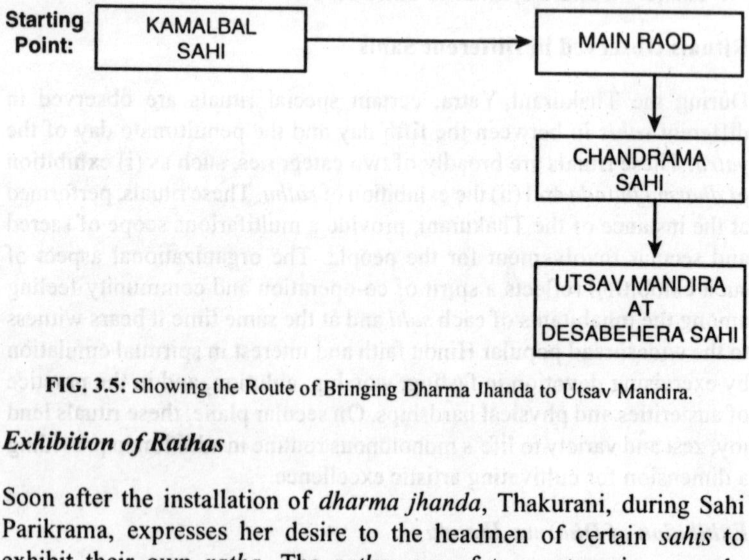

FIG. 3.5: Showing the Route of Bringing Dharma Jhanda to Utsav Mandira.

Exhibition of Rathas

Soon after the installation of *dharma jhanda*, Thakurani, during Sahi Parikrama, expresses her desire to the headmen of certain *sahis* to exhibit their own *ratha*. The *rathas* are of two categories, namely pauranic and non-pauranic. Non-pauranic *rathas* are associated with the *yatra* from the beginning and are exhibited in three important Dera *sahis* such as Bachuari Sahi, Santrani Sahi and Chandrama Sahi where the *Binchana Ratha, Arata Ratha* and *Boita Ratha* are displayed respectively. In a ritual order of merit basing on Thakurani's liking, *Binchana Ratha*, is always first ritually inaugurated followed by *Arata Ratha* and *Boita Ratha*. Pauranic *rathas* were originally held forth during Sitala-Sasthi festival. With a gradual non-observance of this festival some of them have been incorporated in the Thakurani Yatra. In these *rathas* images of various pauranic deities are installed. In the Thakurani Yatra of 1985, six pauranic *rathas*, namely, Jwalamukhi, Kali, Narayan, Laxman, Nagarjuna and Parsurama were placed for exhibition. A brief description of each *ratha* is given below:

Binchana Ratha

This is installed by the inhabitants of Bachuari Sahi in their own locality. Although this is called as a Dera *ratha*, people of other communities equally participate in its organization. It consists of a platform having four wheels. Upon the platform a revolving disc, having sitting arrangements, one at centre and the rest at four corners, is present. On the inaugural day, when the Thakurani and other deities move round the *ratha*, the disc revolves and five Dera boys, within the age-limit of five to ten years, fan the deities with the help of Binchana and, hence, it is named as *Binchana Ratha*. On this day, these boys make some ritual observances involving a complete taboo to non-vegetarian food and in the evening, they take only a portion of *bhoga* priorly offered to the Thakurani.

Arata Ratha

The inhabitants of Santrani Sahi instal the *Arata Ratha* during the Thakurani Yatra. Like *Binchana Ratha*, this is also called as a Dera *ratha*. By status, it is treated as the second most important *ratha*, the first being the *Binchana Ratha*. This *ratha* is shaped like the wheel of an *arata* from which it derives its name. The ritual process of installation of this *ratha* is similar to all others. After its installation, when the Thakurani visits Santrani Sahi, the wheel of this *ratha* is moved round in order to pay respect to the goddess.

Boita Ratha

The inhabitants of Chandrama Sahi organize to exhibit the *Boita Ratha*, a chariot in the shape of a boat. On the platform of this *ratha* a large wooden boat is installed and at the middle of the boat, a bomboo of forty to fifty feet length is placed erect. At the upper portion of this bamboo, three hexagonal wooden plates of different sizes are inserted, each at a distance of three to four feet from the other. These three plates are decorated with electrically-lighted bulbs and flags of both red and black colour. The piece of bamboo is erected at the time of inaugural exhibition of the *ratha* in presence of Thakurani and other deities. Prior to its erection, a *puja* is offered to the Thakurani and *sindur* from the Thakurani *ghata* is smeared to the bamboo and flags.

Jwalamukhi Ratha

This *ratha* is so named because people of Kalupatra Sahi install an image of Jwalamukhi[7] form of goddess Durga, upon the *ratha*. Inaugural exhibition of this *ratha* is done in the Sahi but thereafter it is brought to Badabazar locality. Inaugural ritual is performed in the presence of the Thakurani and other deities and the ritual involves a *puja* to the head of Jwalamukhi with recitation of Durga *staba* and placement of head on the body of deity, Jwalamukhi.

Kali Ratha

At the time of Thakurani Yatra the dwellers of Sandhamana Sahi show off a large wooden image, with 20 feet height of goddess Kali, another form of goddess Durga. Mythically goddess Durga takes to this form after the form of Jwalamukhi. As the myth narrates, in Jwalamukhi form, Durga started killing people and desired to attack gods. Being frightened, the latter prayed for a rescue to Lord Siva, consort of Durga. Siva, in order to refrain Durga from destructive attitude, slept on her way and in consequence, Durga ignorantly kicked him. Immediately he rattled his *dambru* and at its sound, Durga became conscious of her mistake[8] and at once she screamed to protrude her tongue[9] and her body turned black due to shame. Because of her blackness, this form of Durga is popularly referred to goddess Kali. Rituals observed at the time of inaugural display of *Kali Ratha* are same as those observed in case of *Jwalamukhi Ratha*.

Laxman Ratha

This *ratha* is installed by the people of Jena Sahi showing off a twenty feet tall wooden image of Laxman, the great fighter brother of Lord

Rama of *Treteya Yuga*.[10] Construction work of this *ratha* is done at Badabazar locality where it is kept for exhibition during *yatra*. Its inaugural ritual is also performed in the presence of the Thakurani.

Parsurama Ratha

For the last fifteen years, the inhabitants of Mentu road locality have been displaying a *ratha* carrying a twenty feet tall, wooden image of Parsurama, a great Brahmin fighter of early *Treteya Yuga*. In this posture he looks like a *rishi* holding a *kamandalu* in left hand but by right hand he holds a *tangi*. *Parsurama Ratha* is also constructed at Badabazar locality and at the time of its ritual inauguration, Thakurani and other deities visit.

Nagarjuna Ratha

Although organized by the people of Sitarama Sahi, *Nagarjuna Ratha* is installed at Badabazar. The wooden image of Nagarjuna is of about twenty feet height, expressing an attacking posture. The bearded Nagarjuna is the valiant son of Arjuna, the great warrior of *Mahabharata* war.[11] The image is kept open for exhibition only after an inaugural ritual is performed in the presence of the Thakurani and other deities.

Narayana Ratha

This ratha is placed for exhibition at the middle of Pitagundi Sahi. The inhabitants of this *Sahi* have been installing a fifteen feet tall wooden image of Lord Narayana also called as Vishnu. The image is sky-blue-coloured, and has four hands holding a *sankha*, a *chakra*, a *dhanu* and a *sara*. Like all other *rathas*, a ritual is performed in the presence of the Thakurani at the time of inaugural demonstration.

Whether pauranic or non-pauranic, no *ratha* is freshly constructed during each *yatra*. Because of a heavy expenditure incurred in demonstrating a huge image of a deity on a *ratha*, a comparatively permanent wooden structure is built whose parts can be detached and preserved for the next *yatra*. These parts are kept preserved with precautionary measures either in a *matha* or temple of each *sahi*. At the time of *yatra*, those are again arranged, the image is freshly painted and *ratha* is decorated artistically with secular items like electric bulbs, coloured cloth-pieces and papers. Although for construction as well as decorative works, professional carpenters and artists are employed, the organizational leaders and many young boys co-operate and participate in the work jubilantly. These workers feel enthusiastic when a piece of moral encouragement is extended from the elderly persons of their own *sahi*. Day and night, they labour hard and devote themselves with competitive spirit to be applauded by the viewers as regard to the naturality in image placement and artistic excellence in decoration. As numerous devotees, both from outside and within Berhampur, flock to have a *puja* to the Thakurani and *darsana* to these *rathas* during the *yatra*, these *rathas* are continued to be exhibited even two to three days after the completion of *yatra* and thereafter making a *visarjan* ritual, parts of each *ratha* are detached and preserved for the next *yatra*. However, so long as the images of pauranic deities are demonstrated on a *ratha* during *yatra*, everyday at evening, an *arati* is offered to the deity.

DAY OF RETURN

Earlier it has been discussed that Thakurani is believed, as per a widely popular oral tradition, to be a married daughter of Desabehera. In the local social tradition, a married daughter when visits her parental house, is given an affectionate treatment and her days of stay are utilized as an occasion for enjoyment. Her stay may be extended but on the day of return, the atmosphere turns painful and the daughter is given a sorrowful farewell. However, she is presented with a number of gifts and presentations from the parents, relatives and well-wishers. This social situation is best reflected on the Thakurani Yatra. That while the days of *yatra*, which may be extended with Thakurani's desire, are enjoyed amidst splendid arrangements and merry-making, on her day of return, Desabehera, fellow Deras and organizers of *yatra* develop a feeling of departing but at the same time, make all customary arrangements of offering necessary gifts and presentations. Therefore, special rituals, besides daily ritual worship, are observed on the last day of the *yatra*. These rituals are of two categories such as (a) those concerning a ritual offering to the Thakurani, and (b) those for warding off evil spirits.

Ritual Offering to the Thakurani

The ritual offerings including *ghata* or animal are given to the Thakurani. While before the beginning of return procession, *ghatas* are offered, animal, especially a goat, is offered at the end of the procession, i.e. inside the Thakurani temple. Among the *ghatas*, one *Hajare akhi thiba ghata*[12] from Desabehera's family and another from Thakurani's *Mausima* family and thousands of *Sahanika ghatas*[13] from devotees are offered.

Hajare akhi thiba ghata is first offered to the Thakurani and this makes a ritual confirmation to the day of return. The *ghata* is unbaked and porous and prepared hereditarily by R. Krishna Rao's family, a potter from Pankilapalli village. The *ghata* is brought to Desabehera by a married female of the potter's family. At about 11 a.m., following the *tantric samarpana mantra* the Damla priest keeps a *jalanta deepa* inside the *ghata* and thereafter makes a ritual offering to the Thakurani inside Desabehera's house. This *ghata* is, later on, carried over to the Thakurani temple traditionally by a married female[14] of Nala Biswanatham's family of Chandrama Sahi on behalf of the Desabehera along with the return procession.

As soon as the message of the ritual offering of *Hajare akhi thiba ghata* is spread, another such *ghata* by Thakurani's *Mausima* family and many *sahanika ghatas* by her devotees are ritually offered and the ritual is performed by Barber priests of the Thakurani temple on the basis of *wardika*. Inside each of these *ghatas*, a small piece of bamboo, a small model of a bow and an umbrella are kept. These *ghatas* are carried by married female devotees[15] to the Thakurani temple along with the return procession. While devotees from different *sahis* mix, at nearest places on the route, with the return procession, the *ghata*-carrier from *Mausima* family gets into the procession when the Thakurani visits her home on her way to the temple. At *Mausima's* home the Thakurani is offered with *arati* and *pana*. While the female devotees participate in the procession making a queue, their male relatives protect them from stampede. The investigator has observed during the Thakurani Yatra in 1985, a participation of more than fifteen thousand female devotees each carrying on head a *ghata* in the return procession.

As the Thakurani reaches her temple the *mukhya ghata* along with the *ghatas* of Kali and Sata Bhaunis and the *Hajare akhi thiba ghata* are placed in the sanctum sanctorum whereas the *ghatas* from devotees are placed under a neem tree in the temple campus. From the *mukhya ghata, phulamanda* is brought out and placed on the head of the *vigraha* of Budhi Santani Thakurani at sanctum sanctorum. People eagerly await to see the Thakurani's *mahatmya* in keeping the flower afresh. The investigator personally has observed at a distance of three feet during 1985 *yatra* and is convinced about the freshness of flower. But before the opening of *mukhya ghata*, which was sealed since the third day of *yatra*, a goat is sacrificed and her blood and head are offered to the Thakurani. The body of goat is taken by Desabehera to offer a non-vegetarian feast to his relatives.

Rituals to ward off Evil Spirits

There is a popular belief among the local people that when the Thakurani is offered with special ritual worship, other supernatural spirits and deities become jealous and create disturbances in the performance of rituals. Sometimes many sorcerers in order to experiment their strength of sorcery make black magic to the Thakurani, Kali or any of the Sata Bhaunis and that affects the *ghata*-carrier. These sorcerers often send *bhuta* and *preta* to create nuisance during the days of arrival and return of the Thakurani. In order to ward off these malevolent spirits, certain preventive rituals are performed which are described below.

Wearing of Rakshas Munda

One of such rituals is performed hereditarily by T. Satyam, a Dera male of Bada Redika Sahi. The ritual involves a tantric *abahana puja* to an image of a *rakshas munda*. It is believed that when wearing this *munda*, he walks ahead of the arrival or return procession of the Thakurani, the evil spirits sent by sorcerers fail to affect the procession.

Carrying a Barakoli Plant

As a defensive measure another ritual is performed by a male member of Appala Swamy's family, staying at Vijaya talkies area. Although they are cobbler by caste, they have a hereditary role in warding off evil spirits during the return procession of the Thakurani. In 1985 *yatra*, Appala Swamy, a sixty-two years old male, had performed the ritual. Appala Swamy, being a priest in the Manikesvari temple, knows how to perform the ritual by himself. He brought a *barakoli* plant, tied to it certain vegetable fruits like *kakudi, kalara, alu*, certain food materials like *bara* and *pakudi*, a broomstick and a cock. He painted his body with black and red spots, and before attending the return procession of the Thakurani, he made a ritual by offering wine, egg and *jhuna dhupa* to the plant into which he had invoked the spirit of Manikesvari by a tantric *abahana mantra*. In the procession he always remained close to the carrier of the Thakurani *ghata*, so that evil spirits could not effect her anyway.

Thakurani's Body-Guard

Putting on various dresses as that of a King, Minister, Warrior, Police Inspector and Constable, a multi-caste group of men move along with the Thakurani during *Sahi Parikrama* and also at the time of the return procession. These people, sent by the Senapati of Kamalbal Sahi, serve as Thakurani's body guards. It is believed that they safeguard the deity from sorcerous effect.

Pita Khechudi Bhoga

Pita Khechudi is a food item given as a presentation from Desabehera to the Thakurani at the time of her return to the temple. The taste of this food item is deliberately made bitter unlike its usual sweetness. The latent intention is that, when other supernatural spirits and deities shall suspect and envy the Thakurani of getting a nice treatment at her paternal house, she can cheat and give a negative explanation showing *Pita Khechudi* as an example. *Pita Khechudi* is offered ritually to them for their confirmation so that they shall not take any malevolent attitude towards Desabehera and the local people.

To summarize, I have focused in this chapter on various sacred performances, which are essentially observed during the Thakurani Yatra. While describing the ritual organization of the Thakurani Yatra, I have highlighted the occasions, purposes and procedures of observance of different sacred performances. I have also narrated the mythical background of observing this *yatra*, which on the whole reflects the pattern of incorporation of the Thakurani as a member of the society. It also substantiates the logic for celebrating the Thakurani Yatra, which through the religious rituals expresses the customary way in which a social phenomenon exists in the local Hindu social organization. This social phenomenon, as such, explains why and how a married daughter is often invited in a traditional procedure to her paternal house where she gets an affectionate treatment during her short stay not only by her kinsmen but also by the villagers and at the end, returns to her mother-in-law's house as per the customs and traditions. Taking the instance of the Thakurani Yatra, we can opine that the religious phenomena of the Hindu civilization reflect and substantiate, at the same time, certain social phenomena.

Apart from justifying that there exists a relationship between religious phenomena and social phenomena, the Thakurani Yatra also substantiates that the ritual organization in an institution of sacred is patterned by and, hence, reflects the local social organization in the Hindu civilization.

In the analysis of the Thakurani Yatra, it has also come out that there exists, at the contextual level, a coexistence and integration not only among the Saiva, Vaishnava and Shakta sectarian traditions but also in between the Oriya and the Telugu cultural traditions of Hindu civilization. In Chapters 4 and 5, which deal with the typological categories and the study of life of the sacred specialists respectively, I have particularly tested and discussed on this finding.

NOTES

1. Janardana Sharma, *Berhampura Thakurani Yatra* (Berhampur: Ganesha Bhandara, 1933), p. 1.
2. *Ibid.*, p. 2.
3. Madras Hindu Religious Endowment Board, Order No. 2355 dated October 8, 1935 (Management File, Index No. 22-G: Office of the Inspector of Endowments, Berhampur, Orissa).
4. Some years ago, people from Kampa *Sahi* requested the organisers of the *yatra* for a *parikrama* of the Thakurani to their sahi but the request was turned down since Kampa Sahi remains outside the village *sarahada* of Berhampur.
5. In 1985, because of ignorance, the Organising Committee of the *yatra* took a decision to make a route chart of everyday's *Sahi Parikrama* to notify the devotees but it could not be worked out since the Thakurani ventilated her displeasure over it by coming to a devotee's body.
6. The drum-beater is an elderly male member of Elada Basavraju's family of Balinkipeta Sahi. The family has been hereditarily playing this role.
7. Under a conspiracy by *devas* (gods), Goddess Durga had to nude herself for killing Mahishasura (buffalo-demon). But as she became conscious of the fact, she got extremely angry upon such betrayal action of *devas* and her face looked like a burning fire. At this stage, Goddess Durga looked like a ferocious woman and so renamed as Jwalamukhi Goddess with a burning face. But in the image, total body of the Goddess is painted red.
8. As per Hindu *Dharma* kicking one's own husband is considered as a great *papa* (sin).
9. In usual life, a Hindu female protrudes her tongue as an instinctual response to the commitment of any sinful mistake.
10. As per Hindu belief, since inception, human world has passed through four *yugas*, namely, *Satya, Treteya, Dwapara* and *Kali*.
11. *Mahabharata* war between Pandavas and Kaurabs dates back to *Dwapara Yuga* of Hindu chronological classification.
12. Literally this refers to a *ghata* having one thousand eyes, but practically the *ghata*, which is unbaked, has numerous small holes throughout its body excepting only the base and the neck.
13. *Sahanika ghata* is a *ghata* offered to Thakurani by the devotees on the basis of a *Sahanika* or vow.
14. As per the local social tradition, carrying of a *ghata* is the work of a female.
15. These married female devotees make fasting throughout the day and take food only after they reach at the Thakurani temple carrying on head their own *Sahanika ghatas* along with return procession during *yatra* and make a *darsana* to the Thakurani.

Plate 3.1: Budhi Santani as worshipped in the Thakurani Temple at Berhampur

Plate 3.2: The Musicians participating the Invitation Procession along with the Desabehera

Plate 3.3: Desabehera (4th from the left) Meets the Mohuri Raja (2nd from left) to get Blessings for Organizing the Thakurani Yatra Successfully

Plate 3.4: A Scene of Pitha-pratistha performed by the Brahmin (first from left) at Desabehera's Home

Plate 3.5: Desabehera's mother receiving the Phulamanda from the Raula woman (first from left)

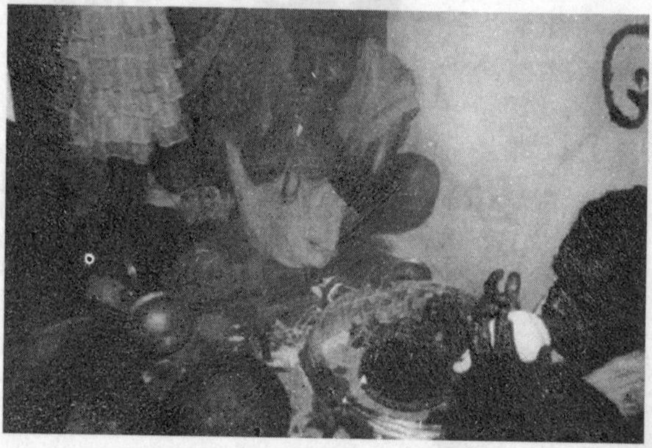

Plate 3.6: A Scene of Changudi Puja performed by the Damla Priests

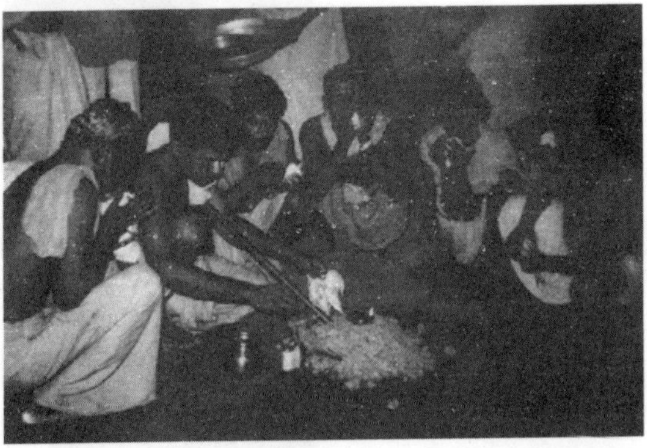

Plate 3.7: Damla Priests are performing the Digabandhana Ritual

Plate 3.8: Potter women, who traditionally prepare the Nine Ghatas and Rukhas for the Desabehera during the Thakurani Yatra

Plate 3.9: A Scene of Desabehera's wife carrying the Mukhya-ghata on head during the Sahi-Parikrama

Plate 3.10: Women carrying on Head the Ghatas of Goddess Kali and the Sata Bhaunis during the Sahi-Parikrama

Plate 3.11: A Scene of Sweeping Type of Action-Oriented Sahanika Sacred Sacrifice

Plate 3.12: A Scene of 'Dandua' Type of Action-Oriented Sahanika Sacred Sacrifice

Plate 3.13: A Devotee in a Tiger besha

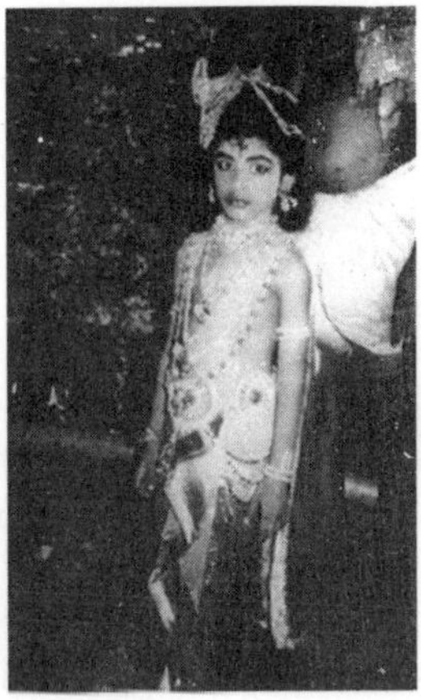

Plate 3.14: A Devotee in the Besha of Lord Krishna

Plate 3.15: A Child in the besha of the Babaji-Rupi Siva

Plate 3.16: A Scene of Non-Sahanika Sacred Sacrifice of Group category

Plate 3.17: Narayana Ratha

Plate 3.18: A Scene of Non-Sahanika Sacred sacrifice of Individual category

Plate 3.19: Arata Ratha

Plate 3.20: Nagarjuna Ratha

Plate 3.21: Boita Ratha

Plate 3.22: Binchana Ratha

Plate 3.23: Damlas making Ritual Worship of the Hajare Akhi Thiba Ghata

Plate 3.24: Some of the Manasika Ghatadharis of the Return Procession

Plate 3.25: The Sliced Head of the Sacrificed Goat is ritually offered to Budhi Santani

Plate 3.26: A Scene of the Placement of the Phulamanda on Budhi Santani's Head at her Temple after the Yatra

Plate 3.27: A Gathering of the Desabehera, his wife, Ghata-Carriers of Kali and Sata Bhaunis, Temple priests and some of the Yatra organizers after the end of the Thakurani Yatra

4

SACRED SPECIALISTS
Their Typology

In the institution of sacred, a number of rituals are performed which provide a scope to the people for participation and involvement at various functional levels. On the basis of such functional involvement, the people can be basically classified as (1) ritual consultants, (2) ritual performers, (3) ritual associates, and (4) ritual observers.

The ritual consultants are those people who act as consultants regarding the performance of rituals. These people are well-versed with the detail procedure of each ritual. The ritual consultants may be further classified as (a) *Shastric*, those who are consultants for Shastric procedure and (b) *Laukik*, those who are consulted for *Laukik* procedure. Among the *Shastric* ritual consultants, a further specialization may be found such as (i) *Vedic* and (ii) *Tantric*, depending upon whether they have mastery over *Vedic* ritual knowledge or *Tantric* procedure of ritual.

The ritual consultants are usually theorists. They are not ritual practitioners. The rituals are rather performed by the ritual performers. On the basis of the procedural difference in ritual performances, the ritual performers are seen to be specialised in *Vedic, Agamic, Tantric* or *Laukik* rituals and, hence, they may be classified accordingly. At the functional level, the ritual performers may further be categorized according to their specific functional role in the performance of rituals.

Ritual associates are persons associated with the performance of rituals directly or indirectly although they themselves do not perform any ritual (A.K. Sinha, 1974). They have peripheral roles without which the completion of a ritual will not be possible. They may not be aware of the details of a ritual but are satisfied with their organizational roles. The florists, the musicians, the ritual-article sellers and the pilgrim-guides are to be regarded as ritual associates (*ibid.*, p. 30). The ritual associates are broadly of two categories, namely (i) professional, those who practise their functional role as a profession and (ii) amateur, those who take up the functional role only during a specific ritual or a festival.

At the time of performance of rituals in a temple, the devotees gather inside the *darsana-griha* to observe the ritual, which is considered by the Hindus to be a pious activity. These devotees are called as 'common observers'. But during the performance of certain rituals, some devotees are regarded as 'special observers' because such rituals are performed by the ritual performers on behalf of these special observers, who are here categorized as the "ritual observers." They form a distinct level in the institution of sacred and, hence, provide a scope to experiment and verify the features of Hindu civilization.

In the institution of sacred at each Hindu sacred centre, these four functional roles are found. While at the sacred centre of universal importance, a clear distinction among these roles are seen and the persons playing the roles too have distinct status, at the sacred centre of local importance, this distinction, however, is not marked. On the other hand, merging of these roles in a single person may be observed here.

Among the four functional categories of people involved in the institution of sacred, the ritual observers do not earn for their livelihood from their functional role whereas the ritual consultants, the ritual performers and the ritual associates make a primary or a secondary income for their living from their direct or indirect participation in the rituals. These latter three categories of persons, who earn their livelihood by being involved, directly or indirectly, in the sacred performances, are commonly termed as the sacred specialists.

On the other hand, the ritual observers are termed as the sacred sacrificers since they always make certain sacrifices to the deities while observing the rituals. In this chapter, I have made a discussion on the typological variation of only the sacred specialists whereas a similar analysis on the sacred sacrificers has been made in Chapter 6.

Typological Variation of Sacred Specialists at the Level of Functional Role

In the sacred performances at Budhi Santani Thakurani Temple of Berhampur, a group of eight families of Bhandari caste officiate as the ritual performers. They are called as the "Thakurani Mandira Pujari". The temple has been declared as the property of these families by the Madras Hindu Religious Endowment Board's order No. 2355-A dated 8-10-1935. For the smooth officiation of the sacred performances, to each family certain days have been assigned for performing all the rituals at the temple, and correspondingly, the family owns the entire income during these days. The days of assignment of rituals rotate after two months. All these *pujari* families stay near the temple and exhibit a keen solidarity among them. These *pujaris* perform the daily rituals and also the rituals for the special observers at the temple.

In the society these *pujaris* enjoy a separate status. At the time of the Thakurani Yatra they perform the rituals related to various sacred sacrifices done by the devotees. The daily rituals at the Utsav Mandira during the Thakurani Yatra are performed by persons belonging to Damla caste. For the purpose of the Thakurani Yatra, two Damla families, one from Pitala village and the other from Ambapua village, are invited traditionally. They have their hereditary roles and both the families are priestly families in the Thakurani temple of their own village. These Damlas at the time of the *yatra* draw maximum respect from all since they are the Utsav Mandira *pujaris*. While the Thakurani Mandira *Pujaris* follow the agamic procedure of rituals, the Utsav Mandira *pujaris* tantrically perform the rituals entitled for them.

The Bhandaris and the Damlas, however, are not entrusted to perform the *Pitha-Pratistha* ritual because they do not have the specialised knowledge in the Vedic procedure of observing rituals. The *Pitha-Pratistha* ritual is done in Vedic way, and a Brahmin *purohita* performs it.

All the three ritual performers, the Bhandaris, the Damlas and the Brahmin, are experts in their own field of specialisation. Whenever any dispute arises regarding the performance of a ritual or any clarification is needed by a devotee with reference to any ritual offerings, the chief Bhandari *pujari* and the chief Damla *pujari* act as ritual consultants, concerning the agamic procedure or the tantric procedure respectively. Apart from them, a Kamma Brahmin named as the *Jyotisha*, an expert in astrology, is consulted by the organizers of the *yatra* with respect to denoting the auspicious time period for the performance of certain rituals. He is especially consulted to find out the auspicious time period and the day for the *Subhakhunti Sthapana*, for the *Barana Puja*, for the reception and the return of the Thakurani, on the occasion of the Thakurani Yatra.

The ritual associates can be classified on the basis of their nature of involvement in the ritual. Among them we may include the Mandira Jhadudar, the florists, the *puja* material sellers, the messenger, the carrier of the *Subhakhunti*, the trumpet player, the drumbeater, the flute player, the conchshell blower, the *changudi* supplier, the *phulamanda* supplier, the *ghata* and *rukha* supplier, the *ghata* and *rukha* painter and the *manasika besa* painter.

Mandira Jhadudari is entrusted hereditarily to a specific family of Hadi caste in the Dhanamera Sahi settled at the western outskirt of the Berhampur Sarahada. The head male member of the family comes to the Thakurani Mandira everyday early in the morning and cleans the *Mandira-agana*. He is not permitted to enter into the *darsana-griha* and the *garbha-griha* for this purpose because he is considered to be an untouchable. The adult males of the same family also perform the function of messenger and the drum-beater at the time of Thakurani Yatra. Likewise, the work of supplying *ghata* and *rukha*, the work of providing *phulamanda*, the duty of *pahadapaka* and the duty to supply the *changudi* and *Subhakhunti* are entrusted hereditarily to a specific family of Kumbhara, Raula, Dhoba and Medri castes of Berhampur respectively. Similarly, the function of the flute-player and the conch-shell blower is done by a Raula family whereas a Medri family acts as the trumpet-player. The specific functional participation of the ritual associates in the ritual organization of the Sacred Complex of the Budhi Santani coincides with their traditional caste occupations as expressed in the arena of the local social organisation. The ritual organisation, thus, involves people according to their traditional caste occupation. But this principle has not been adopted as a binding one.

The ritual associates are not found to be referred with certain classificatory names. They are identified by their caste name and the locality in which they stay. For example, when one enquires about the ritual associate who supplies the *ghatas* and the *rukhas*, the reply from the Desabehera, the patron of the *yatra*, will be that the Kumbhara *ghara* of Pankilapalli is the supplier. When caste and the locality identification do not seem to be sufficient, at that time the family name is utilized. Thus, people say that the Prusti *ghara* of Aga Sahi is the carrier of *Subhakhunti*.

The ritual associates can, therefore, be classified on the basis of caste identity, locality identity and also family identity. Moreover, they can be categorized as those attached to the institution of temple and those having activities in the institution of *yatra*. The florists and the *puja* material sellers attached to the temple have their permanent shops. Some of the owners of these shops belong to the Mandira *pujari*, i.e., Bhandari community whereas others belong to the Brahmins and the Raulas. At the time of *yatra*, the Deras and the Kumutis set up their shops for selling *puja* materials whereas the Raulas have the monopoly over selling the flowers. During the *yatra*, the Bhandaris prefer to act as ritual performers since they have a greater income in this practice than by selling *puja* materials. Some of the Bhandaris distribute the vermillion of the Thakurani to the ritual observers and practise it as a source of income.

There are also ritual associates whose caste occupation is quite different from their ritual roles in the *yatra*. The Devangas at Berhampur, for example, are weavers by profession but they are the carriers of the *Dharma Jhanda*, the *Hajare akhi thiba ghata* and the *ghatas* of the goddesses and apart from it, their Kularaja, the Desabehera, invites Budhi Santani Thakurani for the purpose of *yatra*. These ritual roles are not synonymous to their weaving occupation. Similarly, a Chamara family, whose profession is to produce leather materials, carries a big branch of *barakoli* plant along with the return procession of the Thakurani at the end of the *yatra*. The work of painting the *ghatas* and the *besha-dharis* is also not a caste-ridden occupation. These roles during the *yatra* are done by the ritual associates belonging to different castes. Thus, the *ghata*-painters are Brahmins whereas the *besha*-painters are not necessarily Brahmins. They may be Brahmins, Barbers, Khandayats, Karans and Doluas.

One of the important ritual associates at the time of Thakurani Yatra are the *dootas* of Thakurani. These *dootas* act as the body-guards of the goddesses during the *Sahi-Parikrama* and protect them from the *tantric* effect of the *tantrists* who often visit the *yatra* and experiment their *tantric* learning. These *dootas* are traditionally the inhabitants of Kamalbal Sahi. They are mainly Deras but the Kumutis and the Khaduras also participate along with them.

The ritual associate who acts as the carrier of the *Subhakhunti* is a Tulabhina by caste. His caste profession is to prepare *takia, rejai* and *seja* but his ritual role has nothing to do with this.

Typological Variation of Sacred Specialists on the basis of Linguistic Diversity and Sectarian Division

Apart from the functional role-based differentiation, the sacred specialists may also be classified on the basis of linguistic diversity and sectarian division. Linguistically, all the sacred specialists may be categorized as (1) either Oriya-speaking or (2) Telugu-speaking. Thus, the sacred specialists from Devanga, Chamara, and the Kumuti communities are Telugu-speaking whereas all others are Oriya-speaking.

All the sacred specialists are found to be Hindus but belonging to different sects. Thus, the Thakurani Mandira *pujaris* are Vaishnavas, the *Phulamanda* supplier is a Saivite, the *ghata* suppliers are Vaishnavites but the *ghata carriers* are Lingayats. The *subha-khunti* carrier, the *barakoli dala* carrier, the *changudi* supplier and the Utsav Mandira *pujaris*, on the other hand, are Shaktas.

To summarise, I have found that the Sacred Complex of Budhi Santani exhibits an intermediary stage, as regards the typological classification of the sacred specialists, between the two extremes, i.e. the sacred complex of universal importance, and the sacred complex of local importance. Thus, while in former case, there exists a distinct classification of sacred specialists into three types such as ritual consultants, ritual performers and ritual associates and in latter case, there is a total blending of these three typological categories in one person, in the case of the Sacred Complex of Budhi Santani, I have observed that the sacred specialists can be classified, but not distinctly due to merging, into ritual consultants, ritual performers and ritual associates.

In the analysis of the sacred specialists, I have also found that the functional roles of the sacred specialists generally, but not necessarily, coincide with the occupational roles of their own castes in the local Hindu social organization.

As regards the typological classification, this study brings out that the sacred specialists can be discriminated on the bases of caste, language, sect and functional role. But because of their participation in the institution of sacred, which generates a sense of co-operation and integration among them, they cut across all these discriminations. However, the analysis in this chapter does not speak about the level of cultural integration and compromise which exists among the sacred specialists by their involvement in the institution of sacred for a long time. This has been discussed in the next chapter, which focuses on the style of life of the sacred specialists.

5

SACRED SPECIALISTS
Their Style of Life

In the previous chapter, we have discussed that there exist a number of differentiations, on the basis of caste, language, sect and functional role in the institution of sacred, among the sacred specialists of the Sacred Complex of Budhi Santani. And irrespective of all these differentiations, they are found to make a primary or secondary income by their participation, directly or indirectly, in various sacred performances. However, none of them lives totally on their earnings made from these sacred performances. During the non-*palidinas*, therefore, they earn by pursuing their traditional caste occupations or by doing services, which cut across the caste rigidity. In these days, they maintain the cultural identity of their own communities in their daily life. But during the *palidinas*, when they perform their hereditary sacred performances as the *sevakas* of Budhi Santani Thakurani, their style of life is basically moulded by the institution of sacred into a specific pattern, which can be self-identified as 'Sevaka Culture'. This chapter discusses about the patterned style of life of the sacred specialists.

Settlement and Residence

All the sacred specialists, irrespective of their differences in terms of caste, occupation and role in the sacred performances, live in a linear pattern of settlement. Their houses, which face the *sahi* road, include a frontyard and two to five rooms, arranged in a linear fashion. From the point of view of the structure of house, these sacred specialists may be divided into two broad categories. The *pujaris*, Thakurani *mandira*, the *ghata*-carriers, the carrier of *subhakhunti*, the Mandira *Jhadudar*, the Utsav Mandira *pujaris*, the painters of Thakurani *ghata*, the *Dharma Jhanda* carriers and the flute-player form one category of sacred specialists who have houses made of brick and cement. The roofs of their houses are of asbestos or concrete type. They are also economically richer than the other categories of sacred specialists, which include the trumpet player, the supplier of Thakurani *ghata* and the *pahada pakali*. The houses of the latter categories are thatched and constructed by brick and mud.

On the basis of the pattern of residential location, the sacred specialists may be of three categories, those having residences around the boundary of the Thakurani Mandira, those having residences in the locality of their own community and those whose residences are scattered in multi-ethnic localities. In the first category are the sellers of *puja* materials and the Thakurani Mandira *pujaris*, who reside in the close proximity of the *mandira*. They live in Thakurani Mandira Sahi, Khaspa Sahi and Jeora Sahi.

Most of the sacred specialists fall under the second category. They live in their respective areas of community dominance. For instance, the Utsav Mandira *pujaris* live in Damla Sahi of Ambapura village, the Mandira *jhadudars* and drum-beaters stay in Dhanamera Sahi, the trumpet players and *changudi* supplier live in Medri Sahi, the *ghata* supplier resides in Kumbhara Sahi of Pankilapalli village and the *ghata* carriers live in various *sahis* where the people of their own community are mostly concentrated.

Again, the sacred specialists like the carrier of *subhakhunti*, the *pahada pakalis*, the *jangam*, the *purohita*, the *manasika besha* painters, the *ghata* painters, the flute-player and the carrier of *barakoli-dala* may be grouped under the third category. All of these sacred specialists live in multi-ethnic *sahis*. For instance, the carrier of *subhakhunti* stays in Aga Sahi and belongs to Tulabhina community, which has only two families in that *sahi*. Rest of the eighty-seven families of Aga Sahi belong to the Kumutis, Deras, Sunaris, Doluas and Karanas. Similarly, the *purohita* who performs the *yajna* of *pitha* at Desabehera's house lives in Jena Sahi. In this *sahi*, there are only four Brahmin families whereas the rest twenty-eight families belong to the Teli, Dalua and Sunari communities.

In most cases the sacred specialists have retained their ancestral houses. Among them, the Brahmins, Deras, Tulabhinas, Bhandaris, Damlas, Chamaras, Raulas and Hadis have remodelled their houses with modern equipments whereas the Medris and Kumbharas have not remodelled their houses.

Family and Kinship

As regards their family life, the sacred specialists of Berhampur are more or less homogeneous. For instance, all the sacred specialists lead a patriarchal and patrilineal family life, where joking and avoidance relationship between affines are permitted. The sacred specialists, irrespective of their caste and language, have preserved their traditional custom of inheritance of parental property. In all cases, it is only the sons who have a right over the parental property. Apart from a Jyesthansa given to the eldest son, the rest is shared equally by the sons. Among all the sacred specialists, father is regarded as the headman of the family and only after his death, the eldest male member, *suo motu*, succeeds him. Structurally, lineal extended type of family is more prevalent among them. None of them has a mixed extended type of family. The younger generation of the sacred specialists show an inclination towards nuclear type of family life.

At the kinship level, the sacred specialists of Berhampur too may be divided into two categories, those having *gotra* and family name and those having only *gotra*. In the first category, fall the Devangas, Damla, Medris and Kamma Brahmins. These are originally Telugu-speaking communities who have migrated to Berhampur from various parts of Andhra Pradesh. They have retained their traditional kinship divisions. However, the sacred specialists of this category may be further classified into two groups, those who use family name but not surname and those who use surname but not family name. The Devangas, Medris and Kamma Brahmins may be included in the former group whereas the Damlas may belong to the latter group. The Damlas have only one *gotra*, i.e. Nageswara, which is divided into family names such as Udu, Ipili, Durgasi and Uditandri but currently none of the Damla sacred specialists use these family names. Instead, only one surname, i.e. Patra is in vogue among them. This change is probably due to the influence of Oriya cultural tradition where the use of surname, and not family name, is the practice.

On the other hand, the Bhandaris, Raulas, Tulabhinas, Hadis and Daluas, who form the second category, have kinship divisions in the form of *gotra* and not family names. Furthermore, they use surnames like other Oriya-speaking communities.

To sum up, in their family and kinship life, the sacred specialists exhibit an innate combination and compromise of two cultural traditions, Telugu and Oriya.

Food and Drinks

Despite differences in caste, language, occupation and also cultural tradition, a number of similarities are noticed in the foods and drinks among the sacred specialists. For instance, *bhata, dali* and a vegetable curry are staple food of all the sacred specialists. Similarly, all of them, at present, have the practice of taking tea everyday in the morning. But apart from this, distinct differences in the habit of food and drink are also marked among them. Thus, in their food habit they may have three broad groups, such as completely vegetarian, restricted vegetarian and non-vegetarian. Among the sacred specialists of Berhampur, the Jyotisha, a Kamma Brahmin, and the Lingadhari Devangas are completely vegetarian. Among other sacred specialists, all of whom are non-Brahmins, the Daulas, Kumbharas, Hadis, Medris, Damlas, non-Lingadhari Devangas, Tulabhinas, and Bhandaris from the third group. They consume both vegetarian and non-vegetarian food items. Fish, egg, mutton and chicken are consumed by all of them. The Raulas come under the second group. Apart from their role in the Thakurani Yatra, they serve as *pujakas* in Siva temples of Berhampur. When they have their *pali-dinas* as the *pujakas*, they do not eat non-vegetarian foods. However, in other days they consume fish and mutton but not egg or chicken.

Consumption of liquor is prohibited among most of the sacred specialists of Berhampur. Its practice is limited to the low caste sacred specialists like the Hadis and Medris. With the impact of modern education, the younger generation among the Medris and Hadis are, however, noticed to dislike the consumption of liquor. As mentioned earlier, in taking tea early in the morning, the sacred specialists cut across all barriers of language, caste, profession and sect. The sacred specialists of Tulabhina, Medri and Hadi castes, who were earlier in the habit of drinking *torani* in the morning, have also changed this habit and instead, they take tea. A change from vegetarian to non-vegetarian food habit is marked among the sacred specialists of Berhampur. For instance, among the Devangas, this change may be due to the gradual reduction in the practice of wearing *lingas* whereas among others, it may be mostly owing to the increase in purchasing capacity, the ascending desire to celebrate festive occasions with non-vegetarian food and/or the consequent increase in the availability of non-vegetarian food materials in the market.

Dress and Dialect

The sacred specialists of Berhampur make a distinction, in some way or the other, in the use of dress between the occasion of performing rituals and not performing rituals. The dress, which is used or which has been used for non-ritual activities, is not put on for performing a ritual. In their nature of use of dresses for ritual performances, the sacred specialists may be distinguished as of two categories, those who have a separate dress-type and those who do not have. The sacred specialists of Bhandari, Raula, Tulabhina and Damla communities are *pujakas* in different temples at Berhampur. While performing rituals in their respective temples, they wear a yellow or red silken *dhoti* and keep a yellow or red silken *chaddar* or a towel on their shoulder. The sacred specialists of Kamma Brahmin, Devanga and Dalua communities also put on silken *dhoti* and a *chaddar* while performing rituals in their homes. However, the sacred specialists of Medri, Hadi and Kumbhara communities, who fall under the second category, do not have a separate dress like silken *dhoti* and *chaddar* for performing rituals. On the occasion of ritual performances, they use to wear a white, cotton *dhoti* which is washed and thereafter used for non-ritual purposes. All the sacred specialists, irrespective of caste, language and sectarian differences, do not wear any footwear when they perform rituals.

When the sacred specialists do not perform any ritual, they put on dresses of their own choice. White, cotton *dhoti* and a towel on shoulder are their traditional dresses when they are at home. Sacred specialists of lower castes, namely Hadi and Medri sometimes do not keep a towel. The Bhandari, Damla, Raula and Tulabhina sacred specialists often tie the towel round their waists. When the sacred specialists go out they wear a shirt along with a *dhoti*. During the non-ritual occasions, a change in the style of dress is also noticed among them. In the younger generation, modern dresses like pant, shirt and shoes have become a fashion.

A similar change in dress is also marked among the females. The traditional style of putting on *saree* and blouse is not followed by the unmarried girls who wear *chudidar* or *salwar* and *punjabi*, frocks or a *saya* and blouse. In their style of wearing *saree*, the women may be classified into two categories, those who have *kunchi* and those who do not have *kunchi*. *Kunchi*, being a Telugu cultural tradition, is found among the women of Kumbhara, Devanga and Kamma Brahmin communities. They form the first category whereas women among the Tulabhinas, Raulas, Hadis, Daluas and Bhandaris do not have *kunchi* while wearing *sarees*. The women among the Medris and Damlas, who were earlier Telugu-speakers but now have adopted Oriya cultural tradition, also do not keep *kunchi* while putting on a *saree*. However, irrespective of the differences in their dress pattern, the women of all these communities smear vermillion on forehead and wear toe ring, ear-ring and a *pusta* to identify their marital status.

The sacred specialists of Berhampur may also be divided in the practice of having body markings. Thus, the sacred specialists among the Bhandari, Tulabhina and Damla communities anoint vermillion on forehead after taking bath, whereas those among the Devanga, Kamma Brahmin and Raula communities, smear sandal paste on forehead, arms and chest after the bath. On the other hand, body marking as a practice is not seen among the sacred specialists of Hadi, Medri, Kumbhara and Dalua communities.

The sacred specialists of Berhampur originally belong to two linguistic categories, Telugu and Oriya. The Devangas, Kamma Brahmins and Kumbharas, who claim to have migrated from Andhra Pradesh, speak Telugu among their kinsmen and family members. The sacred specialists of these three communities often talk in Telugu among themselves but in their interaction with other sacred specialists, they converse in Oriya language. Among the other sacred specialists, Raulas, Tulabhinas, Bhandaris, Oriya Brahmins, Hadis and Daluas trace their linguistic origin back to Oriya language. They now use Oriya both as their script and spoken language while interacting with their kinsmen, pilgrims and other sacred specialists. However, the sacred specialists of Damla and Odia Medri communities, who claim to have migrated long ago from Andhra Pradesh, now have totally adopted the Oriya language as their medium of communication among kinsmen and others. Although the sacred specialists have diverse linguistic origin, all of them can speak fluently the Ganjam dialect of Oriya language.

Thus the sacred specialists of Berhampur are found to be at a compromising stage. While they have retained some features of their traditional style of dress, they are also marked to have common consciousness in adopting the modern style of dress. This is particularly noticed among the younger generation. Such compromising and integrational characters of the sacred specialists are again marked in their use of language towards the pilgrims and also among themselves.

Occupation and Income

In the context of their occupation and income, the sacred specialists of

Berhampur exhibit heterogeneity. Most of them have adhered to their respective caste-based occupations as the primary source of income. Thus, as regards the primary occupation, the Kumbhara sacred specialist is a pot-maker, Odia Medri sacred specialist is a basket-maker, Hadi sacred specialist is a scavenger in the Berhampur Municipality, Oriya Brahmin sacred specialist is a *pujaka* in a local Jagannath temple, Damla sacred specialist is a *pujaka* in a village goddess temple, Kamma Brahmin sacred specialist is a *jyotisha*, Dhoba sacred specialist is a washerman and the Raula sacred specialist is a *pujaka* in a Siva temple. The sacred specialists, for whom their caste occupation is not a primary source of income, belong to Oriya Brahmin, Damla, Devanga, Bhandari, Tulabhina and Dalua communities. For instance, although the Dalua is a traditional warrior and agricultural community, the sacred specialists from this community now practice grocery business as their primary occupation. Similarly, the Bhandari is a barber community but for the Bhandari sacred specialists, priesthood in the Budhi Santani Thakurani temple at Berhampur is the primary occupation. The sacred specialists of Tulabhina, a cotton-carding community, primarily earn as *pujakas* in a mother goddess temple. The caste occupation of Devanga community is weaving but most of the sacred specialists of this community have resorted to different kinds of business as their primary source of income. Moreover, contrary to his own caste-occupation, an Oriya Brahmin sacred specialist is found to practise the selling of *puja* materials near the Budhi Santani Thakurani temple as his primary occupation.

While for some of the Damla sacred specialists the caste occupation is their primary source of living, for others, who practise business or work as government or private servants, it is a subsidiary source of income.

Most of the sacred specialists of Berhampur do not completely depend upon their primary occupation for their living. Some of them are also engaged with subsidiary occupations. For instance, some Bhandari *pujakas* have their own shops to sell sacred materials near the Budhi Santani temple. They especially sit in the shops when they do not have *pali-dinas*. During the *pali-dinas* they engage some of their family members or kinsmen to sit in the shop. Some other Bhandari *pujakas* have constructed *prabhas* of different deities like Budhi Santani, Kali and Sapa-Sapuanai. They send these *prabhas*, on hire, for exhibition during various Thakurani Yatras celebrated at different villages. One of the Bhandari *pujakas* also construct images of Ganesh and Saraswati and by selling these images he makes a subsidiary income during

Ganesh *puja* and Saraswati *puja*. An elderly Bhandari *pujaka* has an electronic shop and a *chitralaya* of his own, managed by himself and his sons. Recently he has also temporarily joined in a government service. Like the Bhandari *pujakas*, the Odia Medri sacred specialists, who are adept in music, make a subsidiary income by playing musical instruments when hired by other communities for various festive occasions, especially marriage. The Raula sacred specialists, on the other hand, sell flowers and flower garlands in the local market or go on hire to blow their conch-shell during marriage ceremonies. As such, the Sacred Complex of Budhi Santani of Berhampur provides a primary source of income to the Bhandari *pujakas* and the sacred specialists who sell sacred materials near the Thakurani temple. But for others, this sacred complex is a subsidiary source of income.

Hereditary occupation, primary or secondary, are followed by most of the sacred specialists. However, in the younger generation, many cases are noticed regarding change of occupation. Those, who do not practise their hereditary occupation, are either employed in government services or have undertaken a business.

Thus, irrespective of differences in caste, language, sect and occupation, the sacred specialists, who continue their hereditary occupations, exhibit a distinct style of life. However, in the younger generation, a gradual adoption of new occupations is also marked.

Caste and Caste Council

Since the Independence of India, a number of factors like democratic set-up of government, the Constitution of India, development in science and technology, rapid industrialisation and urbanisation have affected and caused various changes in different aspects of the traditional caste-based living style of the people in general and the sacred specialists in particular. The impact of these factors is also easily noticeable in the life of the sacred specialists of Berhampur, particularly in their own caste and caste council.

All the sacred specialists claim that the people of their own caste have settled at Berhampur for more than two hundred years. Some of these sacred specialists are even unable to speak about the origin and migration history of their own caste whereas those of Devanga, Dalua and Kalinga Kumuti community are well-versed with it. Against all post-Independence factors which have been destabilising the caste-ridden style of life, the caste-men of most of the sacred specialists have expressed a common negative consciousness and they have acted to increase the strength of their caste solidarity. One way of this expression is the continued existence of their caste council, either in the traditional pattern or in a restructured way.

Only except the Kamma Brahmin and Oriya Brahmin sacred specialists, who do not have a caste council but are, *suo motu*, conservative in their style of life, all other sacred specialists have their own caste council in which they are either members or office bearers. On the level of modification of caste council, the sacred specialists of Berhampur may be classified into three categories, those who have preserved their traditional caste council in totality, those who have entirely modernised their caste council and those who have partly modernised their caste council. In the first category, the Devanga, Tulabhina, Damla and Telugu Kumbhara sacred specialists are included. The posts in their caste council are hereditary and bear traditional names. For instance, among the Devangas, the post-bearers are named as Senapati at *sahi* level and Desabehera at community level; among the Damlas, they are named as Behera at village level and Dalabehera at community level; among the Tulabhinas, they are called Behera and Bhaḷabhai at Taluka level and among the Telugu Kumbharas, they are named as Adhikari at village level and Senapati at community level. In the second category, Dalua and Bhandari sacred specialists are included. The office-bearers in their caste council are democratically elected and they do not have traditional naming. For instance, among the Bhandaris, the Office bearers are called as Sabhapati, Upa-Sabhapati and Kosadhaksha at Mandala, Zilla and Pradesh levels. The office-bearers among the Daluas are named as President, Vice-President, Secretary and Treasurers at village, regional and community levels. The caste council among the Raulas, Odia Medris and Hadis has partially modernised. Among them, the Hadis have preserved the traditional naming of their office-bearers, Behera and Choudhury, but they have transformed these posts, which were earlier hereditary, as elected posts. On the other hand, the Raulas and Odia Medris have combined the traditional as well as modern system. Thus, among the Odia Medris, the office-bearers, at *sahi* level are hereditary and they are named as Behera and Prusti whereas at Zilla level, they are named as Sabhapati, Upa-Sabhapati and Kosadhaksha, all of whom are democratically elected. The Odia Medris, thus, exhibit a horizontal merging of traditional and modern system of the caste council. In contradiction to them, the Raulas exhibit a vertical merging of the two systems. Thus, in their caste council at village level, both Behera, a traditional and hereditary office-bearer and President, a modern and elected office-bearer, jointly operate. Similarly at the community level, Dala-Behera, a traditional and hereditary office-bearer and President, a modern and elected office-bearer, officiate.

The above cases speak about the structural modification of the caste councils. Certain modifications at their functional level have also occurred. Among the castes, who have preserved the traditional form of caste council in totality, the caste council has a functional operation only on the aspects of social control and marriage. In those castes, who have partly modernised their caste council, the functional operation touches the field of social reformation along with marriage and social control. Among the castes, who have totally modernised their caste council, the functional operation occurs on the fields of social control, marriage, social reformation and social welfare. Thus, with the impact of modernizing factors, the castes are found to make their caste council an institution of welfare along with social control.

Religious Life

The sacred specialists of Budhi Santani of Berhampur also exhibit a distinct style in their religious life. For instance, although they belong to different sects and are associated with different sacred performances all of them worship the mother goddesses as their *istadevis*. All these goddesses have their sacred centres, which are situated in the Ganjam district. These sacred centres are popular either at local or regional level. However, at their homes, the sacred specialists exhibit homogeneity in worshipping the deities of all the three major sects, Saiva, Vaishnava and Shakta of Hindu religion. The most popular deities propitiated among them are Jagannath, Krishna, Siva, Kali, Durga, Laxmi, Nrushinhanath, Parvati, Tara-Tarini, Budhi Santani, Bhairavi and Narayana. The sacred specialists of Berhampur commonly worship these deities, which are either of local, regional, or universal importance.

The sacred specialists are marked not to make any discrimination on sectarian basis while propitiating the deities at their homes. They are also found not to make this discrimination while visiting different sacred centres. Visiting the sacred centres is a part and parcel of the style of life of all the sacred specialists who are noticed to have visited most of the locally popular sacred centres in Ganjam district among which the sacred centres of the deities Bhairavi at Mantridi, Ganesh at Panchama, Tara-Tarini near Purushottampur, Bagdevi at Kulada, Narayani near

Khallikote, Budhi Santani at Berhampur, Mohuri Kalua near Mohuri Gada, Gokarneswara at Sukunda, Sakaleswara at Bhabinipur and Ishanaeswara at Golanthara are a few. Of the sacred centres of regional or universal importance, the Jagannath temple at Puri, Lingaraj temple at Bhubaneswar, Nrusinhanath temple at Simanchalam are visited by most of the sacred specialists. Among them, only the Kalinga Kumuti sacred specialist has visited the Dwadasa Jyotirlingas and Chaturdhamas. Similarly, the sacred centre of goddess Kamakshi in Assam has been visited by only one Bhandari sacred specialist. The Tirupati temple has been visited by one Dalua sacred specialist. Thus, mostly the sacred specialists of Budhi Santani of Berhampur visit the sacred centres of the Kalinga civilizational region.

The visit of the sacred specialists to different sacred centres is either in connection with marriage, *balapaka* ceremony, *sraddha* or a *darsana* of the concerned deity. A visit to sacred centres in connection with marriage, *balapaka* ceremony or *darsana* is a practice among all the sacred specialists of Budhi Santani of Berhampur. It is only the Kalinga Kumuti sacred specialist who visits the Jagannath temple of Puri every year to perform the *sraddha* ritual of his father. The visit to sacred centres by the sacred specialists may also be categorised as of three types, daily, more than once and only once.

Thakurani Yatras of different Thakuranis like Budhi Santani, Narayani, Gariamma, Bandeswari, Bagdevi, and Brahmanidevi are celebrated at many places of Ganjam and Phulbani districts of Orissa. A visit to the Thakurani Yatras either as a ritual performer or as a ritual observer is a general practice among the sacred specialists of Budhi Santani of Berhampur.

Daily Life

The daily life of the sacred specialists of Budhi Santani of Berhampur revolves round their respective occupational engagements. Among them, who work as *pujakas* in a temple, a homogeneity in the daily life is noticed. In this category, the sacred specialists of Bhandari, Damla, Raula and Tulabhina communities may be included. All of them leave their bed early in the morning and complete the *nityakarmas* prior to 5 a.m. Then they take bath, put on the priestly dress and go to their respective temples where they serve as *pujakas*. They perform the daily rituals at the temple and at the same time, they also perform rituals for the devotees who make offerings to the deity. They take their food in the temple only after ritually offering food to the deity.

In the afternoon, after the *Anna Bhoga* ritual, the deity takes rest and during this time, the *pujakas* either take rest or remain engaged with household or subsidiary occupational works. For instance, the Raula, Tulabhina and some of the Bhandari *pujakas* either take rest or do household works whereas the Damla *pujaka* of Pitala work as a weaver and some of the Bhandari *pujakas* make goddess images. At night, they perform *Pahada Bhoga* for the deity at the temple and after making arrangement for the rest of the deity, they come to home to sleep.

The sacred specialists, who sell flowers and other *puja* materials, also get up early in the morning and after finishing *nityakarmas* and bathing they open their shops. Their shops remain open till the temple gets closed in the night. During this time, they manage among their family members to sit in the shop for selling the *puja* materials and they go one after another to take food at home. All of sacred specialists of this category have the photograph of Budhi Santani in their shop. They offer *dhupa arati* to her in the morning after opening the shop and again in the evening.

The *jhadudar*, who is a sacred specialist from Hadi community, of Budhi Santani temple of Berhampur also gets up from his bed and finishes *nityakarma* and bathing prior to 5 a.m. Then, he comes to the temple to clean its precincts, which he completes within an hour. Then he attends to municipality duty up to 11 a.m. After coming home he again takes bath and then consumes the food prepared for the lunch.

In the afternoon he again goes for Municipality duty and then goes to the temple to clean the precincts. He comes back to home by 6 p.m. and then, remains engaged with household works. Before retiring to the bed, occasionally he reads *Puran* in the night.

The daily life of all other sacred specialists is designed to suit to their own non-religious occupations. This feature is also noticed in the younger generation among the *pujakas* who do not continue their traditional sacred occupations. However, it does not take long to notice that irrespective of the difference in their occupations, homogeneity to some extent, is also clearly visible in their daily routine. For instance, among all these sacred specialists, the daily routine includes three phases of engagements. The first phase, which starts from early morning to 9 a.m., includes activities like completion of *nityakarmas*, bathing, *puja* to household deities and breakfast. In case of Kalinga Kumuti sacred specialist this phase also includes a visit to local temples for a *darsana* of the deities, especially Budhi Santani and Tirupati Balaji. The middle phase includes two shifts of occupational engagement interspersed with lunch break and rest for one or two hours. This phase usually continues from 9 a.m. to 9 p.m. whereafter the last phase starts. The last phase includes dinner and retirement to bed. It may also include, as in the case of a Damla sacred specialist, a *darsana* of deity in its temple.

Life Cycle Rituals

In the observance of life cycle rituals, the sacred specialists of Budhi Santani of Berhampur are found to have followed the traditions and customs of their own caste. Since the people of different castes of Berhampur are noticed to follow a similar pattern of observing the life cycle rituals, therefore, a distinct homogeneity is marked with regard to the observance of the life cycle rituals among the sacred specialists. For instance, it is a common practice with all the sacred specialists that, for the delivery of their first issue, their wives are invited to their respective parental houses in the seventh month of pregnancy. However, for the successive deliveries they may or may not be invited to their parental houses. For a smooth delivery of their wives, the *pujakas*, florists, ritual material sellers and the *jhadudars* make a *puja* near the Budhi Santani Thakurani. Sometimes, for this, they observe *Khandadhuapani* ritual near Budhi Santani and offer *Khandadhuapani* to their women who drink it. This practice is not found among other sacred specialists who, instead, make *manasikas* for this purposes near their own *istadevis*. In these cases, the *manasika* is noticed to be a vow to observe *balapaka* ritual, at the sacred centre of the concerned deity, for the child for whom the manasika is made.

The sacred specialists, irrespective of their differences in caste, language, sect and occupation, follow certain prenatal as well as post-natal restrictions with regard to food, observance of religious rituals and social intercourse. Thus, restrictions for a visit to burial ground, for consumption of dry fish prior to birth and restrictions to cook food, to observe religious festivals, to enter into sacred centres and to consume dry fish till the observance of purgatory ritual after birth are common practices among all the sacred specialists. They also share a common consciousness over the observance of post-natal rituals like *Panchuati* and *Athuari* related to protecting their newly born babies from the evil impact of the spirit, *Sathi*. Birth pollution is observed by the parents for twenty-one days except those who belong to Medri and Dalua communities. The latter observe it for twelve days.

The sacred specialists further exhibit commonness in celebrating the *ekoisia* or name giving ceremony for their babies on the twenty-first day after delivery. All of them, except the *subhakhunti* carrier, invite a Brahmin *purohita* to observe the *ekoisia* ritual at the end of which the *purohita* prepares a *jataka* for the baby and finds out a name for it as per its *jataka*. While selecting a name for the baby, the sacred specialists are also found to choose the names of gods and goddesses. In case of the *subhakhunti* carrier, who belong to Tulabhina community, *jataka* for the baby is not made and Brahmin *purohita* is not invited for *ekoisia* ritual. The *ekoisia* is observed with the performance of a ritual by the parents of the baby near their family deity, at the end of which, a name is given to the baby by the headman of the family.

It is a hereditary practice with all the sacred specialists of Budhi Santani of Berhampur to observe *balapaka* ceremony of their babies at one or more sacred centres. Usually, this ceremony is observed at the nearby temple of their *istadevis*. Apart from this, at times this ceremony is repeatedly observed, as a *manasika*, by them at the temples of other deities of the region. The Nrusinhanath temple at Simanchalam is, thus, found to be popular among these sacred specialists who have repeatedly observed there the *balapaka* ceremony either of their own or of their children.

After the *balapaka* ritual, the Brahim sacred specialists give importance to the *upanayana* ceremony, which is celebrated during the age from 10 to 14 years. Irrespective of their linguistic difference, the Brahmin sacred specialists follow the *shastric* procedure in performing this ceremony. This ceremony, however, is not celebrated among the non-Brahmin sacred specialists of Budhi Santani. On the other hand, the *pujakas* of Budhi Santani, undergo an initiation ritual when he receives a *mantra* from his *guru*. This ritual bears much importance among the *pujaka* community since nobody among them is allowed to perform the daily rituals of Budhi Santani if he has not obtained the *guru-mantra*. This ritual is not felt as a necessity among other sacred specialists of Budhi Santani.

Unlike the *upanayana* ceremony, a distinct homogeneity is observed in the celebration of marriage among all the sacred specialists. They observe the traditional customs in the performance of marriage rituals. However, they enjoy the ceremony by accretion of modern items of decoration and music. At present, marriage among all the sacred specialists of Budhi Santani is strictly monogamous, and post-pubertal. It is settled through parental negotiation. But, at the time of negotiation, the authority of the caste council is invited to be present. This is, however, not the case among the Brahmin sacred specialists who do not have a caste council of their own. While selecting a bride, all the sacred specialists follow the custom of preferential marriage with the cross-cousins, especially the maternal one. Paternal cross-cousins are acquired through exchange marriage among all of them except the Tulabhina and Kalinga Kumuti sacred specialists who consider the paternal cross-cousins as consanguines. Junior levirate and junior sororate forms of marriage, although socially permitted, occur rarely among them. The nuptial ceremony takes place at bride's residence. Kinsmen and others are invited for the nuptial ceremony and are treated with a feast. Prior to the nuptial ceremony, the bridegroom among all the sacred specialists visits the temples of his own locality to have a *darsana* of the deities. Payment of dowry is still in vogue among them. Recently, the caste councils of Bhandari and Dalua sacred specialists have started a campaign against the dowry practice whereas the caste councils of other sacred specialists do not oppose it. Divorce and remarriage, although not socially objected, are not appreciated by all the sacred specialists.

After death, the corpse is burnt among most of the sacred specialists of Budhi Santani. However, the corpse of a one year child is buried by them. The sacred specialists of Devanga and Raula castes, who are Saivites, bury their dead. Among the Hadi sacred specialists, the decision to bury or burn the dead depends upon their financial capacity; those who are poor do prefer to bury. Death rituals are observed for eleven days among the Bhandari, Damla and Dalua sacred specialists whereas among others, the rituals are observed for twelve days. During these days certain social restrictions in connection with death pollution are followed by the sacred specialists irrespective of their professional differences. *Barsikia sraddha*, a ritual performed on the completion of one year of death, is another common observance among the sacred specialists, who are classified into two groups as regard the observance of the ritual related to ancestral worship. The sacred specialists from Devanga, Telugu Kambhara and Kamma Brahmin communities perform this ritual on the Pongal festival whereas all others observe it on the Mahalaya festival.

The analysis of this chapter brings out that irrespective of a number of differences in terms of caste, language, sect and profession, the sacred specialists, because of their functional involvement in the Sacred Complex of Budhi Santani for a long time, have developed a common style of life, which can be self-identified as 'Sevaka Culture'. The commonness and homogeneity in their style of life are found distinct in settlement pattern, family and kinship life. It has been observed in this study that this homogeneity has developed along with a steady process of combination and compromise between two cultural traditions, Telugu and Oriya, which finds its expression especially in the religious life and the languages used towards the sacred sacrificers by the sacred specialists. The Sacred Complex of Budhi Santani has not only developed a process of integration and compromise among the sacred specialists but also among the sacred sacrificers. This phenomenon has been discussed particularly in Chapter 6, which analyses the sacred sacrificers and their sacred sacrifices.

In this chapter, I have also brought out that the elder generation of the sacred specialists mostly adhere to their traditional style of life but the younger generation has shown changes especially in their dress pattern, food habit and occupation owing to an impact of the general development of the Hindu social life in India.

6

SACRED SACRIFICES AND SACRED SACRIFICERS

The Hindus have devised several *margas* to obtain the *Bhagvat-krupa*. Essentially, they give much importance to the *Bhagvat-krupa* because it leads to the attainment of *moksha*, it helps in developing the righteousness and it also fulfils the mundane desires of varied nature such as cure from diseases and other bodily ailments, successful delivery, getting a son, winning a case in the court, success in the examination, fixation of marriage of children, smooth celebration of marriage, success in business, getting a job, getting a promotion in service etc. While Lord Siva and Vishnu are propitiated by the Hindus preferably for the attainment of *moksha* or for developing the righteousness, the goddesses of all kinds are worshipped by them mostly for the fulfilment of the mundane desires.

The Hindus commonly share the belief that all goddesses with various names are different manifestations of the same *Matru-Shakti* called the *Adi-Shakti* or *Adi-Mata*. In one of the famous sacred literatures, *Devi Bhagavata*, there is a narration about how innumerable goddesses are identified with the *Adi-Shakti*. In every creation of the universe, it is narrated, the *Adi-Shakti* assumes the different gradations of *amsa-rupini*, *kala-rupini*, and *kalamsa-rupini* or manifestation in parts, smaller parts and further sub-divisions respectively. In the first grade, she is represented by Durga, Laxmi, Saraswati, Sabitri and Radha; in the second by Ganga, Tulasi, Manasa, Sasthi, Mangala, Chandika and Kali; and in the third by the Gramadevis and by women folk in general. In the *Tantrasastra*, two lists of *mahavidyas* are quoted which depict the nuermous manifestations of the *Adi-Shakti*. These manifestations, as the Hindus believe, are broadly of two categories, mild and fierce. The goddesses, namely Laxmi, Saraswati, Parvati, Ganga, Radha and Sabitri are mild manifestations of the *Adi-Shakti* whereas Kali, Durga, Chandi, Samaleswari, Kichakeswari, Bhairavi and almost all the *grama-devis* are her fierce manifestations.

Whether mild or fierce, these goddesses are propitiated by the people through certain sacrifices. Propitiation of goddesses to fulfil the mundane desires by doing sacrifices is not a new religious tradition among the Hindus. It was a practice even in the epic ages. For instance, in the *Ramayana*, it is narrated how Rama had sacrificed one of his eyes to propitiate goddess Durga, who became pleased and supported him to win the war against Ravana. It is mentioned in the sixth chapter of Birata Parba of the *Mahabharata*, the Pandavas had propitiated Durga. As per the thirteenth chapter of Bhisma Parba of the *Mahabharata*, Arjuna had also propitiated Durga to win his fight against Bhisma. This tradition was also followed by many kings of the feudatory states. All these kings had their own *istadevis*, who were propitiated with various sacrifices with the hope that the goddess would protect the people and the kingdom from the enemy. Now, the worship, through sacrifices, of goddesses as the *Raksha-Kartris* has become a feature common with the people of all villages and traditional towns of India.

At Berhampur, Pitala and Boirani, the people propitiate their *Raksha-Kartri*, the goddess Budhi Santani, by making varieties of sacrifices, both at her temple and at her Utsav Mandira. The range of these sacrifices becomes wider especially during the Thakurani Yatra. It may vary from simple material-sacrifice of flowers, cocoanut and banana to spending for one day's *puja* materials of the Thakurani; from the ordinary action-sacrifice of a mere *darsana* or a sweeping of the frontyard of the Utsav Mandira to the carrying of the *manasika ghatas* and from traditional individual-oriented *besha*-sacrifice to a modern, group-oriented *besha*-sacrifice. Within these extreme types of sacrifices, there are numerous varieties of sacrifices, which may exhibit a regional and also a local uniqueness in the context of the Hindu universe. Since these sacrifices are made in connection with a sacred complex, these may be kept under a generic term, sacred sacrifices. In the context of the Sacred Complex of Budhi Santani, a wide range of sacred sacrifices are sacrificed by various categories of sacred sacrificers which have been typologically analysed in this chapter to test the hypotheses concerning Hindu civilization.

TYPOLOGICAL CLASSIFICATION OF SACRED SACRIFICES

All the sacred sacrifices which are made in connection with the Sacred Complex of Budhi Santani may be categorized into two broad groups, *Sahanika* sacred sacrifices and non-*Sahanika* sacred sacrifices (Fig. 6.1). The former type of sacred sacrifices are made on the basis of a

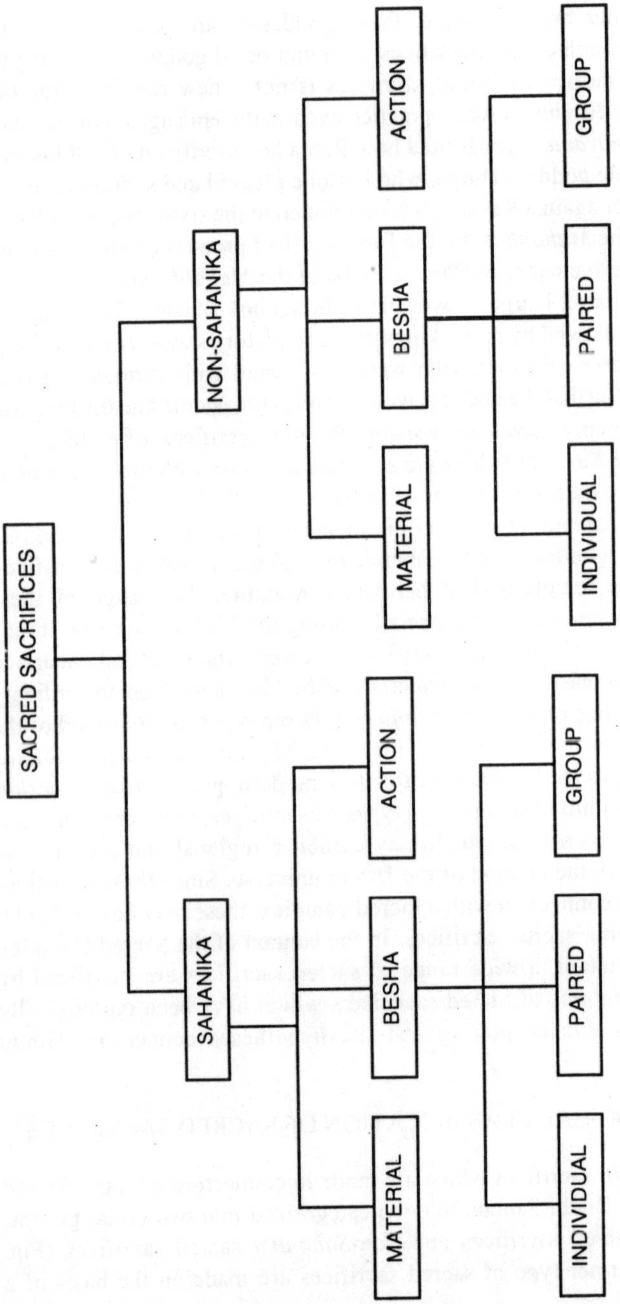

FIG. 6.1: Broad Typological Classification of Sacred Sacrifices

sahanika. The *sahanikas* are made by the people long before the sacred sacrifices are given. These may also be called as conditional sacred sacrifices since these are promised earlier with a condition to fulfil the mundane desires. The non-*sahanika* sacred sacrifices may, therefore, be termed as the non-conditional type. People make these sacred sacrifices with non-*a priori* condition but to exhibit their *sraddhaa* to the goddess, who is believed as the *Raksha-Kartri*. Within the *sahanika* as well as the non-*sahanika* categories, the sacred sacrifices may further be classified as of three types, material, action and *besha*.

Sahanika Sacred Sacrifices

Material

It is a popular tradition among the devotees of Budhi Santani to offer material objects as *sahanika* sacred sacrifices. These may be a body-part like the tongue or eye of the goddess, or a food item like the *muan* or the entire *bhoga* of one day for the goddess, or a dress item like the *saree* or an ornamental item like the '*tilaka*' or an item like the *ghata*, for the abode of the goddess or an item like the *Dharma Jhanda*, for the store house of the goddess.

Among these objects, the body-part and the ornamental ones are made of silver, gold or tin coated with silver or gold. The rich devotees usually offer the materials made of gold or silver whereas the poor and the middle class devotees prefer to offer the materials made of silver or gold coated tins. The body-part material items are noticed to be associated with the mundane desire to cure the corresponding body-part of the relatives of the Sahanikakari. All other material items, unlike the body-part ones, are not associated with such specific mundane desires. The *ghatas*, made of clay, are mostly offered as sacrifices but a significant number of *ghatas* made of steel or brass are also sacrificed by the people. While the metallic *ghatas* are preferred by the rich devotees, the clay *ghatas* are preferred by the poor and middle class devotees. The devotees often sacrifice *sarees*, which are black and cotton-made, to the Thakurani. It is believed that these *sarees* are mostly appreciated by her. Some of the devotees also make food sacrifices, as their Sahanikas, to the Thakurani. Both at the Thakurani temple and the Utsav Mandira, conical *muan* is commonly offered as a Sahanika food sacrifice. Sometimes, especially during the Thakurani Yatra, certain devotees, as their Sahanika, bear the expenses of all the food items, required for one day's *bhoga* of the Thakurani. Similarly, the devotees also make Sahanika to bear the expenses of making a new *Dharma Jhanda* for the Thakurani.

Action

The action-oriented Sahanika sacred sacrifices are of two categories. In one category the sacred sacrifices are meant to serve the Thakurani, whereas in the other category, the sacred sacrifices are meant to take severe pain for expressing their *sraddhaa* to the Thakurani.

Sweeping and then making *jhoti* on the frontyard of the Utsav Mandira at the early morning is a popular sacred sacrifice of the first category. This is mostly practised by the married women. Similarly, serving the Thakurani as her *doota* during the Thakurani Yatra is another sacred sacrifice of the first category. This sacrifice is done only by the males. Another sacred sacrifice, which is done only by the females, of this category is the carrying of the *ghata* of Budhi Santani or of Kali during their *sahi bhramana* in the Thakurani Yatra.

On the last day of the Thakurani Yatra, Sahanika *ghatas* are sacrificed to Budhi Santani Thakurani by males and females at their homes. These *ghatas* are then carried on head by them to the Thakurani temple along with the return-procession of Budhi Santani. The sacred sacrifice of carrying these Sahanika *ghatas* may be included in the second category. The *ghata*-carriers maintain the ritual purity by observing *opasa* till they complete the sacrificial action. *Dandua* is another sacred sacrifice of the second category. This is done by the males who observe *opasa*, close their mouths by biting a piece of straw and then go to the Utsav Mandira by stepwise prostrating themselves from their own houses.

Besha

A large number of devotees make the Thakurani Yatra colourful and entertaining by coming to the place of Utsav Mandira in different *beshas* or *rupas*. Many among them make Sahanikas for putting on these *beshas*. All the Sahanika *beshas* are put on only after the fulfilment of the mundane desires. While wearing these *beshas*, the *besha-dharis* follow a strict ritualistic procedure. On the very day when they are to wear the *besha*, they take bath early in the morning, observe *opasa* and then go to the Chitralaya for wearing the *besha*. Thereafter, they visit minimum seven houses of their kinsmen who receive them, appreciate their *beshas* and then offer some rupees and *pana* to drink. Those who put on *beshas* of the deities are forbidden to pay respect to others. After visiting the houses of kinsmen, they go to the Utsav Mandira, make *puja* of Budhi Santani by offering *bhoga* and then come to the Chitralaya to return the *besha*. The Chitralaya owner also receives some money against the hire of *beshas* from them. Thereafter, they distribute the Thakurani *bhoga* among the kinsmen whom they have visited and take food. Among all the *beshas*, the *Bagha besha* differs in that, unlike all others, *pranapratistha* is made first to this *besha* at the Utsav Mandira and then it is put on by the *besha-dhari*. The Sahanika *beshas* are of various types which include the *beshas* of different deities, namely Naba-Durga, Jwalamukhi, Siva, Yama, Krishna, Babajirupi Siva and Balarama; different epic characters such as Rama, Laxmana, Arjuna, Bhima, Hanumana, Sita, Radha, Biswamitra, Narada, Laba and Kusha; different occupational status such as a doctor, sorcerer, lady teacher and Alekha Babaji; spirits such as Pila-Khai Dahani and animals, namely *Bagha*. All these *beshas* may be classified into three categories; individual, paired and group. Among these three categories, the Sahanika *beshas* mostly belong to the first category. The Yama and Naba-Durga are group *beshas* and the Radha and Krishna, Arjuna and Krishna, Rama and Laxmana, Laba and Kusha, Rama and Balarama and the Kabali are paired *beshas* whereas all others are usually individual *beshas*. Further, among the Sahanika *beshas*, the Krishna and Babaji *beshas* are mostly put on by the devotees, because the former is considered to be the most beautiful *besha* and the latter is regarded as the most economic *besha*. *Bagha besha* is the most painful and costliest among all the individual *beshas*. It is believed that the Krishna, Babaji and Bagha *beshas* are appreciated most by the Thakurani. The *besha-dharis* belong to both the sexes. While the male *besha-dharis* range from the age group of three to forty years, the female *besha-dharis* belong to the age group of three to ten years.

Non-Sahanika Sacred Sacrifices

Materials

The materials, which are offered as non-Sahanika sacred sacrifice are broadly of two types, *ahara* and *archana*. In the first type, *nadia, kadali* and *pana* are the main materials. Sometimes, *muan* is also offered as non-Sahanika sacred sacrifice. These sacrifices are meant for the *ahara* of the Thakurani. In the second type, materials like *deepa, dhupa, puspa* and *haladi-pani* may be included. These materials are meant for the *archana* of the Thakurani. Moreover, during the *archana* of the Thakurani, it is noticed that the devotees prefer to sacrifice only *mandara* and *itamala puspas* because these two varieties are liked by her.

Action

The action oriented non-Sahanika sacred sacrifices include the *darsana* of the Thakurani and her *puja* at her temple, Utsav Mandira as well as during her *sahi-bhramana*. The sweeping of the courtyard and the frontyard of the Utsav Mandira is also done by the devotees as a non-Sahanika sacred sacrifice and, hence, it may be included in this category. This sweeping sacrifice, which is done by the married females, is mostly done to maintain the family tradition. It is noticed that all action oriented non-*sahanika* sacred sacrifices may be included in the service category, since these are meant to serve the Thakurani.

Besha

During the Thakurani Yatra, many devotees are also noticed to put on various non-*sahanika beshas*. The strictness in following the ritualistic procedure, which is associated with the *sahanika beshas*, is not adhered to in case of these *beshas*. For instance, the non-*sahanika besha-dharis* do not observe *opasa* like the *sahanika besha-dharis*. Further, like the latter, the former are not forbidden to pay respect to others and are allowed to visit houses of any number, both of kinsmen and others. The primary aim of the non-*sahanika besha-dharis* is to express *saraddhaa* to the Thakurani. Apart from it, many *besha-dharis* also intend to wear different kinds of *beshas* which may entertain others. By entertaining others, the *besha-dharis* also derive personal pleasure. While entertaining, the people offer money to them, who spend it against the cost of *besha*, the *puja* to the Thakurani and their food.

There are a large number of non-*sahanika beshas*, which may be called as occupational *beshas*, put on by the devotees during the Thakurani Yatra to exhibit the roles of various occupational status. These include the *beshas* of Doctor, *Gunia*, Master and *Mastrani, Sapua* and *Sapuani, chasa-dala, dera* weavers and *chadeia* and *chadeiani, khurdha paikas* and *nabikas* with their *boita*. These *beshas* exhibit the occupations of the past and also of the present. These broadly give a picture of the various occupations, which are in vogue at the local as well as regional level. Among all the categories of *beshas*, the *beshas* of some specific communities illustrate maximum typological variation. In includes the *beshas* of *Dhobani, Keutuni*, leper, *Chhota, Gauduni, Landa Brahmana, Sabara, Chhodagajia, Adi-Manaba, Kaudinaki, Saheb, Sadhu, Irani stri, Dakshini stri*, and *Odia stri*, which are put on by the devotees to entertain people by exhibiting the typical behaviour of these communities.

On the basis of the number of individuals participated in a *besha*, the non-*sahanika beshas* may further be classified into three categories such as, individual, paired and group. Most of the non-*sahanika beshas* belong to the group category. For instance, the beshas, namely Dhangda dance, Jahni Osha, Kapurusha Raja and his *patuara, Ramalila*, Krishna *lila, Khurdha Paikas, Saba-Yatra, Chasa-dala, Dera* Weavers and *Adi-Manaba* require participation of more than two individuals and hence, these may be included in the group category. In the case of *Sapua* and *Sapuani, Master* and *Mastrani, Chadeia* and *Chadeiani*, Krishna and Arjuna, Rama and Laxmana *beshas*, only two individuals participate and, hence, these may be included in the paired category. The non-*sahanika beshas* of individual category are of large variety, such as *Chhodagajia, Kaudinaki, Mankada, Dakshini stri, Irani stri, Saheb, Pilakhai-Dahani, Sadhu, Bhalu, Baradangua, Dhampamali*, Leper, *Chhota, Dhobani* and *Keutuni*.

Typological Composition of Sacred Sacrificers

The wide range of sacred sacrifices made in connection with the Sacred Complex of Budhi Santani, thus speaks about how the Hindus adopt varied means to propitiate their deities. Although these sacred sacrifices exhibit heterogeneity, none of these can be categorically identified with any specific group of sacred sacrificers. In making a specific sacred sacrifice to Budhi Santani the sacred sacrificers are not found to differentiate among themselves in terms of caste, language, occupation and education.

Here an attempt has been made to analyse the composition of the sacred sacrificers in terms of their sex, age, *varna*, language and profession. Attempt has also been made to classify them on the basis of their level of education, the reason of making sacred sacrifice, the kind of sacred sacrifices made by them, the locality from where they have visited, the type of accommodation chosen by them to make the sacred sacrifices, the nature of their dependence on the sacred specialists and the motivating persons for their sacred sacrifices. For this, a sample of 500 sacred sacrificers has been drawn up from the Thakurani temple on various occasions and from the place of Utsav Mandira during the Thakurani Yatra.

Composition according to Sex, Age, Profession, Varna and Level of Education

As shown in Table 6.1, both males (31.8%) and females (68.2%) make sacred sacrifices to Budhi Santani. These sacred sacrificers are represented from different age-groups (Table 6.2), although majority (68.0%) of them belong to the middle age-group (21-40). In so far as the *varna*, level of education and profession are concerned, the sacred sacrificers exhibit a heterogeneous composition. Thus, as shown in Table 6.3, they are represented from such professional categories as peasant (5.2%), artisan (15.0%), business (21.8%), higher profession (9.4%), menial

TABLE 6.1: Showing the Sex Composition of the Sacred Sacrificers

Sl. No.	*Sex*	*No. of Sacred Sacrificers*	*Percentage*
1.	Male	159	31.8
2.	Female	341	68.2
	Total	500	100.0

TABLE 6.2: Showing the Age Composition of the Sacred Sacrificers

Sl. No.	*Age Group in Years*	*No. of Sacred Sacrificers*	*Percentage*
1.	0 - 10	64	12.8
2.	11 - 20	31	6.2
3.	21 - 30	187	37.4
4.	31 - 40	153	30.6
5.	41 - 50	41	8.2
6.	51 - 60	17	3.4
7.	61 - Above	7	1.4
	Total	500	100.0

TABLE 6.3: Showing Professions of the Sacred Sacrificers

Sl. No.	*Profession*	*No. of Sacred Sacrificers*	*Percentage*
1.	Peasant	26	5.2
2.	Artisan	75	15.0
3.	Business	109	21.8
4.	Higher Professions (Doctor, Lawyer, Engineer etc.)	47	9.4
5.	Menial Services	135	27.0
6.	Housewife	92	18.4
7.	Other Professions	16	3.2
	Total	500	100.00

services (27.0%), housewife (18.4%) and other professions (3.2%). It is noted that the sacred sacrificers of lower professions make a larger proportion of the sample. Similarly, it came out (Table 6.4) that majority of the sacred sacrificers do not have education above the matriculation level. Thus, only 9.4 per cent of them are graduates whereas only 4.2 per cent are post-graduates. While 36.4 per cent of the sample have primary level of education and 21.6 per cent have education up to matriculation. A significant percentage (28.4%) of them are found to be illiterates. The sacred sacrificers of Vaishya (37.2%) and Sudra (28.6%) *varnas* are found (Table 6.5) to be more in number than the Brahmins (12.0%) and Kshatriyas (14.8%). Participation of the untouchables with a very limited percentage (7.4%) is noticed probably due to certain social restrictions.

TABLE 6.4: Showing the Level of Education among the Sacred Sacrificers

Sl. No.	*Level of Education*	*No. of Sacred Sacrificers*	*Percentage*
1.	Illiterate	142	28.4
2.	Primary	182	36.4
3.	Matriculation	108	21.6
4.	Graduation	47	9.4
5.	Post-Graduation	21	4.2
	Total	500	100.0

TABLE 6.5: Showing the *Varna* Composition of the Sacred Sacrificers

Sl. No.	*Varna Sacrificers*	*No. of Sacred Sacrificers*	*Percentage*
1.	Brahmin	60	12.0
2.	Kshatriya	74	14.8
3.	Vaishya	186	37.2
4.	Sudra	143	28.6
5.	Untouchable	37	7.4
	Total	500	100.0

Composition according to Language and Geographical Distribution

The goddess Budhi Santani of Berhampur is not a deity of universal importance like Lord Jagannath at Puri or Lord Siva at Kashi where sacred sacrificers of various languages, congregate to make sacrifices. As shown in Table 6.6, sacred sacrificers of only two regional languages, Oriya (61.6%) and Telugu (38.4%), visit the Thakurani to make sacrifices.

The sacred sacrificers are found (Table 6.7) to have represented from a limited geographical region, which spreads through two States of the country, namely Orissa and Andhra Pradesh. Out of the 500 sacred sacrificers interviewed, 238 have come from Berhampur city, 184 from outside the Berhampur city but within the Ganjam district, 57 from the districts other than Ganjam of Orissa State, 21 from Andhra Pradesh and none from places other than Andhra Pradesh and Orissa.

TABLE 6.6: Showing the Language Composition of the Sacred Sacrificers

Sl. No.	*Language*	*No. of Sacred Sacrificers*	*Percentage*
1.	Oriya	308	61.6
2.	Telugu	192	38.4
	Total	500	100.0

TABLE 6.7: Showing the Geographical Distribution of the Sacred Sacrificers

Sl. No.	*Geographical Distribution*	*No. of Sacred Sacrificers*	*Percentage*
1.	Within Berhampur City	238	47.6
2.	Outside Berhampur City but within Ganjam District	184	36.8
3.	Districts other than Ganjam inside Orissa	57	11.4
4.	Andhra Pradesh	21	4.2
5.	States other than Andhra Pradesh inside India	0.0	00.0
	Total	500	100.0

Composition according to the Types and Purposes of making Sacred Sacrifices

An assessment on the choice of sacrifices made by the sacred sacrificers has also been done. It is found that non-*sahanika ahara* and *archana* type materials are sacrificed by all the sacred sacrificers. But, apart from it, they also make other kinds of sacred sacrifices. Among the other broad categories of sacred sacrifices, *besha* type (54.4%) is found to be preferred more than the action (19.0%) and material (26.6%) categories of sacred sacrifices. The sacred sacrificers are noticed to make sacrifices for various purposes, on the basis of which a classification has also been made. It is found (Table 6.9) that out of the 500 sacred sacrificers, 171 have made sacred sacrificers for protection of life or cure from diseases of their own or relatives; 76 to express *sraddhaa* to Budhi Santani; 68 to maintain the family tradition; 37 for settlement of marriage of their family members, 23 for success in examination, business, court case etc.; 29 to have a son; 16 for maiden use of a vehicle or a *saree*; 31 to raise funds; 45 as personal hobby and only 4 because of the direction from Budhi Santani through dream.

TABLE 6.8: Showing the Types of Sacred Sacrifice made by the Sacred Sacrificers

Sl. No.	*Sacred Sacrifice*	*No. of Sacred Sacrificers*	*Percentage*
1.	*Besha*	272	54.4
2.	Action	95	19.0
3.	Material	133	26.6
	Total	500	100.0

TABLE 6.9: Showing the purposes of making Sacred Sacrifices by the Sacred Sacrificers

Sl. No.	*Purpose of Making Sacred Sacrifice*	*No. of Sacred Sacrificers*	*Percentage*
1.	Protection of life or cure from diseases of their own or relatives	171	34.2
2.	To express *sraddhaa* to Budhi Santani	76	15.2
3.	To maintain the family tradition	68	13.6
4.	Settling marriage of family members	37	7.4
5.	Success in examination, court case, business etc.	23	4.6
6.	To have a son	29	5.8
7.	For maiden use of a vehicle or a *saree*	16	3.2
8.	To raise funds	31	6.2
9.	Personal hobby	45	9.0
10.	Direction from Budhi Santani through dream	4	0.8
	Total	500	100.0

Composition according to Persons motivating for making Sacred Sacrifices

It is noticed during the interview with the 500 sacred sacrificers that all of them have decided to make a sacred sacrifice only after being motivated by ownself or other persons who may be family members, kinsmen, neighbours, friends or the sacred specialists of Budhi Santani Thakurani. Accordingly an analysis has also been made as shown in the Table 6.10 among the sacred sacrificers. And it has been found that the sacred specialists do not play a significant role in motivating people for making sacred sacrifices to the Thakurani for fulfilment of their mundane desires. Out of the 500 sacred sacrificers, 126 are motivated by themselves, 87 by family members, 91 by kinsmen, 119 by neighbours and 77 by friends.

TABLE 6.10: Showing the Persons motivating the Sacred Sacrificers to make Sacred Sacrifices

Sl. No.	*Motivating Persons*	*No. of Sacred Sacrificers*	*Percentage*
1.	Self	126	25.2
2.	Family members	87	17.4
3.	Kinsmen	91	18.2
4.	Neighbours	119	23.8
5.	Friends	77	15.4
	Total	500	100.0

Composition according to Nature of Dependence on Sacred Specialists and Type of Accommodation

At all Hindu sacred complexes, there develops an inter-dependence between the sacred specialists and the sacred sacrificers. It is because the sacred sacrificers primarily depend on the sacred specialists for religious guidance and knowledge and also for making sacred sacrifices. On the other hand, the sacred specialists depend on the sacred sacrificers for their economy. In this way, three types of dependence, such as hereditary, temporary and no dependence, exist between them. By interviewing the 500 sacred sacrifices it has been found (Table 6.11)

TABLE 6.11: Showing the Nature of Dependence on the Sacred Specialists by the Sacred Sacrificers

Sl. No.	*Nature of Dependence*	*No. of Sacred Sacrificers*	*Percentage*
1.	Hereditary	149	29.8
2.	Temporary	314	62.8
3.	No dependence	37	7.4
	Total	500	100.0

TABLE 6.12: Showing the Type of Accommodation made by the Sacred Sacrificers

Sl. No.	*Type of Accommodation*	*No. of Sacred Sacrificers*	*Percentage*
1.	House of Sacred Specialists	14	2.8
2.	Lodging	22	4.4
3.	*Dharmashala*	28	5.6
4.	House of relatives	179	35.8
5.	Did not stay	69	13.8
6.	Own house	188	37.6
	Total	500	100.0

that 149 have a hereditary and 314 have a temporary dependence with the sacred specialists. Only 37 have not depended on the sacred specialists in making their sacred sacrifices. Moreover, the type of accommodation made by the sacred sacrificers speaks about the wideness in importance of a particular sacred centre. In case of a sacred centre of universal importance like Jagannath temple at Puri, the sacred sacrificers, in large number make arrangement of accommodation other than their own house and this may be at lodging, *dharmashalas*, house of relatives or house of the sacred specialists. But, this type of arrangement of accommodation by the sacred sacrificers is found less in number at sacred centres of lesser importance. As studied among the 500 sacred sacrificers, it has been found (Table 6.12) that more than half have not made such arrangement of accommodation since they have their own houses (37.6%) or have not stayed (13.8%) for the purpose of sacred sacrifice. Of the rest, majority (35.8%) have stayed at the houses of their relatives. While 5.6 per cent have stayed at *dharmashalas* and 4.4 per cent have stayed at lodging, only 2.8 per cent have preferred to stay at the houses of the sacred specialists.

7

SACRED SYMBOLS AND SACRED BELIEFS

All the sacred performances, observed at the Sacred Complex of Budhi Santani, are found to be associated with certain sacred symbols and sacred beliefs. These sacred symbols exhibit a wide range of variation, from a shapeless stone smeared with vermillion to an image decorated with gold ornaments; from an image carved on the wall of the temple and, hence, fixed to different *ghatas*, which are not static, rather go on Sahi-Parikrama; from inanimate objects like flag and bamboo pole to flowers and living man dressed with different *beshas*; from sliced body-parts of a deity to a complete image; from sacred symbols, which exhibit features of only little or great tradition to sacred symbols, which exhibit features of a combination and coexistence of both little and great traditions; from sacred symbols of structural nature to sacred symbols of functional nature; and from sacred symbols of unitary nature to sacred symbols of collective nature. Despite their varied nature, these sacred symbols provide a scope for a classification as has been made below.

TYPOLOGICAL CLASSIFICATION OF SACRED SYMBOLS

Broadly, all the sacred symbols of the Sacred Complex of Budhi Santani may be classified into two groups, those which are associated with the Thakurani temple and those which are associated with the Thakurani Yatra. Thakurani temple is the abode of Budhi Santani. Here a sliced portion of her total figure is worshipped. For instance, at Berhampur her head is worshipped, at Pitala her trunk is worshipped and at Boirani her feet are worshipped. At the Thakurani temple, apart from Budhi Santani, other deities are also worshipped in certain symbolic forms. These deities include the Naba-Grahas, the Dasa-Mahavidyas of Budhi Santani, Sitala, Siva, Parvati, Durga and Baidhara.

Certain sacred symbols have been specially associated with the Thakurani Yatra, which occurs regularly at Berhampur and irregularly at Pitala and Boirani. For instance, during the Thakurani Yatra, Budhi Santani, her Sata Bhaunis, Kali and Baidhara are worshipped with their sacred symbols, which are of mystical nature inside the Utsav Mandira. Deities, namely Kali, Jwalamukhi, Narayana, Krishna, Radha, Siva and epic heroes like Rama, Laxmana, Sita, Parsurama, Nagarjuna and Hanuman are also symbolically worshipped during the *yatra*. Certain sacred symbols such as *dharma-jhanda* and *subha-khunti*, are noticed only during the Thakurani Yatra.

The sacred symbols associated with the Sacred Complex of Budhi Santani may also be classified as of two types, mystical and anthropomorphic. Mystical as well as anthropomorphic sacred symbols are noticed not only in the Thakurani temple but also during the Thakurani Yatra. Mystical sacred symbols are found more in number during the Thakurani Yatra than in the Thakurani temple. At the Thakurani temple, the deities Baidhara and Sitala are worshipped as stone pieces smeared with vermillion. However, the sacred symbols of Budhi Santani, her Bije Pratima, her Dasa-Mahavidyas and Naba-Grahas are of anthropomorphic in nature in the Thakurani temple. During the Thakurani Yatra, the Thakurani *ghata* containing the *phulamanda* represents the symbolic abode of mystical nature of Budhi Santani inside the Utsav Mandira. This *ghata* is comparatively larger than other eight *ghatas*, which represent the symbolic abodes of mystical nature of Kali and Sata Bhaunis of Budhi Santani. To mark its dominant character, the Thakurani *ghata* is decorated with a *prabha*. The *dharma-jhanda* and *subha-khunti*, which are placed during the Thakurani Yatra, are also of mystical nature whereas the sacred symbols of Kali, Jwalamukhi, Laxman, Narayana, Nagarjuna, Parsurama, Rama, Siva, Sita, Radha and Krishna are of anthropomorphic nature.

The sacred symbols may further be classified as of two categories, movable and immovable. For instance, the Bije Pratima of Budhi Santani at her temple, the *ghatas* worshipped at Utsav Mandira, the photos of different deities hanged on the inner wall of *darsana-griha* of the Thakurani temple and people wearing *beshas* of gods, goddesses and epic heroes may be regarded as sacred symbols of movable type. On the other hand, the anthropomorphic body of Budhi Santani at her temple, her Dasa-Mahavidas, which are images carved on the outer wall of the temple, Naba-Grahas, which are images also carved on the wall of the Thakurani temple, the mystical idol of Baidhara and Sitala at the

Thakurani temple, the images of Kali, Jwalamukhi, Parsurama, Narayana, Laxmana and Nagarjuna, the *subha-khunti* and the *dharma jhanda* may be considered to be sacred symbols of immovable type. At the Thakurani temple, the immovable sacred symbols outnumber the movable sacred symbols whereas during the Thakurani Yatra, a reverse situation is noticed.

Among the sacred symbols, some are found to be propitiated individually whereas others are noted to be worshipped in group. Basing on this feature, the sacred symbols may also be classified as of two categories, unitary and collective. The *subha-khunti*, the *dharma-jhanda*, the images of deities and epic heroes exhibited on *rathas*, the *beshadharis* of Krishna and Siva represent the sacred symbols of unitary nature. On the other side, the Naba-Grahas or the Dasa-Mahavidyas of Budhi Santani or the nine *ghatas* at the Utsav Mandira or the *besadharis* of Rama, Laxman and Sita or Radha and Krishna are sacred symbols of collective nature. Similarly, at the Thakurani temple, the anthropomorphic body-part of Budhi Santani, her Bije Pratima and the mystical idol of Baidhara are collectively worshipped. These sacred symbols, unlike those of unitary nature, are identified only in groups. Thus, one cannot find the sacred symbols of only two or three *grahas* or Mahavidyas because it may amount to incompleteness.

A further classification, basing on the presence or absence of life, may be made among the sacred symbols as animate and inanimate types. Thus, among the sacred symbols found in the Thakurani temple, the Neem tree is of animate type. Apart from this, all other sacred symbols present in the Thakurani temple are of inanimate type. Among the sacred symbols, which are associated with the Thakurani Yatra, the *manasika beshadharis* of different gods and goddesses, *ghata* carriers of Budhi Santani, Kali and her Sata Bhaunis and the Thakurani *dootas* may be categorized as animate type whereas the *subha-khunti*, the *dharma-jhanda*, the images of gods, goddesses and epic heroes exhibited on *rathas* and the *ghatas* of Budhi Santani and her Sata Bhaunis may be classified as inanimate sacred symbols and these outnumber the animate ones. The inanimate sacred symbols are made of bamboo, stone, metal or clay. The animate sacred symbols are represented either by trees or human beings.

Among the sacred symbols associated with the Sacred Complex of Budhi Santani, a sectarian classification may also be made, such as Shakta, Vaishnava and Saiva. For instance, the sacred symbols of Budhi Santani, her Dasa-Mahavidyas, her Bije Pratima and Sitala, which exist in the Thakurani temple fall under the Shakta category. The *ghatas* of Budhi Santani, her Sata Bhaunis and Kali, the *subha-khunti*, the *dharma-jhanda*, the images of Kali, and Jwalamukhi, which are exhibited on *rathas* may also be included in this category. The image of Narayana, which is exhibited on a *ratha* and the Krishna and Rama *beshadharis* are sacred symbols which may be placed in the Vaishnava category. In the Saiva category, the sacred symbols represented by the Siva and Babaji *beshadharis* may be included. Thus, in the Sacred Complex of Budhi Santani, a co-existence of the sacred symbols of the three major sects, Shakta, Saiva and Vaishnava of Hindu civilization is noticed.

All the sacred symbols associated with the Sacred Complex of Budhi Santani are not believed to be the direct representations of gods or goddesses. While some sacred symbols are direct representations of gods and goddesses, other sacred symbols identify their link with gods and goddesses indirectly. Basing on this feature, the sacred symbols may be classified as primary, secondary and tertiary type. Primary sacred symbols are believed to be the direct representations of gods and goddesses. For instance, the head of Budhi Santani, which is worshipped at her temple, is believed to be a direct representation of her head and, hence, a primary sacred symbol. In the category of primary sacred symbol, the mystical idols of Baidhara and Sitala, which are worshipped at the Thakurani temple, may also be included. The Neem tree at the Thakurani temple, the images of the deities and epic heroes exhibited on *rathas* during the Thakurani Yatra and the *beshadharis* of different deities, epic heroes and heroines may also be treated as primary sacred symbols.

Moreover, certain sacred symbols in the Sacred Complex of Budhi Santani are believed to be the representations of deities because these are either derived from or associated with the primary sacred symbols of these deities. Such sacred symbols may be called as the secondary sacred symbols. For instance, the *phulamanda* and the *subha-khunti* derive their sacredness from the head, a primary sacred symbol of Budhi Santani, which is worshipped at her temple at Berhampur. Hence, these may be called as secondary sacred symbols of Budhi Santani. Similarly, the Bije Pratima of Budhi Santani of Berhampur does not possess the figure of her head nor of her total body but has the image of goddess Durga in her posture of killing Mahisasura, the bufallo-demon. This Bije Pratima is believed to be a representation of Budhi Santani only through its association with her head and, hence, it may be treated as a secondary sacred symbol. In the same principle, the Dasa-Mahavidyas, and the *manasika ghatas* of Budhi Santani may also be included in the category of secondary sacred symbol. At the Utsav Mandira, Budhi Santani, her Sata Bhaunis and Kali are worshipped symbolically. These deities have their primary sacred symbols, which are of anthropomorphic forms at their own temples, but at the Utsav Mandira, they are represented by *ghatas*, the secondary sacred symbols. During the Thakurani Yatra, the *ghatas* are carried on head by the *ghatadharis* for the Sahi Bhramana. While carrying the *ghatas*, the *ghatadharis* also derive sacredness and they are reverred by the devotees. For instance, during the Sahi Bhramana, the devotees wash the feet of the Thakurani *ghatadhari* with turmeric water and offer *pana* at her feet. This ritual is done with the belief that the Thakurani *ghatadhari* represents the moving sacred symbol of Budhi Santani and a reverence to the *mukhya ghatadhari* means a reverence to her. The *ghatadharis* are, thus, considered to be the sacred symbols only by their association with the *ghatas*, the secondary sacred symbols and, hence, they may be treated as the tertiary sacred symbols. Sometimes, the Thakurani *dootas* may also be included in the category of tertiary sacred symbols, since they also derive sacredness by their association with the Thakurani ghata.

The sacred symbols, which are associated with the Sacred Complex of Budhi Santani may further be classified as of two types, those which represent the little tradition and those which represent the great tradition of Hindu civilization. Thus, the sliced body-parts of Budhi Santani, which are worshipped at her temples, at Berhampur, Pitala and Boirani, the mystical idols of Baidhara and Sitala, which are worshipped at the Thakurani temple, the *subha-khunti*, the *dharma-jhanda*, the *phulamanda* and the *ghatas* and *ghatadharis* of Budhi Santani, her Sata Bhaunis and Kali, all these may be treated as sacred symbols of little traditional type. In their form, these sacred symbols have a local origin. On the other hand, the sacred symbols of the Bije Pratima and Dasa-Mahavidyas of Budhi Santani and the sacred symbols of the Naba-Grahas, which are found at the Thakurani temple may be treated as the sacred symbols of great traditional type. By forms these sacred symbols are universally accepted among the Hindus. In the great traditional type of sacred symbols, the images of deities and epic heroes, which are exhibited on *rathas* during the Thakurani Yatra and the *manasika beshadharis* of different deities, epic heroes and heroines may also be included. Thus, in the Sacred Complex of Budhi Santani, a combination of sacred symbols of little as well as great traditional type is noticed.

All the sacred symbols, which have so far been discussed, represent

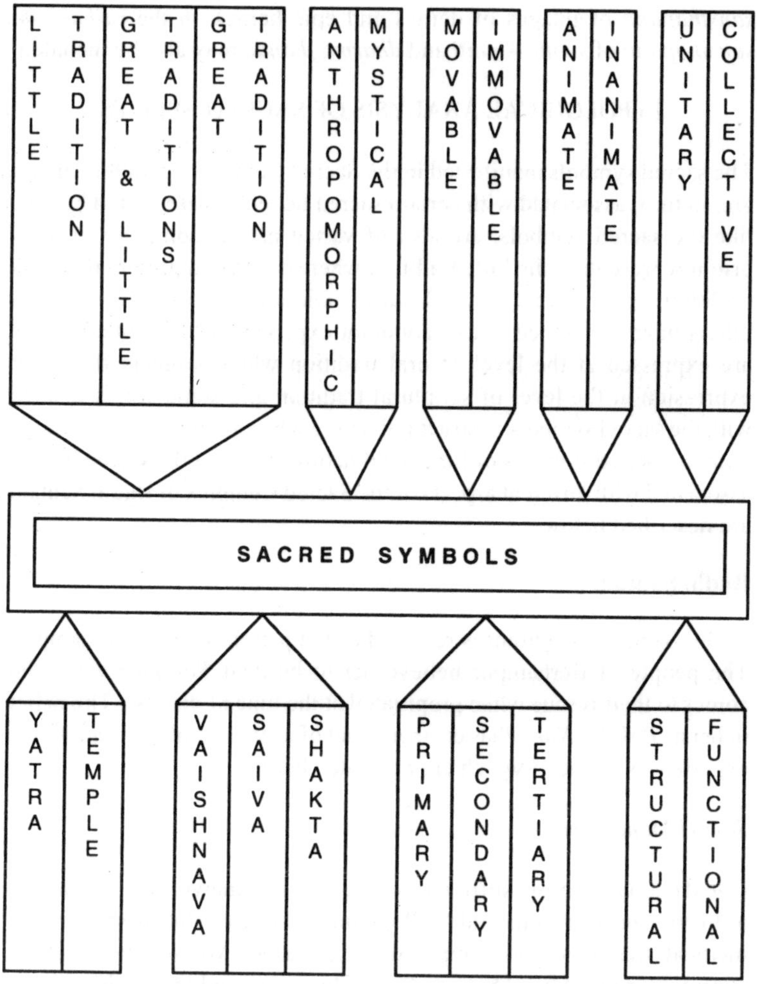

FIG. 7.1: Broad Typological Classification of Sacred Symbols.

one or the other forms of the deities or epic heroes and heroines. Broadly, all of these may be regarded as of structural nature. But in the Sacred Complex of Budhi Santani, a number of sacred symbols of functional nature are also noticed. For instance, all the rituals connected with the daily worship of Budhi Santani at her temple and her Utsav Mandira are symbolically done and, hence, these may be called as functional sacred symbols. In the category of functional sacred symbol, the ritual performances associated with *ghata sansthapana, Digabandhana, sansthapana* of images of deities and epic heroes on the *rathas* and *sansthapana* of *subha-khunti* and *dharma jhanda* may also be included.

TYPOLOGICAL ANALYSIS OF SACRED BELIEFS

The sacred symbols manifested in the Sacred Complex of Budhi Santani are, in turn, associated with certain sacred beliefs. These sacred beliefs, like the sacred symbols, are also of varied nature; some are of local origin representing the little tradition whereas others represent the great tradition; some have emanated out of individual experiences whereas others have developed out of common experiences of devotees; some are expressed at the level of oral tradition whereas others find their expression at the level of scriptural tradition and some are associated with the sacred symbols of structural nature whereas others are associated with the sacred symbols of functional nature. Some of the sacred beliefs associated with different aspects of the Sacred Complex of Budhi Santani are described below.

Budhi Santani

Budhi Santani Thakurani is reverred as the patron deity of Berhampur. The people of Berhampur believe her to be their *Raksha-Kartri* who comes to their rescue when propitiated at the time of distress. The belief in her as *Raksha-Kartri* has emanated out of a large number of individual experiences, some of which are presented below.

Savitri Mohapatra

One day, my third son suffered from fever of unknown type. I called on a doctor and kept him under allopathic treatment. But in spite of the medical treatment, his temperature increased. My son was getting enormous pain. After 15 days, the doctor suggested to take him to the Medical College Hospital. With this, I was shocked but kept patience and admitted him to the Medical College Hospital. There also a number of doctors examined him for three days but still there was no sign of cure. On the night of fourth day, the temperature of my son suddenly increased and he vomitted and started shouting out of pain. This became unbearable for me and I felt hopeless. At that moment, one of my female kins suggested me to pray Budhi Santani to save my son. This was the only alternative for me. I propitiated Budhi Santani in my mind and promised to make her *puja* by taking my son in a Krishna *Besha* for her *darsana* on three occasions of the Thakurani Yatra. To my surprise, the temperature of my son started reducing from the next day morning and he became completely cured after two days. Earlier, I had heard about Budhi Santani Thakurani as the *Raksha-Kartri* but my own experience strengthened my belief. In the successive three *yatras*, I immediately fulfilled my vow.

N. Amulu: My faith in Budhi Santani Thakurani as the *Raksha-Kartri* developed out of my personal experience with her in connection with the illness of my son, who was four years old at that time. The event took place 17 years ago, when my son suffered from small-pox. After a few days, the disease aggravated and none of my family members and neighbours were hopeful of his living. They started making the necessary arrangement for his funeral ceremony. Observing this in the evening, I could not control my anguish. At midnight, I alone went to the temple of Budhi Santani Thakurani but found its doors were locked. At the door, I cried a lot and prayed the goddess to protect the life of my son. In that moment, an old woman came to me and went away after telling me not to be worried. Thereafter, two policemen came and told me that my son would be recuperated because Budhi Santani in the guise of the old woman had given me consolation. They also brought me back to my house.

At home, I kept 25 paise, a small amount of vermillion and non-parboiled rice mixed with turmeric in a piece of cloth and then tied the cloth, in the name of Budhi Santani, to the hand of my son. In the night, I felt through dream that an old woman, wearing a red *saree* with unbraided hair, patted my son with a broom-stick. In the morning, I found my son to make movement of his body. He also took some food. This strengthened my belief in Budhi Santani's *mahatmya*.

I immediately anointed my son with turmeric and oil and then collected the dirt on his body. I took the dirt to the Thakurani temple and placed it near the Neem tree present inside the temple precinct. I, then, offered a *deepa* to Budhi Santani and took her refuge by prostrating myself at her front and by teething a piece of straw. In mind, I vowed to the Thakurani to bring my son in *Jeelapi Besha* for her *darsana* during five Thakurani Yatras if his life is protected by her.

After a couple of days, my son became completely cured, for which I developed faith in the Thakurani as the *Raksha-Kartri* and later on, I also fulfilled my vow.

L.M.: On two occasions I have tested and found Budhi Santani Thakurani to come to my rescue at the time of distress. Now I am fully convinced that she is our *Raksha-Kartri*.

My first experience with her took place when my second son, Surendra, suffered from acute stomach pain and dysentery at the age of ten. He was given medicines but did not recupe. I was frightened and became worried. At that moment his father was out of home for three days. My neighbours were consoling me. Among them, two women suggested me to make *Sahanika* before Budhi Santani to save my son. Earlier, I had seen how one among these two women could save the life of his son by making *sahanika* before Budhi Santani. As per their suggestion, I came along with Surendra to the temple of Budhi Santani in the evening. I was ignorant of the ritual procedure of making *sahanika* and, hence, I took help of the temple priest. According to his instruction, I rolled my son on the ground before the goddess, made ritual worship to her and spoke, "O, Mother, Surendra is your son, not mine. He is suffering from illness. You take care of him and I am just to guard him. If you cure him I shall bring him in a *besha* for your *darsana* on three Thakurani Yatras. This is what I want to say you." I alongwith my son, then, came to home. In that night, I did not give him any medicine but in the next morning, he became completely cured and attended his school. I was astonished but convinced that the Thakurani cured my son. As per my vow, later on, I took my son in a *besha* for the *darsana* of the Thakurani during three successive Thakurani Yatras.

My second experience with Budhi Santani was during the occasion, when both my third and fourth sons suffered from para-typhoid. At that time, my third son was 11 years old and fourth son was nine years old. Both of them were medically treated but instead, the disease aggravated. Hence, I decided to make *sahanika* before Budhi Santani which I did in the earlier manner. Thereafter, both the sons gradually recuperated. Later on, I fulfilled my *sahanika*.

Now it has become a tradition in our family to make *sahanika* before Budhi Santani if any of our family members suffer from illness.

Narayanamma: I believe that Budhi Santani is our *Raksha-Kartri* since she had once saved the life of my son. Seven years ago, my son, Laxmana, at the age of 12 years suffered from small-pox. He was given medical treatment but did not recupe. As I became worried, my neighbours suggested me to make *sahanika* before Budhi Santani.

As per their suggestion, I kept Rs. 1.25 in the name of Budhi Santani in a piece of yellow cloth and tied it to the hand of my son. At home, I made a *sahanika* remembering Budhi Santani in mind to take my son, if cured by her, in a *besha* for her *darsana* during three successive Thakurani Yatras. Thereafter, I found my son to recuperate.

He became completely cured within three days. This no doubt strengthened my belief in Budhi Santani as the *Raksha-Kartri*. Later on, I fulfilled my *sahanika*.

H. Tarini: I have developed faith in Budhi Santani because she had come to my rescue. Earlier, I was having two daughters and no son. When my wife conceived for the third time, I prayed Budhi Thakurani to give me a son this time. I secretly made *sahanika* before the goddess that if I get a son, then I shall take him in Krishna *besha* for her *darsana* during the Thakurani Yatra. Fortunately, my third issue was a son and I became convinced that it was due to the mercy of Budhi Santani. Later on, I had also fulfilled my *sahanika*.

H. Senma: My second son, Apanna, had suffered from small-pox when he was one year old. In spite of the medical treatment, he could not be cured. Instead, the disease aggravated. With this, I became worried and made *sahanika* before Budhi Santani to take Apanna, if cured by her, in a Krishna *besha* for her *darsana* during her *yatra*. In fact, from next day onwards, my son started recuperating and he became completely cured within five days. This made me believe that the Thakurani was the *Raksha-Kartri* of my son and, hence, later on, I also fulfilled my *sahanika*.

Analysis

The above-mentioned sacred beliefs are of 'individual-experience' type. It is noticed that *sahanikas* are associated with such type of sacred beliefs. These sacred beliefs are also found to be expressed at the level of oral tradition. Since these sacred beliefs are of local origin, they represent the little tradition. These sacred beliefs also depict the functional and not structural character of Budhi Santani.

Origin and Structure of Budhi Santani

There is a popular sacred belief with regard to the origin and structure of Budhi Santani who is also named as *Mahamayee*. This sacred belief was initially expressed at the level of oral tradition but, at present, it has found its place at the level of scriptural radiation. This sacred belief is presented here as narrated in the *Shri Mahamayee Purana* written by Acharya Tarini Charan Patra.

As the sacred belief goes, Budhi Santani Thakurani was initially worshipped by a tribal man. The Thakurani was having her *pitha* in the house of this tribal man. As this *pitha* of the Thakurani became popular in the mass, a large number of devotees came for her *darsana* daily. Gradually, her popularity also increased as the *Raksha-Kartri*.

Madhaba Sahu, a business man, came to know this. He met the tribal man and approached him to be his *sisya*. The tribal man first cautioned him regarding the difficulties of worshipping a goddess, but since Madhaba was sincerely interested, then he accepted him as the *sisya*.

After some years, the wife of Madhaba expired and hence, whenever Madhaba was coming to Boirani in connection with his business in the weekly market, he was bringing his only son along with him. Some years later, Madhaba's tribal *guru* also died leaving aside the goddess in unworshipped condition. Hence, the goddess desired to remain along with Madhaba, who may serve her.

One day, while alongwith his son and goods carried on bullock-cart, Madhaba was coming to Boirani, he saw a tribal belle, embellished with various ornaments, following him along. Madhaba could not control his curiosity and enquired about her whereabout. She replied that she did not wish more to stay at her paternal house in Mala area. Therefore, she had come out to stay in the plain. Since she had no relatives in the plains she desired to stay along with Madhaba if she was accepted as his daughter. From that day onwards, Madhaba adopted her as his daughter. In the guise of this tribal belle was the Thakurani to whom Madhaba failed to recognise.

With son and the Thakurani in the guise of daughter, the days of Madhaba passed away smoothly. Earlier, at Boirani, the *padapitha* of goddess Parvati was established in the name of *Mahamayee*. The Thakurani desired for the revival of this *pitha*. For this purpose she selected the day of *Maha Ashtami* when she wished to leave her human form and stay in the *padapitha*. Therefore, she made a plan as per which she started beheading the son of Madhaba on the day of *Maha Ashtami*. When Madhaba saw it, he got annoyed. He scolded her and out of anger sliced her into three pieces, head, trunk and feet. He throw the head with force so that it fell at Berhampur.[1] Similarly, he also threw her trunk in such a manner that it fell at Pitala.[2] However, in the mean time, the Thakurani with her Devirupa had gone away to space leaving aside her *manaba-* or *maya-rupa*, which was sliced by Madhaba.

After losing his son and adopted daughter, Madhaba felt extremely sorry and desired to commit suicide out of anguish. At that moment, he heard a *sunya-bani* from the *Devi-rupi Mahamayee*, that "Dear father, have patience, I was *Mahamayee* in the guise of the tribal belle. I did all these things for a good purpose which was a secret all along but now I would divulge it to you. Long long ago, the king Daksha Prajapati was celebrating a *yajna*. He invited many but not his eldest son-in-law, Siva. Siva's wife, Sati Parvati felt insulted with this type of behaviour from her father and consequently sacrificed herself in the *yajna-kunda*. Hearing the death of the Sati, Lord Siva became terribly annoyed. He carried on shoulder the dead body of his wife and danced to make destruction all round. All deities felt panic and requested Lord Vishnu to find out a solution. Vishnu, then, sent his *Chakra*, which sliced the Sati's body into 108 parts. These parts fell down at different places where they are now worshipped. All these 108 places were regarded as sacred centres by the people. Among these, except Boirani, where Sati's *pada* had fallen, the rest 107 sacred centres gained popularity. I felt that the *pada pitha* of *Sati* at Boirani should also gain popularity and be worshipped by people. Hence, while searching a befitting *sadhaka* for this purpose, I found you. I stayed along with you as your daughter. The rest was planned deliberately by me so that you would slice me and my feet would remain here being merged with Sati's *pada*. So do not be worried for your son. Sprinkle *mantra-jala* over him so that he will get up. Listening the *sunya-bani* from the goddess, Madhaba cooled down and paid reverence to her.

Analysis

This sacred belief is also an 'individual experience' type. It speaks about the context in which the Thakurani took its origin at Boirani, Pitala and Berhampur. It also narrates the background of its structural variation at the three places. It helps to make a structural co-relation among the three sacred segments, Berhampur, Boirani and Pitala. Hence, this sacred belief may be included in the 'structural' category. Apart from this, both little and great traditions are found to be in a compromising state in it. Thus, in the first phase, the sacred belief narrates the Thakurani as a tribal deity, which was worshipped by a tribal priest. Later on, she remained as a tribal belle, adopted by casteman. This part of the sacred belief is of local nature and, hence, may be treated as little traditional type. The second part of the sacred belief narrates how Boirani became the *pada-pitha* of Sati Parvati. This part of the sacred belief is universally popular among the Hindus and, hence, may be treated as of great traditional nature. The last part of the sacred belief depicts about the merging of the *maya-pada* of the Thakurani in the *sati-pada* so as to popularise the former. This part of the sacred belief may, therefore, be regarded as an expression of compromise between the little tradition and the great tradition.

Displacement of the Sacred Centre of Budhi Santani at Berhampur

While translating the book, *Berhampura Thakurani Yatra—Deshabhakti* and *Daibabhakti*, written by M.V. Narayana Rao and Janardana Sharma depicts a sacred belief with regard to the displacement of the sacred centre of Budhi Santani from the hilly area near the ancient Mohuri Gada to its present place at Berhampur. As the sacred belief goes, the sacred centre of Budhi Santani was, at first, situated on the hill near the Mohuri Gada, where the King of Mohuri estate was staying. The goddess was worshipped at that place and the Thakurani Yatra was also celebrated there. But in 1832 A.D., when the king and his people revolted against the British-India Government, the Mohuri gada was obstructed by the latter. This created trouble in the daily worship of the goddess. Hence, the King brought the *Chakra* of the goddess to the place at Berhampur, where she is now worshipped. The king appointed Patrala Peraya as the *Desabehera* and permitted him to make the *puja* of the goddess. He also gave the Svikara Patra to the *Desabehera* to celebrate the Thakurani Yatra as the patron biennially.

Analysis

This sacred belief finds its expression at the level of scriptural description. However, this does not represent the great tradition. Rather it depicts the local situation regarding the displacement of the sacred centre of Budhi Santani. Hence, it may be included in the little traditional category.

Budhi Santani, Desabehera and Thakurani Yatra

Dr. Beni Madhaba Padhi, in his article 'Bramhapura Thakurani Yatra', has depicted a sacred belief that Desabehera was the first priest of Budhi Santani, the presiding deity of Berhampur. It was a Tuesday late night in the month of Chaitra, that Desabehera, while coming out of his home for urination, saw a girl of 17 or 18 years old, unbraided and dressed with a black saree, crying at a distance. Listening to her cry, he asked about her village and enquired of her trouble. The girl replied that she had desired to go to her paternal house but, somehow, missed the route, and for this, she felt helpless. Desabehera consoled her and asked to stay in his house for the night. He told her to be fearless since he is father-like. Further, he told to help her reaching at her paternal house in the next day morning. Desabehera then asked her to bring her baggage. On hearing this, the girl moved towards the nearby bush, Desabehera also followed her to give company. But as soon as he came near the sacred centre of the Grama-devati, he could not see the girl. He became astonished and puzzled. He thought the entire event to be either dreamy or magical. He came to home and tried to sleep but failed.

Next morning, Desabehera completed his *nityakarma* and went to make the morning *puja* of Budhi Santani. But when he placed flowers on the forehead of the goddess for her *puja*, the flowers fell down. He tried again and again but failed. He got surprised to find the goddess not receiving the *puja*. He thought that, perhaps, he might have done somewhere a mistake. Thinking this, he prostrated before the goddess. In mind, he told the goddess that he would remain in this position so long as she would not divulge the fact. After a while, the goddess made a *sunya-bani* speaking to Desabehera that she did not receive puja from him since she had been accepted as a daughter by him last night. Desabehera then asked her that if that was her desire, then how would she get her *puja*. The goddess replied that she would get *puja* from the person, whom he would see first while going back from that place. Listening this, Desabehera could not control his tears and asked her whether that would be the last meet between them. The goddess consoled him and told that she would visit his house, by invitation, biennially to spend some days merrily and then would come back.

In the mean time Desabehera's Bhandari, who had come to shave him, waited for his arrival for some time at his house. But after finding him late, he came to the sacred centre of Budhi Santani. The Desabehera, after his conversation with the goddess, while coming back to his house, saw the Bhandari first and asked him to make the *puja* of the goddess. Initially, the Bhandari was not willing but Desabehera narrated everything and told that the goddess desired him to make *puja*.

Since this event, Padhi narrates, the Bhandari and his descendants have been serving the goddess as *pujakas* and the Desabehera and his descendants have been inviting the goddess, biennially, for the celebration of the Thakurani Yatra.

All the sacred specialists commonly share this belief and claim that the Thakurani Mandira is the *sasu-ghara* of Budhi Santani and the house of Desabehera is her *bapa-ghara*. Further, the Thakurani Yatra is commemorated during the visit of Budhi Santani, after an invitation by the Desabehera, to her paternal house. The people of her paternal village make *puja* to exhibit their reverence to her.

Analysis

This sacred belief has emanated out of Desabehera's personal experience and, hence, it may be included under the individual experience category. Further, this sacred belief, which was earlier an oral tradition, now finds its expression at the level of scriptural tradition. It also gives a narration regarding the origin of the functional roles of the Bhandaris as the Mandira *pujakas* and the Desabehera as the patron of the Thakurani Yatra. Hence, it may be treated as a functional type of sacred belief. This sacred belief also speaks about the characters who are not universally popular among the Hindus. Rather, they obtain recognition locally. Hence, this may also be regarded as a little traditional type of sacred belief.

Budhi Santani and Dasa-Mahavidyas

At Berhampur, in the temple of Budhi Santani, there are images of ten goddesses, which are carved on the outer wall of the temple. These ten goddesses are Kali, Tara, Sodasi or Tripura-Sundari, Bhubanesari, Chhinnamastika, Bhairavi, Dhumabati, Bagalamukhi, Matangi and Kamalatmika. The symbolic structure of each goddess is different from others. These structures have been constructed as per the scriptural description. Devotees, who come to propitiate Budhi Santani, also pay regards to these goddesses. As per the scriptural description, these ten goddesses are referred to be the Dasa-Mahavidyas of the Adi-Shakti or Adi-Mata. Some of the devotees and sacred specialists were interviewed regarding their belief in the relation between Budhi Santani and the Dasa-Mahavidyas. All of them replied that these Dasa-Mahavidyas are ten *avatars* of Budhi Santani, i.e., the Adi-Mata.

Analysis

This sacred belief exhibits a compromising state between the little tradition and the great tradition. While Budhi Santani is a deity representing the little tradition, the concepts of Adi-Shakti or Adi-Mata and Dasa-Mahavidyas represent the great tradition of Hindu civilization. Here, by their sacred belief that Budhi Santani is the Adi-Shakti or Adi-Mata the people have developed a compromise between the two traditions.

Budhi Santani and Durga

The goddess Durga is also equated by the people with Budhi Santani.

The Mandira *pujakas*, when interviewed, told that they believe Budhi Santani and Durga as the same goddess. For this, at the temple, the *Bije Pratima* of the Thakurani structurally represents the Mahisamardini Durga.

Analysis

Here also the sacred belief strengthens the compromise between the little and great traditions by equating Budhi Santani, a deity of little tradition, with Durga, a deity of great tradition.

Budhi Santani, Kali and Baidhara

Budhi Santani, Kali and Baidhara are three deities who are commonly propitiated at the Utsav Mandira during the Thakurani Yatra. Moreover, at the Thakurani temple, Baidhara is worshipped along with Budhi Santani whereas Kali has a separate temple. The sacred specialists have developed certain sacred beliefs in their mind regarding the relationship among these three deities. They also transmit these sacred beliefs to the people.

1. The Thakurani Mandira *pujakas* believe that the deity, Baidhara is the son of Budhi Santani and hence, is worshipped at the Thakurani temple. As regards the relation of Budhi Santani with Kali a difference is marked in their beliefs. While some of them claim that Kali is the *bohu* of Budhi Santani, others believe that Kali is one of her sisters.
2. The Desabehera believes that Kali and Baidhara are the daughter-in-law and son of Budhi Santani respectively.
3. The Damla *pujakas* of Utsav Mandira also regard Kali and Baidhara as Budhi Santani's daughter-in-law, and son respectively.
4. The *kahali*-blower of Raula community claims that Kali and Baidhara are two Hindu deities worshipped along with Budhi Santani at the Utsav Mandira during the Thakurani Yatra. However, he is ignorant about the nature of relationship among these three deities.
5. Among the sacred specialists of Dalua community who hold the hands of the Thakurani *ghata*-carrier during the Thakurani Yatra, there is variation in their belief regarding the relationship among these three deities, Budhi Santani, Kali and Baidhara.

An old sacred specialist among them expressed his ignorance about the relationship among these deities. But the two young sacred specialists who, at present, are playing their roles in the Thakurani Yatra, believe that Baidhara is the son of Budhi Santani. However, as regards the relation between Kali and Budhi Santani, both differ in their belief. While one believes that Kali is the daughter-in-law of Budhi Santani, the other believes the two deities to be the sisters.

6. The *jhadudar* of the Thakurani temple, believes Kali as the daughter-in-law of Budhi Santani. But as regards the relation between Baidhara and Budhi Santani, he expressed his ignorance.

Analysis

These sacred beliefs aim at establishing a relationship among the three deities, Budhi Santani, Kali and Baidhara. The nature of relationship among them, as depicted in these sacred beliefs, is not universally accepted by the Hindus. But instead, the beliefs are locally claimed since they have indigenous origin. Hence, they may be included in the structural as well as little traditional category. They also find their expression at the level of oral tradition.

Phulamanda

Phulamanda is a bundle of Itamala flowers. This is used as a sacred symbol of Budhi Santani during the Thakurani Yatra. It is also associated with certain sacred beliefs.

1. There is a popular belief that the *phulamanda* jumps from the Thakurani's head down to Desabehera's hand expressing the Thakurani's willingness to visit her paternal house. The *phulamanda* is believed to have the power of the goddess and hence, it represents her sacred symbol during the Thakurani Yatra. The *phulamanda* is also believed to maintain its freshness till the end of the *yatra* because,it carries the power of Budhi Santani.
2. Another belief depicts that the *phulamanda* is to be prepared only of the brick-red variety of Itamala flowers because its brick-red colour is very much appreciated by the Thakurani. The *phulamanda* supplier of Raula community narrates that

once she could not collect the brick-red variety of Itamala flowers and hence, she prepared the *phulamanda* out of the yellow variety of Itamala flowers. She then took the *phulamanda* and submitted to the Desabehera's wife but the latter refused to accept it since she has the belief that the goddess would not be pleased without the brick-red variety of Itamala flowers. When the *phulamanda* supplier expressed her inability to get the flowers, the Desabehera's wife sent her to a person's house to get the flowers. She did it and brought another *phulamanda* of brick-red Itamala flowers.

Analysis

Both of these sacred beliefs find their expression at the level of oral tradition. As the two beliefs are of local origin and are not universally popular among the Hindus, these may be included in the 'little tradition' category. Among these two sacred beliefs, the first one speaks that the jumping of *phulamanda* and its maintenance of freshness till the end of the *yatra* is due to the Thakurani's power. People have believed it since they have observed it; hence this belief may be treated as a 'common-experience' type. On the other hand, the second sacred belief speaks about the experience of the *phulamanda* supplier and so it may be treated as an 'individual-experience' type.

Subha-khunti

Subha-khunti or the auspicious pole is a piece of bamboo which is ritually made auspicious at the Thakurani temple prior to the commencement of the Thakurani Yatra. It is then placed at the spot where the Utsav Mandira is constructed later on. The placement of *subha-khunti* is also associated with certain sacred beliefs, which are claimed by the sacred specialists.

1. The Thakurani Mandira *pujakas* believe that the placement of *subha-khunti* amounts to the *subha sthapana* of the Utsav Mandira.
2. The Thakurani Mandira *jhadudar*, the *phulamanda* supplier, the Damla *pujakas* of Utsav Mandira and the *kahali* blower believe that the placement of *subha-khunti* indicates confirmation as regards the beginning of the Thakurani Yatra.
3. The Dalua sacred specialists believe that the placement of *subha-khunti* means the *subharambha* of the Thakurani Yatra.

Analysis

These beliefs have developed out of the general experiences that the Thakurani Yatra commences only after the placement of *subha-khunti*. Further, the people have observed that the construction of the Utsav Mandira, which is done after the placement of *subha-khunti*, has been taking place without any trouble and, hence, their belief has been strengthened. This belief is orally expressed by the sacred specialists who have commonly experienced it. Hence, this sacred belief may be treated as a 'common-experience' and of 'functional' type, which finds its expression at the level of oral tradition.

Dharma Jhanda

Certain sacred beliefs, as narrated below, are associated with the *dharma jhanda*, which is placed a few yards in front of the Utsav Mandira during the Thakurani Yatra.

1. One hundred years ago, a little boy of Desabehera Sahi stroke at the *dharma jhanda*, during the Thakurani Yatra, by a stick while playing around it in the morning. Some people had seen it but had not given much importance and, therefore, they had not informed his parents. But when, in the evening the boy died with diarrhoea and vomitting they informed this event and thereafter, people developed a fear towards the *dharma jhanda*. As a result, their belief that *dharma jhanda* also possesses the *shakti* of Budhi Santani was strengthened.
2. All the sacred specialists commonly share the belief that *dharma jhanda* is the store house of Budhi Santani. Hence, the devotees, who intend to offer *pana* and *sankhudi bhoga* to the goddess, place them near the *dharma jhanda*.

Analysis

These two sacred beliefs have a local origin and speak about the function of the *dharma jhanda*. Hence, these may be included in the 'little traditional' and 'functional' categories. Further, both of these find their expression at the level of oral tradition.

Thakurani Dootas

The Thakurani *dootas* are persons wearing the dresses of king, minister, soldiers and police men. During the Thakurani Yatra, while Budhi

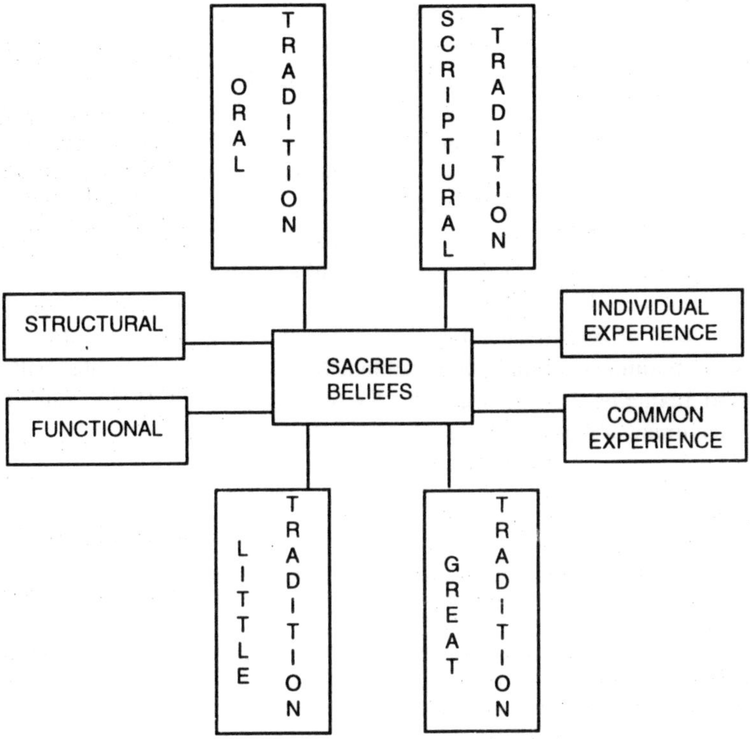

FIG. 7.2: Broad Typological Classification of Sacred Beliefs.

Santani goes on a *sahi-bhramana*, these *dootas* also go as her body-guards. People, who serve the goddess as her *dootas*, follow certain rules. They believe that violation of these rules amounts to enraging the goddess who may harm them. It is said that once, a person, who had made *manasika* to serve the goddess as her *doota* during the Thakurani Yatra, did not keep purity in mind. On the day when he was to serve as the *doota*, he had visited a prostitute's house. Hence, he invited the wrath of the goddess and as a result, he died of diarrhoea and vomiting on the next day.

Analysis

This sacred belief finds its expression at the level of oral tradition. Further, it may also be treated as a little traditional type since it has popularity only at the local level.

To sum up, I have observed that the sacred symbols, with a wide range of typological variations, bring out a continuity and integration among various elements of the sacred complex. The sacred beliefs, which are associated with these sacred symbols, substantiate and strengthen this continuity and integration.

In the Sacred Complex of Budhi Santani a combination and coexistence of the Saiva, Vaishnava and Shakta traditions as well as of little and great traditions of Hindu civilization, which has been verified and proved in earlier chapters, is also marked to exist contextually at the level of sacred symbols. At the level of the sacred beliefs of the Sacred Complex of Budhi Santani, a coexistence and compromise of little and great traditions of Hindu civilization is found to exist both contextually and textually. In this way, the Sacred Complex of Budhi Santani Thakurani strengthens the solidarity of Hindu civilization.

NOTES

1. The befallen head is now worshipped in the Thakurani temple at Berhampur.
2. The befallen trunk is now worshipped in the Thakurani temple at Pitala.

8

SUMMARY AND CONCLUSIONS

Ever since the sacred complex model has been formulated by Vidyarthi (Gaya, 1961), some Indian anthropologists (Jha, 1971; Narayan, 1972; Upadhyaya, 1974 and Vidyarthi, Saraswati and Jha, 1974) have applied it in their study at different ancient textual Hindu places of pilgrimage. As a result of all these studies, a number of hypotheses could be developed and proved with reference to the core of Hindu civilization. Some of these hypotheses have been tested against the empirical data collected in the present study on the Sacred Complex of Budhi Santani of Berhampur as follows:

> That the sacred complex of a Hindu deity reflects a level of integration and continuity among its various elements, namely sacred centres, sacred performances, sacred specialists, sacred sacrificers, sacred sacrifices, sacred symbols and sacred beliefs.

It has been observed in the study on the Sacred Complex of Budhi Santani that a large number of sacred centres coexist on the basis of either structural integration or organisational linkage. These sacred centres are not mere geographical spots. Rather, these are symbolically expressed so as to represent specific deities. The typological variation of these symbolic expressions has been discussed in Chapter 7, which highlights that sacred centres are identified with either a piece of stone smeared with vermillion or an image decorated with ornaments or a *ghata* or a tree or a bamboo pole. As it has been discussed in Chapters 2 and 3, these sacred centres irrespective of the variations at symbolic levels are spots where sacred performances are performed. Like the sacred centres, the sacred performances are also noted to be symbolic in nature. In the context of the Sacred Complex of Budhi Santani all the rituals connected with the daily worship of Budhi Santani in her temple and her Utsav Mandira are symbolically performed. Moreover, the rituals associated with *ghata sansthapana, digabandhana, sansthapana* of images of deities and epic heroes on *rathas* and *sansthapana* of *subha-khunti* and *dharma jhanda* during the Thakurani Yatra are also symbolically performed. All these signify the existence of a combination and integration among such elements as the sacred centres, sacred performances and sacred symbols in the Sacred Complex of Budhi Santani. To further focus on the integration among the various elements of sacred complex, the data analysed in Chapters 4 and 5 about the essentiality of the sacred specialists for the observance of sacred performances at different sacred centres may be specially noted. Thus, it is observed at the contextual level that the sacred sacrificers take the help of the sacred specialists while ritually offering their sacred sacrifices to the deities. However, the factor which strongly integrates the elements like sacred centres, sacred performances, sacred specialists, sacred sacrificers, sacred sacrifices and sacred symbols is the sacred belief. In the context of the Sacred Complex of Budhi Santani the sacred beliefs, vividly discussed in Chapter 7, not only logically explain but also help in sustaining the integration among the different elements of the sacred complex. On the other hand, the consolidation of these sacred beliefs among the people is the result of organised effort of the sacred specialists. The present study, therefore, clearly shows that in a sacred complex there exist integration and continuity among its various elements. Thus, the hypothesis that the sacred complex of a Hindu deity reflects a level of integration and continuity among its various elements, namely sacred centres, sacred performances, sacred specialists, sacred sacrificers, sacred sacrifices, sacred symbols and sacred beliefs holds good with reference to the Sacred Complex of Budhi Santani Thakurani of Berhampur.

> That the sacred complex of a Hindu deity reflects a level of compromise and combination between great and little traditions and also among Saivic, Vaishnavic and Shakti cults.

In his study at Gaya (1961) Vidyarthi tested and proved, for the first time, that the sacred complex of a Hindu place of pilgrimage reflects a level of continuity, compromise and combination between great and little traditions. This hypothesis was later on tested at other sacred cities by many scholars (Jha, 1971, 1973; Upadhyaya, 1974; Narayan, 1972 and Vidyarthi, Saraswati and Jha, 1979) and was found to hold good as far as ancient and textual Hindu places of pilgrimage of India are concerned. For instance, Jha (1973: 56) after reviewing the materials on the Sacred *kshetra* of Ratanpur stated that the Sacred Complex of Ratanpur may be considered to be sanskritic and great traditional in character, it also includes several sacred centres which have grown out of little traditions. The interaction between great and little traditions was also analysed and proved by Goswami and Morab (1974: 121) not in a sacred city but with regard to the Chamundesvari temple of Mysore. It may also be pointed out here that while analysing the integrational character of a sacred complex, scholars have also proved how does a sacred complex make a combination and compromise among different Hindu cults such as Saiva, Vaishnava and Shakta. Thus, in the context of sacred centres, B.N. Sahay (1974: 16) proved that the sacred city of Kashi exhibits a combination and compromise of Saiva, Vaishnava and Shakta sacred centres. Narayan (1983: 89) again proved it with reference to the Sacred Complex of Basukinath.

The data obtained with regard to the Sacred Complex of Budhi Santani also corroborates, both at textual and contextual level, that there exists a level of compromise and combination between the great and little traditions and coexistence among the Saiva, Vaishnava and Shakta cults. Thus, at the level of sacred centres, the deities of these three cults are found to be represented in the precinct of the temples of Budhi Santani and Kali. Apart from it, the sacred centres of these Saiva, Vaishnava and Shakta deities are also noted to be installed during the Thakurani Yatra. To further attest the combination and co-existence of these three cults, the findings of Chapter 6, under "Sacred Sacrificers and Sacred Sacrifices", may be taken into consideration. Thus, Chapter 6 focuses that, at the level of *besha*-sacrifice, the sacred sacrificers put on *beshas* of Siva, Krishna, Naba-Durga, Jwalamukhi and Balarama, which justifies that there exist combination and co-existence among Saiva, Vaishnava and Shakta cults so far as the sacred complex of a deity is concerned.

The empirical data with regard to the Sacred Complex of Budhi Santani point out that there is a co-existence of the sacred centres of both great and little traditional deities (see Chapter 1). This feature is, further, substantiated at the level of sacred symbols (see Chapter 7) and sacred sacrifices (see Chapter 6). The facts delineated and analysed in Chapter 7 as regards the sacred beliefs also establish that there exist combination and compromise between great and little traditions at the level of scriptural tradition as well as oral tradition. Thus, the hypothesis that the sacred complex of a Hindu deity reflects a level of combination and compromise between great and little traditions and also among

Saivic, Vaishnavic and Shakti cults is proved beyond doubt with reference to the empirical data collected from the study of the Sacred Complex of Budhi Santani of Berhampur.

> That the sacred specialists of a Hindu sacred complex develop a common style of life because of their functional involvement in the institution of sacred either by popularising certain texts and myths as the ritual consultants or by officiating as the ritual specialists or by serving as the ritual associates.

In his study among the Gayawals, Vidyarthi (1961) first proved that the Gayawal as a caste of priestly specialists have their own orthodox style of life, which finds expression in their social usages, their exclusiveness from the urban population, their ritual performances and above all in their attitude to modern development. Later on, Vidyarthi, Jha and Saraswati (1974: 110) again verified this finding in the context of the Sacred Complex of Kashi and found that although the sacred specialists in Kashi come from different castes, belong to different linguistic and geographical regions and are functionally heterogeneous, they themselves share a common cultural consciousness so as to lead a style of life that can be identified as the "*Panda culture*". These two studies point out that at Hindu sacred complexes of universal importance, the sacred specialists maintain a common style of life by popularising certain texts and myths and by officiating as ritual specialists and temple priests.

In the present study, I have also tested this hypothesis with reference to the sacred specialists who are part and parcel of the Sacred Complex of Budhi Santani of Berhampur. The empirical data collected in this regard are analysed in Chapters 4 and 5. The facts delineated and analysed in Chapter 4 establish that as like the pauranic sacred complexes at Kashi, Gaya and Vaidyanathdham, the sacred specialists at the non-pauranic Sacred Complex of Budhi Santani are also discriminated on the basis of caste, language, sect and functional role. But due to their hereditary participation in the institution of sacred, a sense of co-operation and integration has developed among them for which they cut across all these discriminations. As projected in this chapter, these sacred specialists are observed to be functionally involved in the institution of sacred either as the ritual consultants who popularise certain texts and myths or as the ritual specialists who perform rituals at the Thakurani temple and also during the Thakurani Yatra or as ritual associates who assist the ritual specialists in the performance of rituals or provide the sacred sacrificers with sacred materials for sacrifices. The analysis of Chapter 5, further, brings out that because of their hereditary functional involvement in the institution of sacred, they have developed a common style of life, which can be self-identified as *sevaka culture*. The facts of this chapter also attest that the homogeneity in their style of life is reflected in settlement pattern, family and kinship life, religious life and the languages used towards the sacred sacrificers. Hence, it goes without saying that as like the sacred specialists at pauranic Hindu sacred complexes, which are universally popular, the sacred specialists of the Sacred Complex of Budhi Santani of Berhampur, which is non-pauranic in nature and has a regional level of importance, also develop a common cultural consciousness due to their functional involvement at different levels in the institution of sacred. Thus, the hypothesis that the sacred specialists of a Hindu sacred complex develop a common style of life because of their functional involvement in the institution of sacred either by popularising certain texts and myths as the ritual consultants or by officiating as the ritual specialists or by serving as the ritual associates holds good with reference to the Sacred Complex of Budhi Santani of Berhampur.

That the nature of organization of sacred performances reflects the local pattern of Hindu social organization.

I have tested this hypothesis especially by the data analysed and delineated in Chapters 2 and 3. The Hindus in their social life follow certain customs and traditions, which reflect an ideal pattern, when they serve their respectable personalities. This ideal pattern is also followed while the sacred specialists serve Budhi Santani Thakurani through various sacred performances during the daily ritual worship at her temple. The data presented in Chapter 3 also highlights that when Budhi Santani visits her father's house during the Thakurani Yatra, she is also served as per the customs and traditions of the local pattern of Hindu social life. Moreover, in the distribution of functional roles among the sacred specialists of various castes, this principle is also followed. Thus, the role of priesthood is offered to the Bhandaris and the Damlas because these communities nourish priesthood at mother-goddess temples as their caste occupations in many villages in Ganjam. Similarly, only basing upon their traditional caste occupations, the Hadis are permitted to serve as the Mandira *jhadudar* and the drum-beater, the Raulas are appointed to supply the *phulamanda* and blow the flute, the Medris are asked to supply the *changudi* and to serve as the musicians, and

Kumbharas are allowed to supply the *ghatas* and *rukhas*. All these facts attest that during the organization of sacred performances in the Sacred Complex of Budhi Santani, the local pattern of Hindu social organization has been taken into consideration. Thus, the hypothesis that the nature of organization of sacred performances reflects the local pattern of Hindu social organization is proved in the context of the present study.

> That the sacred complex, in general, and the sacred specialists, in particular, have been in the process of modification and transformation as a result of a general development in the larger universe of Hindu civilization of which they are a part.

Vidyarthi for the first time tested this hypothesis in the context of the Sacred Complex of Hindu Gaya and observed that under the impact of Western civilization, the sacred complex is witnessing a transformation. With the adoption of industrial technology and new means of transportation and with the acceptance of the principles of secularization and democracy, India, as a whole, is undergoing a series of social and economic changes. With all these changes, the sacred complex, which constitutes an integral part of civilization, is also in the process of change. The three elements of the sacred complex—the sacred geography, the sacred performances and the sacred specialists—are under a process of adjustment to the changing situation (1961: 113). Narayan also studied on the changing aspect of the Sacred Complex of Basukinath and found that the sacred complex acts as a balancing force between the modernity and the tradition of sacred performances while changing substantially in dress, food habits and residential pattern (1983: 90).

In the present study, I have also made a contextual analysis on the level of transformation and modification undergone in the life style of the sacred specialists, in particular, and the Sacred Complex of Budhi Santani, in general. I found that as regards the sacred centres, sacred symbols, sacred sacrifices and the sacred performances, earlier customs and traditions are continued and strictly followed. I have also noted that the sacred beliefs greatly contribute in the continuity of these traditions. The families of the sacred specialists have also not given up their hereditary involvement in the institution of sacred. But many members, especially the younger ones, of these families have declined to be involved in the institution of sacred for the maintenance of their livelihood. Being affected by the factors like modern sources of income, limitation of income from the institution of sacred and higher education, the sacred specialists are found to have engaged themselves in different government services, private services and business. In addition to this, the sacred specialists of the younger generation are also found to have adopted the modern dresses, medicare and education. Some of them have also decorated and designed their houses with modern equipment. The earlier restrictions with regard to food habit and inter-caste social intercourse are not strictly followed. All these facts, which are presented in Chapter 5, attest that the factors causing the general development in the larger universe of Hindu civilization have also affected the style of life of the sacred specialists. Thus, in the context of the Sacred Complex of Budhi Santani, it can be said that the sacred complex in general and the sacred specialists in particular, have been in the process of modification and transformation as a result of a general development in the larger universe of Hindu civilization of which they are a part.

GLOSSARY OF LOCAL TERMS

Local Term		*English Meaning*
Abharana	:	Ornamenting
Achamana	:	Washing face and hands after meal
Adi-Manaba	:	Primitive man
Adi-Mata	:	Primordial Mother
Adi-Shakti	:	Primordial Power
Ahara	:	Food
Akhanda deepa	:	Unbroken lamp
Alu	:	Potato
Anna Bhoga	:	Food offerings to a deity
Arata	:	Spinning wheel
Archana	:	Worship
Artha	:	Wealth
Asana	:	Seat
Ashanti	:	Discontentment
Aswina	:	Name of a month (September-October)
Atma	:	Self
Avahana	:	Invocation
Bagha	:	Tiger
Balapaka	:	Hair-sacrifice
Bapa-ghara	:	Paternal house
Bara	:	Kind of cake fried in oil
Barakoli patra	:	Jujube leaf
Barana puja	:	Engagement worship
Barsikia sraddha	:	Annual death ritual
Belapatra	:	Bael leaf
Bena	:	Flag
Besha	:	Dress
Besha-dhari	:	Person wearing a dress
Bhagavat-krupa	:	Divine blessings
Bhalu	:	Bear
Bhata	:	Boiled rice

Local Term		*English Meaning*
Bhuta	:	Ghost
Bije pratima	:	Moving image
Binchana	:	Hand-made fan
Bisarjana	:	Abandonment
Bohu	:	Daughter-in-law
Boita	:	Boat
Brahma-Muhurta	:	Early morning
Bundi	:	A kind of sweet
Chaddar	:	Bed sheet
Chadeia	:	Bird-catcher
Chadeiani	:	Lady bird-catcher
Chakra	:	A wheel like weapon
Changudi	:	Wicker
Chasa-dala	:	A group of peasants
Chaula	:	Rice
Chhota	:	Lame
Chuda-ghasa	:	A powder mixture of flattened paddy and sugar
Dahi	:	Curd
Dahi-bhata	:	A mixture of boiled rice and curd
Dakshina	:	Gift given to a person as a mark of respect at parting
Dakshini Stri	:	South Indian woman
Dali	:	Soup made of split pulse
Dambru	:	A small double-faced drum with its middle part narrower than the faces
Darsana	:	Visit
Darsana-griha	:	Visiting room
Dasa-Mahavidyas	:	Ten great incarnations
Deepa	:	Lamp
Dera ratha	:	Chariot of the Dera community
Desabeherani	:	Wife of Desabehera
Devi-rupa	:	Goddess-appearance
Dhanu	:	Bow
Dharma Jhanda	:	Pious banner
Dhobani	:	Woman of washerman community
Dhoti	:	A cloth to wear
Dhupa	:	Incense
Digabandhana	:	Constructing and tyling the place of worship

Local Term		*English Meaning*
Doota	:	Messenger
Durganama	:	Various names of goddess Durga
Durga-Staba	:	Praise of goddess Durga
Garbha-griha	:	Sanctum Sanctorum
Gauduni	:	Woman of milkman community
Ghata	:	Pitcher
Ghata sansthapana	:	Establishment of earthen pitcher
Ghara	:	House
Ghodani	:	Cover
Gobara-pani	:	Water mixture of cow-dung
Gota gua	:	Unbroken betel nut
Gota haladi	:	Unbroken turmeric
Graha	:	Planet
Graha-shanti	:	Pacification of planet
Gramadevis	:	Village goddesses
Gunia	:	Sorcerer
Guru	:	Teacher
Haladi	:	Turmeric
Haladi-pani	:	Water mixture of turmeric
Harida	:	Pegion pea
Irani Stri	:	Iranian woman
Itamala	:	A kind of plant whose flowers are specially utilised for the ritual worship of Budhi Santani
Istadevi	:	Tutelary deity
Jalanta deepa	:	Burning lamp
Japa	:	Repetition of incantations
Jataka	:	Horoscope
Jhoti	:	Floor designs
Jhuna dhupa	:	Resin incense
Zilla	:	District
Jyesthansa	:	Extra share of the eldest son from paternal property
Kadali	:	Banana
Kahali	:	Trumpet
Kakudi	:	Cucumber
Kalakunchi	:	A piece of black cloth
Kalara	:	Bitter gourd
Kama	:	Desire

Local Term		*English Meaning*
Kamandalu	:	A water pot
Kapurusha Raja	:	A coward king
Keutuni	:	Woman of fisherman community
Khandadhua pani	:	Water used to wash a sword
Khichri	:	Fried rice
Khurda Paika	:	Warrior of Khurda locality
Kosadhyaksha	:	Treasurer
Kula-Raja	:	Caste-King
Kula-Rani	:	Caste-Queen
Kumbha	:	Pitcher
Kunchi	:	Crimped folded part of a cloth
Landa Brahmin	:	Bald Brahmin
Madhuparka	:	An offering made by mixing together ghee, honey, curd, sugar and water
Maha-deepa	:	A large lamp
Mahatmya	:	Greatness
Mala	:	Garland
Malasri Mantra	:	A hymn to worship goddesses
Manaba-rupa	:	Human-appearance
Manasika besha	:	Desired dress
Manasika ghata	:	Desired pitcher
Mandala	:	Regional
Mandara	:	China rose
Mandira-agana	:	Temple-courtyard
Mandira Bedha	:	Compound wall round a temple
Mandira Jhadudar	:	Temple-Sweeper
Mandira Jhadudari	:	Sweeping of Temple
Mangala Arati	:	Preliminary waving of lamp
Mangala bandana	:	Preliminary obeisance
Mantra-jala	:	Water consecrated by means of incantations
Mankada	:	Monkey
Master	:	Teacher
Masterani	:	Lady teacher
Matangini Mantra	:	A hymn to worship goddesses
Matha	:	Monastery
Matru-Shakti	:	Mother-Power
Mausima	:	Maternal aunt
Maya-rupa	:	Illusory appearance

Local Term		English Meaning
Mohuri-gada	:	Fort of ex-Mohuri estate
Mohuri Raja	:	King of ex-Mohuri estate
Moksha	:	Salvation
Muan	:	A ball of fried paddy seasoned with treacle
Muga	:	A kind of pulse (Phaseolus mungo)
Mukhya ghata	:	Chief pitcher
Nabata pana	:	Sweet drink prepared of refined molasses
Nabikas	:	Boatmen
Nadia	:	Cocoanut
Naivedya	:	Anything dedicated to a deity
Nari-rupi Thakurani	:	Goddess in appearance of a woman
Non-Palidina	:	Day when one does not have his turn of assignment
Odia Stri	:	Oriya woman
Opasa	:	Abstinence of food
Pada pitha	:	Foot seat
Padya	:	Water given to wash the feet
Pahada bhoga	:	Food offering given prior to sleep
Pahada-paka	:	Spreading the cloth over the road on which a deity or king will pass
Pahada-pakali	:	Person who spreads the cloth over the road on which a deity or king will pass
Pakudi	:	A kind of food
Pana	:	Sweet drink
Panchamrita	:	A mixture of curd, milk, ghee, honey and molasses
Panchopachara	:	Worshipping with five kinds of oblations
Panchopachara puja-paddhati	:	Procedure of worshipping with five kinds of oblations
Panchopachara upasana	:	Worship by offering five kinds of oblations
Parikrama	:	To circumambulate
Patuara	:	Procession
Pauranic	:	Mythological
Phulamala	:	Garland
Phulamanda	:	Flower-bundle
Pita Khechudi	:	Fried rice having bitter taste
Pitha Pratistha	:	Foundation of seat

Local Term		*English Meaning*
Pitha sthapana	:	Establishment of seat
Prabha	:	Crown worn to the pitcher of Thakurani ghata
Pradesh	:	State
Prana pratistha	:	Establishment of life
Preta	:	Spirit
Pujaka	:	Priest
Puspa	:	Flower
Pusta	:	A small piece of gold tied to neck as mangala sutra by married women
Raksha-Kartri	:	Saviour
Rakshas-munda	:	Demon-head
Ratha	:	Chariot
Rejai	:	Quilt
Rukha	:	Lamp-stand
Rupas	:	Appearances
Saba-yatra	:	Procession carrying a dead body
Sabhapati	:	President
Sadhaka	:	Man practising austerities
Sadhu	:	A religious mendicant
Sahanika	:	Forbearing
Sahanikakari	:	Person who forebears
Saheb	:	An European
Sahi	:	Part of a village or town
Sahi Parikrama (Sahi Bhramana)	:	Walking through a part of a village or town
Shakti	:	Power
Samarpana mantra	:	Hymns for a ritual offer
Samkalpa	:	Mental resolve
Sandhya Arati	:	Waving of lamp in the evening
Sankha	:	Conch-shell
Sankhudi	:	Food boiled in water
Sankranti	:	The day of passage of the Sun from one sign of zodiac to another
Saparivara	:	Having a family
Sapua	:	Snake-charmer
Sapuani	:	Lady snake-charmer
Sara	:	Arrow
Sarahada	:	Boundary

Local Term		*English Meaning*
Sasu-ghara	:	Mother-in-law's house
Sata Bhaunis	:	Seven sisters
Seja	:	Bed
Senapati	:	Headman of a Devanga Sahi
Sevaka	:	Servant
Sindur	:	Vermillion
Sisya	:	Disciple
Sitala Mantra	:	Hymns of pacification
Snana	:	Bathing
Sraddha	:	Death ritual
Sraddhaa	:	Reverence
Subha Khunti	:	Auspicious pole
Subha Khunti Sthapana	:	Establishment of the auspicious pole
Subharambha	:	Auspicious beginning
Subha-Sthapana	:	Auspicious establishment
Sunya-bani	:	Divine message
Svikara patra	:	Letter of consent
Takia	:	Pillow
Tangi	:	Battle-axe
Thakurani Mandira Pujari	:	Priest of the Thakurani temple
Thakurani Yatra	:	Goddess fair
Tilaka	:	A mark of sandal or other paste on forehead
Torani	:	Cold rice gruel
Ukhuda	:	Fried paddy seasoned with molasses or sugar
Upakarana	:	Ingredients
Upanayana	:	Ceremony of investiture of the sacred thread
Upa-Sabhapati	:	Vice-President
Utsav Mandira	:	Ceremonial temple
Utsav Mandira Pujari	:	Priest of the ceremonial temple
Vastra	:	Dressing
Vigraha	:	Body
Visarjan	:	Abandonment
Vivaha-yatra	:	Marriage procession
Wardika	:	Regular service relationship
Yajna	:	Vedic sacrifice
Yajna-kunda	:	Pyre of vedic sacrifice

APPENDICES

APPENDIX-I

SCHEDULE (SACRED SPECIALISTS)

Serial No. ________________ *Code No.* ______________ *Date* ________

1. Name :
2. Age :
3. Sex :
4. Caste :
5. Linguistic group :
6. Education :
7. Sect :
8. *Istadevi* :
9. Profession :
10. Family background :
    (a) Family of orientation : Members and relations
    (b) Family of procreation : Members and relations
    (c) Religious influence from family members
11. Married life :
    (a) Age at marriage
    (b) Type of acquiring mate
    (c) Religious rituals associated with marriage
12. Education :
    (a) Level of education
    (b) Reason of drop out
13. Profession :
    (a) Primary profession
    (b) Professional attachment with the Sacred Complex of Budhi Santani
14. Religious life :
    (a) Daily life

(b) Visit to different shrines and *yatras*
(c) Purpose of such visits
(d) Role in the Thakurani Yatra at Berhampur

15. Supplementary Questions
(a) What is your idea about Mother goddesses?
(b) Can you speak about the relationship that exists among the deities, Budhi Santani, Kali and Baidhara?
(c) What do you know about the structure of Budhi Santani?
(d) Photos of which deities are hanged on the walls of the *darsana-griha* of the Thakurani temple?
(e) Why the Thakurani Yatra is celebrated?
(f) Why *itamala* flowers are used to make the *phulamanda* during the Thakurani Yatra?
(g) Why *subha khunti* is placed during the Thakurani Yatra?
(h) Why *dharma jhanda* is placed during the Thakurani Yatra?
(i) Why do people of various castes participate as sacred specialists in the Thakurani Yatra?
(j) What are the implications of *ghata sansthapana* in the Thakurani Yatra?
(k) Why do people put on *beshas* during the Thakurani Yatra?
(l) What are the materials offered to Budhi Santani Thakurani?
(m) Why do the goddesses go on *shai-bhramana* during the Thakurani Yatra?
(n) Why are *rathas* exhibited during the Thakurani Yatra?

SCHEDULE

SOCIAL LIFE OF THE CASTES OF SACRED SPECIALISTS

Serial No. ***Date:***

1.00 *General Information*

1.01 Naming, origin history and migration history of the community.
1.02 Village-wise population distribution of the community.
1.03 Natural environment.
1.04 Language spoken and script used in relation to kinsmen and others.

2.00 *Food Habits*

2.01 Vegetarian, non-vegetarian or both.
2.02 Food items of ordinary days and on special occasions.
2.03 Alcoholic and non-alcoholic drinks.
2.04 Change in food habits.

3.00 *Social Divisions*

3.01 Social divisions, hierarchy and its basis (religious, economic, territorial, social, occupational, etc.).

4.00 *Marriage*

4.01 Rules and forms of marriage.
4.02 Rules regarding dowry/bride price, divorce and remarriage.
4.03 Any changes that have occurred in the above aspects.

5.00 *Family*

5.01 Forms of family.
5.02 Inter-personal relations, rules of inheritance and succession pattern in the family.
5.03 Changes noticed in these aspects.

6.00 *Status of Women*

6.01 Participation in social, ritual, religious, economic and political activities.
6.02 Overall status in comparison to men.
6.03 Changes noticed in above-mentioned aspects.

7.00 *Life Cycle Rituals*

7.01 Rituals and taboos related to birth, childhood, adolescence, marriage and death.
7.02 Any major changes noted in these ritual performances.

8.00 *Occupation*

8.01 Primary and subsidiary occupations.
8.02 Traditional and modern occupations.
8.03 Nature of exchange, labour and wage payment.
8.04 Any changes in occupational pattern.

9.00 *Social Control*

9.01 Composition and function of caste council, village council and modern statutory council.
9.02 Nature of crime and punishment.
9.03 Changes that have occurred since Independence in these aspects.

10.00 *Religion*

10.01 Household, village, regional and community deities worshipped.

10.02 Fairs and festivals observed.

10.03 Changes in these aspects.

11.00 *Art, Craft and Oral Traditions*

11.01 Any art or craft practised as a profession.

11.02 Oral traditions of the community.

11.03 Any changes noted in above aspects.

12.00 *Inter-Ethnic Relationship*

12.01 Traditional inter-ethnic relationship (social, ritual, religious, occupational etc.).

12.02 Modern inter-ethnic relationship.

13.00 *Development Programmes*

13.01 Educational, health care and family welfare programmes.

13.02 Employment, agricultural and nutritional programmes.

13.03 Banking and public distribution system.

13.04 Electricity and mass media communication facilities.

14.00 *Scriptural References*

15.00 *Name, Sex, Age and Address of Informants*

APPENDIX-II

ORAL QUESTIONNAIRE (SACRED SACRIFICERS)

Serial No. _______________ *Code No.* ______________ *Date* ________

1. Name :
2. Sex :
3. Age :
4. Residential address :
5. Caste :
6. *Varna* :
7. Primary profession :
8. Education :
9. Linguistic group :
10. What was the sacred sacrifice made by you during your visit to the Thakurani temple or the Thakurani Yatra?
11. What was the purpose of making this sacred sacrifice?
12. Who motivated you to make this sacred sacrifice?
13. Did you make any arrangement for your accommodation during the occasion of making this sacred sacrifice?
14. If yes, what was the type of accommodation arranged for you?
15. Did you depend on the sacred specialists in order to offer the sacred sacrifice to the Thakurani?
16. If yes, then, what was the nature of your dependence?

APPENDIX-III

LIFE HISTORY NO. 1

Name	:	Kaira Patra
Age	:	42 years
Sex	:	Male
Caste	:	Damla
Linguistic group	:	Oriya
Education	:	Class-III
Sect	:	Shakta
Istadevi	:	Budhi Santani Thakurani
Profession	:	Betel Shopkeeper

Family Background

I, Shri Kaira Patra, am the son of the Late Shri Chhota Patra, who died twenty years ago. My father after marriage stayed as *ghara-jwain* at his father-in-law's house in the village Ambapua, where I am now residing. My father had come to this village sixty years ago. He begot two sons, among them I am one and my brother has died thrity-two years ago. My mother, Late Shrimati Badi Patra, could not survive for many years after the death of my father. Now I have four daughters, Indu, Susama, Hira and Jayanti. Of them, I have completed marriage of Indu and Susama. I have also a son, namely Sankar. Unfortunately, Sankar has absconded from my house for the last eight years. I have celebrated the name-giving ceremony for all my children and their names have been given as per their horoscope.

Marriage

My marriage was arranged by my father. I have married to my maternal uncle's daughter. Before the nuptial ceremony, I have visited the temples of Jagannath and Raghunath at my village for a *darsana* of these deities.

Education

I have read only up to the lower primary level. I was not at all sincere to my study. Neither my parents were imposing on me for study. I was rather swayed by the priestly profession of my father who inherited this hereditary profession from his maternal uncle. Gradually I went along with my father to learn the priestly profession and, hence, I left my school.

Profession

My hereditary profession is *pujaka* of various Thakuranis of Berhampur, Pitala, Chatrapur, Gopalpur, Gopalpur Pentha and Bahadur Pentha during the celebration of Thakurani Yatra at these places. I am not a *pujaka* of any Thakurani Mandira. Moreover, my services during the Thakurani Yatras give me short-term income. Therefore, at Berhampur Bus-stand I have opened a betel shop from which I make a few earning everyday.

Religious Life

Daily Life

Everyday I wake up before 5.30 a.m. and complete my *nityakarma* and bathing within an hour. Then I make *puja* to the household deities. After having *pakhala* and vegetable fry as my breakfast, I go to my shop where I stay up to 8 p.m. During the day I take my lunch at nearby hotel. When I come back to home I read the Thakurani *stuti* and then go to bed.

Deities Worshipped at Home

At home I have kept photos of deities such as Krishna, Vishnu, Siva, Durga, Nrusinhanath, Kali, Ganesha, Saraswati, Laxmi and Budhi Santani Thakurani. Whenever I stay at home, I offer *arati* to these deities in the morning and also at evening. In my absence, my wife performs this ritual.

Visit

I have visited the temples of Bhairavi at Mantridi, of Tarini near Purushottampur, of Ganesh at Panchama and of Mahuri Kalua near Mahuri gada. Besides that, I have gone along with my father to the Nrusinhanath temple at Simanchalam for the observance of my *Balapaka* ceremony. Among the Thakurani Yatras celebrated in the Ganjam district, I have participated in the *yatras* at Berhampur, Pitala, Chatrapur, Gopalpur, Gopalpur Pentha and Bahadur Pentha. In these *yatras* I have worked as *pujaka* of Thakurani at Utsav Mandira.

Role in Thakurani Yatra at Berhampur

I play the hereditary role of *pujaka* at the Utsav Mandira during the

Thakurani Yatra at Berhampur. Along with other Damla *pujakas*, I also perform the rituals of *changudi puja*, *digabandhan* and *sansthapana* of Thakurani *ghatas* as well as the *Hajare akhi thiba ghata*.

Supplementary Questions

Among all the goddesses, Jwalamukhi, Kali, Budhi Santani, Bhairavi, Tarini, Durga, Chandi and Hingula are of one category whereas Laxmi and Saraswati are of other categories.

Budhi Santani, Kali and Baidhara

As I know, the deity Baidhara is treated as the son of Budhi Santani whereas Kali is regarded as the daughter-in-law.

Budhi Santani

I have heard that during the legendary Daksha *yajna*, which I do not know in detail, Vishnu sent the *chakra* which sliced Budhi Santani, conceived as Parvati, the wife of Siva, into three pieces, head, trunk and feet which fell at Berhampur, Pitala and Boirani respectively. People, later on, constructed temples to worship these parts at these places.

Thakurani Yatra

The Thakurani Yatra is organized to please Budhi Santani, lest cholera should spread at Berhampur due to her anger.

Itamala Flower

The *phulamanda* is made of *itamala* flower as per the custom. The *phulamanda* is kept inside the Thakurani *ghata* because it is not to be shown to public.

Subhakhunti

The placement of *subhakhunti* implies inauguration of the Thakurani Yatra. By doing this, people become confirmed about the commencement of the *yatra*.

Dharma Jhanda

At the place of *dharma jhanda*, people offer *pana-pani* to please Budhi Santani, Chandi and Chamunda.

Ghata Sansthapana

All total nine *ghatas* are placed among which one represents the *ghata* of Budhi Santani, another to Kali and the rest belong to the seven sisters of Budhi Santani.

Participation of Castes in the Yatra

Participation of specific families of certain castes in the Thakurani Yatra is based on their traditional caste occupation.

Besha

The *beshas* of Krishna, Radha, Babaji and Rama are put on by the children on the basis of *sahanikas* made by their parents. *Bagha besha* is an important *sahanika besha* but there are many *beshas* which can be categorized as non-*sahanika beshas.*

Offerings

At the Utsav Mandira, devotees come for a *darsana* of Budhi Santani and offer *nadia, kadali* and *muan* for her *bhoga. Deepa, dhupa* and *puspa* are also offered to please the goddess. Black *saree*, metallic tongue and eye are offered as *sahanika* offerings.

Sahi Bhramana

During the *yatra*, Budhi Santani makes *sahi bhramana* to enable people of different *sahis* to have a *darsana* of her.

Ratha Exhibition

Rathas are exhibited to attract more people to the *yatra*.

LIFE HISTORY NO. 2

Name	:	K.P.
Age	:	42 years
Sex	:	Male
Caste	:	Damla
Linguistic group	:	Oriya
Education	:	Matriculation

Sect	:	Shakta
Istadevi	:	Budhi Santani Thakurani
Profession	:	Private Accountancy and *pujaka* of mother goddesses during *yatra*

Family Background

My grandfather was Late Shri Bhagaban Patra and my father was late Shri Kalu Patra, who died in the year 1971. My mother is also no more in this world. Now I stay along with my wife, Usha, three sons, Trilochana, Kailas and Tarakeswar and three daughters, Namita, Sarada and Vina. My paternal house is at the Babaji Tota Sahi of Berhampur where my paternal family has resided for the last six generations. But after my marriage, I have been staying at my father-in-law's house.

Marriage

I got married at the age of twenty. My marriage was arranged through negotiation by my parents. They arranged my marriage with my matenal uncle's daughter. Before the nuptial ceremony, I have visited the Raghunath temple of Berhampur for a *darsana* of the deity.

Education

While I was continuing my school education, my family suffered from severe financial crisis for which I could not continue my study beyond matriculation. Instead, I entered into the *pujaka* profession to earn and support my family.

Profession

My paternal family has a hereditary share as the *pujaka* during the Thakurani Yatras at Chatrapur, Gopalpur, Gopalpur Pentha, Bahadur Pentha, Berhampur and Pitala.

Religious Life

Daily Life

Everyday I finish bathing and *nityakarma* before 6 a.m. Then, I put on a yellow silk dhoti, keep a yellow towel on my shoulder and worship the deities who are kept in my house. After taking my meal, I go out of my house for occupational pursuit by 10 a.m. At the evening, *sandhya arati* to these deities is given by my wife for me since it almost turns 8 p.m. while coming back to house. At home, I again take bath and have a *darsana* to the deities. Then I go to the bed after consuming the food prepared for the dinner. I do not find time to read *puranas*.

Deities worshipped at Home

At home, photos of Siva, Parvati, Laxmi, Ganesh, Narayana, Rama, Jagannath, Durga, Tara-Tarini, Bhairavi and Budhi Santani Thakurani are worshipped twice daily. In the morning the *mangala arati* is given by me and at the evening, my wife performs the *arati* ritual.

Visit

During my childhood, I had gone along with my father to the Nrusinhanath temple of Simanchalam for the observance of my *balapaka* ceremony. Both to the Jagannath temple at Puri and Tara-Tarini temple near Purushottampur, I have gone to celebrate the *balapaka* ceremony of all my children. But to the Lingaraj temple at Bhubaneswar, Bhairavi temple at Mantridi, Ganesh temple at Panchama and Siva temple at Dhabaleswar near Gopalpur, my visit was to have a *darsana* of the deities.

Among the Thakurani Yatras celebrated in the Ganjam district, I have participated in the Thakurani Yatra at Chatrapur, Gopalpur, Gopalpur Pentha, Bahadur Pentha, Berhampur and Pitala as the *pujaka* of the Thakuranis.

Role in the Thakurani Yatra at Berhampur

I enjoy a hereditary share of playing the role of a *pujaka* of the Budhi Santani Thakurani during the Thakurani Yatra. The ritual services which I do along with other Damla *pujaka*s include *diga bandhana, changudi puja, sansthapana* of *ghatas* at Utsav Mandira, daily rituals at the Utsav Mandira and *sansthapana of Hajare akhi thiba ghata*. Against my services, I receive a part of the total income made out of the *dakshinas* given by the devotees.

Supplementary Questions

Mother Goddess

I believe that all goddesses are one but they are worshipped by different names at different historical times.

Budhi Santani, Kali and Baidhara

Baidhara is the same of Budhi Santani Thakurani. His image is worshipped along with the Thakurani both at the Thakurani Mandira and the Utsav Mandira. Goddess Kali is reverred as the daughter-in-law of Budhi Santani. While inviting the Budhi Santani to visit his house, Desabehera conveys his desire to goddess Kali and seeks her willingness.

Budhi Santani

Although I cannot say the myth but I know that Budhi Santani has been sliced into three parts, head, trunk and feet. Her head is propitiated at Berhampur whereas her trunk and feet are worshipped at Pitala and Boirani respectively. Budhi Santani has a dreadful appearance and, therefore, she is of red colour having a protruded tongue.

Itamala Flower

I do not know why the *phulamanda* is exclusively made of *itamala* flower.

Subhakhunti

The placement of *subhakhunti* implies the foundation of the Thakurani Yatra.

Dharma Jhanda

I do not know why *dharma jhanda* is placed but I have seen devotees offering *pana-pani* at the *dharma jhanda*.

Thakurani Yatra

It is traditionally observed. Budhi Santani is invited to her paternal house and the *yatra* is held on this occasion. People propitiate her by making various offerings so that small-pox disease may not break out in future.

Ghata Sansthapana

The need of keeping the *phulamanda* inside a container has caused *sansthapana* of *ghatas*. The *sahi bhramana* of these *ghatas* creates faith among people since it adheres to the tradition. All total nine *ghatas* are placed among which, one, in which the *phulamanda* is kept, is called Thakurani *ghata* and the rest belong to her eight sisters.

Ratha Exhibition

The exhibition of *rathas* during the Thakurani Yatra is meant to make it colourful and crowded.

LIFE HISTORY NO. 3

Name	:	Rama Krushna Gantayat
Age	:	23 years
Sex	:	Male
Caste	:	Bhandari
Linguistic group	:	Oriya
Education	:	Class-IX
Istadevi	:	Narayani
Profession	:	*Pujaka* of Budhi Santani Thakurani Mandira.

Family Background

I, Shri Rama Krushna Gantayat, working as a *pujaka* in the Budhi Santani Thakurani temple, am a grandson of Late Shri Krupasindhu Gantayat. My grandfather, Krupasindhu, had two sons, Kampo and Baraja. Elder of the two, late Shri Kampo Gantayat, had a son from his first wife Radha. After the premature death of Radha, he remarried Subasini and produced five sons, Babu, Narana, Bijaya, myself and Mangulu. I was born in Berhampur city 23 years ago.

Education

I was sincere to my study at the primary level. I have passed up to ninth class without a failure. But due to a sudden death of my father, I switched over to priesthood profession and left my school.

Profession

My primary profession is to serve as a *pujaka* at the Budhi Santani Thakurani temple of Berhampur. This profession is hereditary and to my knowledge it has been continuing for the last six generations. At the Thakurani temple, every *pujaka* has his own *palidinas* to perform the daily rituals. During my *palidinas* I perform the daily rituals but in order to assist me I take help of my cousin brother. Since I am unmarried my mother helps me by preparing food items which are to be offered to the Thakurani as *bhoga*.

I do not sit idle during the days when I do not serve as the *pujaka* at the Thakurani temple. In these days I engage myself in the construction of *devi-prabhas* of Budhi Santani Thakurani, Kali, and Sapa-Sapuani, which are hired by people for the Sitala of the deity through exhibition of their *prabhas* during marriage ceremony and Thakurani Yatras. Apart from this, I also prepare the *murty* of Lord Ganesh and goddess Saraswati which are purchased by the local people at the time of Ganesh *puja* and Saraswati *puja* respectively.

Religious Life

Daily Routine

As a practice, everyday I remember my *istadevi*, goddess Narayani after getting up from the bed. Soon after finishing my *nityakarma* in the morning, during my turn of priesthood, I come to the Thakurani temple. There I offer salutation to the goddess and then perform the daily rituals. In these days, I stay at the temple day and night and remain busy in attending to the devotees. On the days when I do not act as the temple priest, I make ritual worship to the family deities at house and then visit the temple of Budhi Santani Thakurani, Jagannath and Nrusinhanath which are located nearby my house, for a *darsana* to these deities. In the day time, I engage myself in constructing *devi-prabhas*. Before taking rest in the night, occasionally I read *Devi-Puranas* and *Sankranti Granthabali*.

Deities at Home

Although I belong to the Shakta sect and a *pujaka* of Thakurani, I worship the deities of all the three major sects of Hinduism Shakta, Saiva and Vaishnava. At home I have kept the photos of Lord Krishna, Badri Narayan, Ganesha and Siva along with those of mother goddesses, namely Narayani, Budhi Santani Thakurani, Ambika, Kali, Laxmi, Bhairavi, Parvati, Durga and Radha.

Visit

I have visited along with my parents, at the age of three, the Narayani temple near Khalikote in order to observe my *balapaka* ceremony. Besides this, in the Ganjam district, I have also visited the Tara-Tarini temple near Purushottampur, Bhairavi temple at Mantridi, Ganesh temple at Panchama, Bankeswari temple at Bada Dumula, Bagdevi temple at Kulada and Mohuri Kalua temple near Mahuri. I have also visited the Lingaraj temple at Bhubaneswar, and Jagannath temple at Puri. To the Nrusinhanath temple at Simanchalam, I had visited in connection with a vow to sacrifice the hair of my head. At Bhanjanagar, Chatrapur, Chikiti, Purushottampur, Boirani, Pitala, Lathi, Gopalpur, Gopalpur Pentha in the Ganjam district of Orissa and at Palasa and Udankoitha in Andhra Pradesh, Thakurani Yatras are popularly celebrated. I had attended all these *yatras* when my *devi-prabhas* were hired by devotees for exhibition in these *yatras*.

Role in the Thakurani Yatras

Besides exhibiting *devi-prabhas* during Thakurani Yatras at different places, I play the role of a *pujaka* at the time of the Thakurani Yatra celebrated at Berhampur. At the Utsava Mandira, a temple constructed only for the yatra where sacred symbols of the Budhi Santani Thakurani and other mother goddesses are installed and worshipped everyday, the *puja-pali* for twelve hours is auctioned among the Bhandaris and Damla priests. Since a large amount of money as *dakshina* is earned by the priests from the devotees, there takes place a strong competition among the priest-groups to win in the auction. I along with my four brothers make a group and have won several times in the auction. Besides this, on the last day of the Thakurani Yatra when the goddess returns to her temple, several female devotees make vow to carry on head to the temple along with the Thakurani, a *ghata* and a *chhati* which are priorly worshipped at their houses in the name of the Thakurani. I have the *wadika* over a member of devotees at whose homes I go to perform the ritual worship to the *ghatas* and for this I receive *dakshina*, both in cash and kind from them.

Supplementary Questions

Mother Goddess

I believe that all Thakuranis whether Budhi Santani, Durga, Parvati,

Laxmi, Saraswati, Bhairavi, Chandi, Kanyaka Parameswari or Tara and Tarini are different *avataras* of one *shakti*, which is called as Matru-Shakti. These *avataras* can be classified as *ugra avataras* and *santa avataras*. Budhi Santani, Durga, Bhairavi, Chandi and Kali are *ugra-avataras* of the Thakurani whereas Laxmi, Saraswati, Parvati and Kanyaka Parameswari are her *santa-avataras*.

Budhi Santani, Kali and Baidhara

Budhi Santani Thakurani is regarded as the Adi-Mata. However, to Goddess Kali, I believe as one of the seven sisters of Budhi Santani. Baidhara is the son of Budhi Santani and his image is always placed and worshipped near her mother.

Photos of different Deities at Budhi Santani Temple

The devotees sometimes make vows to donate photos of different deities for placement at the *darsana-griha* of the Thakurani temple. Most of these donated photos are of different Thakuranis whereas some photos of Siva and Parvati, Laxmi and Narayan and Radha and Krishna are also donated. These Photos are hanged on wall in the *darsana griha* for a couple of days but afterwards these are removed since a permanent placement of photos of the deities other than Thakurani, shall demand a *puja* according to *bidhi* which is not practically possible for us.

Budhi Santani

Budhi Santani Thakurani has been sliced into three pieces, head, trunk and feet, but I do not know the myth behind it, what I know is that her head is worshipped at Berhampur but her trunk and feet are propitiated at Pitala and Boirani respectively. The head of the goddess is made of sila (stone). At the beginning the Thakurani was having a *bruddha-rupa* for which she was named as Budhi Thakurani. During festive days like, Sankranti, Deepavali, Durga *puja*, and Thakurani Yatra, she is embellished with ornaments to have a *jaubana-rupa*. The *pratima* of the Thakurani is of red colour and she is found to have a protruding tongue because the *pratima* represents her *ugra-avatara*.

Thakurani Yatra

The people of Berhampur have been celebrating the Thakurani Yatra for more than one hundred years. Today Thakurani Yatra is celebrated at different places of south Orissa but the Thakurani Yatra of Berhampur is the biggest among all. Here at Berhampur, the *yatra* is held for more number of days and it attracts more number of devotees than any other places. On the basis of a belief, the houses of the Desabehera is regarded as the *bapa-ghara* of Budhi Santani Thakurani. Basing on a myth, she is invited to her paternal house by the Desabehera in every alternative year. An Utsav Mandira is constructed for her in front of Desabehera's house and there she stays for three to four weeks. Hundred years ago, she was staying only for a week or ten days. At Utsav Mandira, people of Berhampur treat the deity with various offerings so as to pacify and retreat her for causing them suffer from small-pox and diarrhoea. Now-a-days devotees not only from Berhampur and neighbouring villages but also from distant places turn up to propitiate the goddess during the *yatra*.

Itamala Flower

Itamala phulas are flowers with brick-red colour which are believed to be appreciated by the Thakurani most. A *phulamanda* of these flowers is brought by the Desabehera's wife on the calling-day of Thakurani Yatra. It is placed on the head of the Thakurani and then a ritual is performed by the Mandira *pujaka* on behalf of the Desabehera so as to invite the goddess for the *yatra*. As the *phulamanda* falls down, it is believed that the goddess symbolically expressed her willingness. It is further believed that Thakurani's power comes into the *phulamanda*, which is carefully taken as her sacred symbol and worshipped during the *yatra*. The *phulamanda*, which is usually expected to wither within a week, keeps its freshness till the end of the *yatra*, i.e. more than three weeks since the power of Thakurani remains within it.

Subhakhunti

Subhakhunti is nothing but a bamboo pole of a specific size which is made auspicious before the Thakurani at her *mandira* and then taken by a Tulabhina man on behalf of Desabehera to be placed at the place where the Utsav Mandira is to be constructed. This is done for the *subha-sthapana* of the Utsav Mandira.

Ghata Sansthapana

Ghata, a specially designed earthen pitcher, is treated as a symbolic abode of a deity. During the Thakurani Yatra at Berhampur, *sansthapana* of nine *ghatas* are made, one, which is little larger than others, is called as Thakurani *ghata*. In this ghata, the *itamala phulamanda* is kept sealed till the end of *yatra*. This *ghata* is regarded as the abode of the goddess. There are eight other *ghatas* of same size and these *ghatas* are believed to be abodes of eight sisters of Budhi Santani Thakurani.

Dharma Jhanda

It is a red-coloured flag tied at the top of a very long bamboo pole. On the fifth day of Thakurani Yatra, this pole is placed a few yards in front of the Utsav Mandira. This pole is treated as the *bhandara ghara* of deities like Chandi and Chamunda. During the Thakurani Yatra, devotees offer *pana* and smear turmeric paste at the bottom of this *dharma jhanda* for the propitiation of these deities.

Participation of Castes in Yatra

Although the Thakurani Yatra is patronized by a particular community, i.e. Devanga, people of other communities also play significant roles in it. In the organization of *yatra* various roles are distributed among communities, namely Bhandari, Damla, Raula, Tulabhina, Kumbhara, Medri, Dhoba and Hadi. Persons of specific families of these communities play their roles hereditarily. These roles have been given to them by the Raja of Mohuri estate on the basis of the traditional occupation of the community.

Besha

During the Thakurani Yatra, children, young boys and adult males attire themselves with different *beshas* and comes to the Utsav Mandira for a *darsana* to the Thakurani. Some of them make *sahanika* to put on *beshas* and others dress with *beshas* just for a fun. The children usually put on Krishna, Radha, Rama, Laxman, Sita, Siva and Babaji *beshas*. Among all the *beshas* put on by men, the *Bagha besha* is most popular and it is liked most by the Thakurani.

Offerings

Nadia, kadali, muan, phula, deepa and *dhupa* are offered to the Thakurani by almost all the devotees. A few among them also make *sahanika* and offer eye, tongue or *tilaka* prepared of silver or tin and black *saree*.

Sahi Brahmana

As per the local custom, when a married woman comes to the village of her father, she visits people of different *sahis* of the village where she gets a warm reception. Similarly, Thakurani's *sahi brahmana* during Thakurani Yatra is construed as her visit to people of different *sahi* of her paternal village. In each *sahi* she visits, she receives a traditional welcome. The devotees wash the feet of Thakurani *ghata*-carrier with *haladi pani* and make *puja* by offering *phula, dhupa, deepa* and *naivedya* which normally includes *nadia, kadali* and *muan*.

Ratha Exhibition

During the last part of the Thakurani Yatra, *rathas* carrying different Hindu deities are exhibited. As far as I know, these *rathas* are exhibited for the entertainment of the devotees.

Experiences with Budhi Santani Thakurani

I have a number of experiences with Budhi Santani Thakurani. Here, I wish to present only one among them. As a *Mandira Pujaka* of the deity, I have faith in her existence. In fact, my faith in her has steadily strengthened due to my experiences with her at various occasions of distress.

It was 13th March of 1982, when I was busy in celebrating my sister's marriage. In the absence of my father, who expired two years ago, my paternal aunt's son was officiating the marriage ceremony. Unfortunately, at that moment his little daughter became seriously ill and was admitted to the hospital. I felt extremely upset to hear this news at home and prayed Budhi Santani to save her. I also took a vow to offer a goat, to the goddess if she would protect her life. After the marriage I came to know that she was out of danger and two days later, she was relieved from hospital. I have not, so far fulfilled my *manasika* but I want to do it this year.

LIFE HISTORY NO. 4

Name	:	G.R.
Age	:	50 years
Sex	:	Male
Caste	:	Raula

Linguistic Group	:	Oriya
Education	:	Nil
Sect	:	Saiva
Istadevi	:	Nidravati
Profession	:	*Pujaka* of Balunkeswara temple and Chandrasekhara temple.

Family Background

My father late Shri Bhaiga Raula was a *pujaka* at Chandrasekhara temple of Berhampur. My paternal grandfather Late Shri Bauria Raula and his father Late Shri ·Mina Raula, both were also *pujakas* of this temple. Thus, the *pujaka* profession is hereditary for me. My mother, Late Shrimati Rukuna Raula, who died only three years ago, was the daughter of Late Shri Narana Raula, a *pujaka* at Balunkeswara temple of Berhampur. I have married to Saraswati Raula, who is daughter of my maternal uncle, as per the practice of maternal cross-cousin marriage. Since my father-in-law was having no male offspring. I succeeded him as the *pujaka* of Balunkeswara temple. At the beginning, I, no doubt, was facing trouble to officiate as *pujaka* at both the temples but now my sons have already come of age to share my burden.

I have four sons, Simanchala (married, 28 years old), Ramesh (unmarried, 24 years old), Surya (10 years old) and Santos (3 years old). I have also three daughters, namely Jhuna (married, 20 years old), Sumati (17 years old) and Jayanti (13 years old). My eldest son, Simanchala was named by my mother-in-law, who was a devotee of Lord Nrusinha and named him after Simanchalam, the most famous sacred centre of Lord Nrusinha in the east-coast of India. Rest of my children were named as per their horoscope. I have celebrated the *balapaka* ceremony of all my children at the sacred centre of our *istadevi*, goddess Nidradevi, at home. But for the eldest son I have repeatedly observed the ceremony at Nrusinhanath temple of Simanchalam now in Andhra Pradesh.

Married Life

My marriage was arranged at the parental level. My wife was known to me since her childhood as she was the daughter of my maternal uncle. I have been enjoying a very cordial married life. Our marriage ceremony took place at my wife's paternal residence. Before the commencement of the nuptial ceremony, I have visited the temples of Jagannath,

Chandrasekhara, Nrusinhanath, Narayana and Budhi Santani Thakurani to obtain blessings.

Education

I have not taken admission into any school since my birth. From the beginning, I rather developed interest in the priesthood profession. I remained along with my father always and from the age of eight, I started learning the techniques of this profession from him. When I grew up to my youth, I had already mastered over these techniques. At the age of twenty, I took the precepts from a Brahmin priest of Belagaon and then was appointed as *pujaka* at Chandrasekhara temple.

Profession

My primary profession is to serve as *pujaka* both at Balunkeswara and Chandrasekhara temple. Besides this, I make subsidiary income as 'conchshell blower' in the marriage ceremonies of other communities.

Religious Life

Daily Life

During the days when I serve as *pujaka* I wake up at 4 a.m. and finish my *nityakarma*. Thereafter, I bathe at the tank of Balunkeswara temple and put on my priestly dress which includes a long yellow silken dhoti to cover the lower half of my body and a yellow 3 feet breadth and 5 feet long silken *chaddar* to cover the upper half of the body. I smear sandal paste on my forehead, chest and upper hands and then come to the temple to perform the daily rituals. During these days, bhoga for the deity is prepared at the temple by my wife. The *bhoga*, after being offered to the deity is consumed by my family members at the temple. Hence, cooking at home is stopped for these days. Only at night after the *pahada bhoga* of the god, I come back to my home to sleep at night.

During the days when I do not serve as *pujaka*, I get up at 4 a.m., complete my *nityakarma*, take bath and then, putting on a priestly dress, I visit both Chandrasekhara and Balunkeswar temple for a *darsana*. Therefore, I come back to home and take my breakfast. Throughout the day, I spend the time either by sitting at home or at the temple.

Deities at Home

There is acute shortage of space in my house. Therefore, apart from our *istadevi*, Nidravati, I am unable to keep images of other Hindu gods and goddesses at home.

Visit

I have visited Nrusinhanath temple at Simanchalam to perform the *balapaka* ceremony of my eldest son. My visit to Jagannath temple at Puri, and Lingaraj temple at Bhubaneswar was purely for a *darsana*. Within the Ganjam district, I have gone to the temples of Bhairavi and Mantridi, Tara-Tarini near Purushottampur, Ganesh at Panchama, Mahuri Kalua near Mahuri Gada, Gokarneswara at Sukunda, Sakaleswar at Bhabinipur and Ishaneswar at Golanthara. Apart from the Thakurani Yatra at Berhampur, I have not visited any other *yatras*.

Role on Thakurani Yatra at Berhampur

I have a traditional role to blow Kahali during the Thakurani Yatra at Berhampur. At the time of reception procession and *sahi parikrama* procession, I remain ahead of the procession and blow the Kahali. During my life time, I have performed this role for the last 30 years. Before the commencement of *yatra*, Desabehera invites me for this purpose and pays me a *chhancha* (ration given to a person for cooking) against my service in the *yatra*.

Supplementary Questions

Mother Goddess

There are numerous mother goddesses worshipped in different names at various places. They have different forms and thus, some look ferocious whereas others affectionate. Some have full figures while others have sliced body-parts. However, what I find, all mother goddesses are nothing but various forms of the same, *Matru-Shakti*.

Budhi Santani, Kali and Baidhara

As far as I know the Kali and Baidhara are two Hindu deities worshipped along with Budhi Santani Thakurani at the Utsav Mandira during the Thakurani Yatra at Berhampur. However, I am ignorant of the relationship among these three deities.

Budhi Santani

At Berhampur, only the head of Budhi Santani Thakurani is worshipped whereas her trunk and feet are worshipped at Pitala and Boirani respectively. I do not know how Thakurani could be sliced into three parts which are now placed at three different places. As I have marked at the Thakurani temple at Berhampur, the goddess keeps a red colour and a protruding tongue. This expresses her ferocious nature.

Thakurani Yatra

Budhi Santani Thakurani is believed to be the married daughter of Desabehera family. In every alternative year at Berhampur, Thakurani Yatra is organized by the Desabehera to invite the Thakurani to her paternal house for a couple of days. She is kept in an Utsav Mandira where her devotees come to make *puja* and *darsana*.

Itamala Flower

Before inviting the Thakurani a *phulamanda* is placed on her head. The Thakurani's willingness to Desabehera's invitation is expressed by the fall of *phulamanda* from her head. It is believed that Thakurani's power comes through this *phulamanda* for which it maintains its freshness till the end of the *yatra*. This is done as a traditional practice. The *phulamanda* is prepared of *itamala* flowers as per the tradition. During each *yatra*, this *phulamanda* is hereditarily given to Desabehera for this purpose from my family. And against this service, I receive a *chhancha* from him.

Subhakhunti

Approximately fifteen days before the commencement of *yatra*, a bamboo *khunti* of specific size is taken in a processing to Budhi Santani Thakurani's temple where the *khunti* is made ritually *subha*. This is, then, called as *subhakhunti* which is placed at the place where the Utsav Mandira is to be constructed for the yatra. The placement of *Subhakhunti* indicates confirmation with regard to the beginning of *yatra*.

Dharma Jhanda

Dharma jhanda is a long bamboo pole on the top of which a red flag is tied. This pole is placed a few yards in front of the Utsav Mandira. The devotees, who come to worship Budhi Santani Thakurani during the Thakurani Yatra, offer *pana-pani* and *deepa* near the *dharma jhanda*.

Participation of Caste in Yatra

A large number of castes participates in the Thakurani Yatra as per their traditional roles. Thus Bhandari and Damla communities participate as *pujakas*, the Raula community as flower supplier and Kahali-blower, the Medri community as *changudi*-supplier, the Kumbhara community as *ghata*-supplier and the Hadi community as drum-beater. Besides, other people from different communities also flock to the Utsav Mandira to have a *darsana* of the Thakurani. Many of them also make a number of offerings to the goddess to fulfil their *manasikas*.

Ghata Sansthapana

In the Thakurani Yatra the Thakuranis are worshipped in the form of *ghatas*. All total nine ghatas are placed, among which one represents the *ghata* of Budhi Thakurani another goddess Kali and the rest seven *ghatas* represent seven goddesses who are treated as seven sisters of Budhi Santani Thakurani.

Beshas

During the Thakurani Yatra, devotees fulfil their vows in a number of ways, *beshas* is one among them. As per the vow, devotees are found to put on *beshas* of Lord Krishna, Rama, Siva, Radha, Sita and also the *besha* of a Tiger. Certain *beshas* are put on by the people for the sake of entertainment.

Offerings

The devotees who come for a *puja* of the Thakurani at the time of *yatra* usually offer *nadia, kadali, muan* along with *deepa, dhupa* and *puspa*. But some of them also offer metallic eye, tongue and black *saree* as per their *sahanikas*.

Sahi Bhramana

At the time of Thakurani Yatra, the Thakuranis are taken for a *sahi bhramana* everyday. People propitiate there by offering *pana-pani* and other items. This is done as per the tradition to please the goddess, who, in turn, will not cause harm to the people.

Ratha Exhibition

Rathas carrying different Hindu gods and goddesses are exhibited in the

Thakurani Yatra to make it more attractive. People after making *puja* to the Thakurani go round to have a *darsana* of these *rathas*.

Visit to Mausima Ghara

The *ghatas* of the Thakuranis are taken to the Mausima *ghara* of Budhi Santani Thakurani, two to three times during the *yatra*. As I know, this is a traditional practice, but I am ignorant of the myth behind this tradition.

LIFE HISTORY NO. 5

Name	:	K.R. K.S.
Age	:	68 years
Sex	:	Male
Caste	:	Kalinga Kumuti
Linguistic Group	:	Telugu
Education	:	Matriculation
Sect	:	Vaishnava
Istadevi	:	Budhi Santani Thakurani
Profession	:	Private Accountancy.

Family Background

I am the Senapati of the Kalinga Kumuti community at Berhampur. My house is considered to be the 'Mausima *ghara*' of Budhi Santani Thakurani. I, Sri Kota Ramamoorty Kuvera Senapati, son of Late Shri Kota Suryanarayan Kuvera Senapati and grandson of Late Shri Kota Chandraswami Kuvera Senapati and great grandson of Late Shri Kota Balaji Kuvera Senapati, stay at my house at Jeora Sahi, Berhampur along with my wife, daughter, son-in-law, three granddaughters and one grandson. Soon after the death of my father in 1937, I took the responsibility of family management. My mother expired in 1948. Both my father and mother were religious in their attitude and behaviour. With their influence, I have also developed a religious bent of mind.

Married Life

At the age of seventeen I got married to my maternal uncle's daughter. My marriage was arranged through negotiation at the parental level. As per the tradition of our family, on the day before my marriage, a Sitala *puja* was performed to pacify Budhi Santani Thakurani at her temple.

Education

I have studied upto matriculation in a Telugu-medium school. I could not continue my study due to sudden demise of my father, for which I left school and learned accountancy privately to earn for the family. Side by side, I also learned Oriya language to make me conversant with the Oriya-speaking people. This helped me in my occupational practice, especially when many Oriya businessmen came to me to seek assistance in accountancy.

Profession

My only profession is private accountancy. Earlier my father was also doing this profession. I have learnt to some extent from him. But at the beginning stage of my learning he died and then, I learnt from Patnaik Babu who was working as an Assistant to my father.

Religious Life

Daily Life

It is an everyday habit with me to visit Budhi Santani Thakurani temple and Tirupati Balaji temple, which are close to my house, after completing *nityakarma* and bath early in the morning. Thereafter, I take food and go for occupational pursuit. I come back to home at about 1 p.m. to have my lunch. I take rest upto 4 p.m. and then, remain busy with my occupational engagement upto 9 p.m. Then, I take my dinner before going to bed.

Visit

I have visited a number of temples and *tirthas* both in and out of Orissa. Inside Orissa, the Lingaraj temple at Bhubaneswar, Surya temple at Konarka, Tara-Tarini temple near Purushottampur, Bhairavi temple at Mantridi, Ganesh temple at Panchama and Mahuri Kalua temple near Mahuri Gada have been visited by me. I also go to Jagannath temple at Puri every year in connection with the observance of *sraddha*. I have also visited the Chaturdhamas and Dwadasa Jyotirlingas in the year 1976. During my visit to all these sacred places I have taken my wife along with.

Role in Thakurani Yatra at Berhampur

I have known from my father that the temple of Budhi Santani Thakurani is her mother-in-law's house and our house is her Mausima-*ghara*. Earlier, our house was regarded as her Bapa-*ghara* and our forefathers were patronizing the Thakurani Yatra by inviting the goddess to our house. But gradually it became difficult for our family to manage the *yatra* and subsequently, the responsibility was given to Desabehera, headman of Devanga community by the Raja of the then Mahuri estate. Later on, Desabehera's house was considered to be the Bapa-*ghara* of Budhi Santani and ours as her Mausima-*ghara*.

As Mausima-*ghara*, during the *yatra*, we invite the goddess two to three times to our house and pay due honour to her. On the last day of *yatra*, we, further, invite her and make ritual worship of the deity. One *Hajare akhi thiba ghata* is offered on this day to her on behalf of our house.

Supplementary Questions

Mother Goddess

All mother Goddesses, called as Thakuranis, no doubt, represent only one power but are manifested in various forms and called by different names at different regions.

Budhi Santani, Kali and Baidhara

Goddess Kali is treated as the sister of Budhi Santani Thakurani. Baidhara is a deity whose image is propitiated near the image of Budhi Santani Thakurani but I do not know the relationship between them.

Budhi Santani

I have heard that the body of Budhi Santani Thakurani has been sliced into different parts which are now worshipped at different villages but I cannot explain how this came to be. The colour of Budhi Santani is red and her tongue is found protruding because she exhibits the Jwalamukhi *rupa*.

Photos of different Deities at Thakurani Mandira

At the *mandira* of Budhi Santani, photos of deities like Durga, Bhairavi, Jwalamukhi, Kali, Radha, Laxmi, Krishna, Siva, Parvati and Santoshi Maa are often found to be hanged on the walls of *darsana-griha*. These photos are donations on the basis of vow of the devotees and hence, these are not hanged permanently.

Thakurani Yatra

On the basis of a myth, which I do not know, Desabehera's family invites their married daughter, Budhi Santani Thakurani from her mother-in-law's house, i.e. the temple, for certain days in every alternative year. For this occasion a *yatra* is organised so as to enable the devotees to offer ritual honour to the Thakurani in various ways.

Itamala Flower

I do not know why the *phulamanda*, used in the Thakurani Yatra, is preferably made of *itamala* flower but I have seen during my life span that this flower has been traditionally used for making the *phulamanda*.

Subhakhunti

Subhakhunti is a ritually-made auspicious bamboo pole placed about a fortnight before the commencement of Thakurani Yatra. Its placement means an auspicious beginning of the *yatra*. It also makes people certain about the commencement of the *yatra*.

Dharma Jhanda

Dharma jhanda is a red flag tied to a long bamboo pole beneath which the devotees offer *pana-pani* and *deepa*. *Pana-pani* is not offered at the Utsav Mandira because it might make the place muddy.

Participation of various Castes in Yatra

Depending on the traditional occupation of various castes, certain families of these castes have been hereditarily entrusted with specific roles, which are congenial to their caste's traditional occupation, to play during the Thakurani Yatra. These families are treated as Thakurani Sevaka families, whose services are rendered only at the time of *yatra*. Apart from that, since Budhi Santani is regarded as the saviour-deity of the entire community, therefore, her devotees of different communities come to the Utsav Mandira to make *puja* and have a *darsana* of their reverred goddess.

Ghata Sansthapana

It is a tradition that the image of Budhi Santani is not brought to the

Utsav Mandira for the *yatra*, rather a flower bundle, which is believed to be her symbol, is brought for this purpose. The *ghatas* are symbolic abodes of the deities. There are nine *ghatas*, whose *sansthapana* is made on the third day of the *yatra*. Among these nine *ghatas*, one, which is larger than others, is the *ghata* meant for Budhi Santani whereas other eight *ghatas* are meant for her sisters, whose names are not known to me.

Besha

Beshas, which are put on by people during the Thakurani Yatra, are broadly of two categories such as *manasika beshas* and non-*manasika beshas*. Among the *manasika besha*s, Krishna, Babaji and Bagha *beshas* are more familiar. Krishna *besha* is mostly put on by the children because they look beautiful with their *beshas*. Babaji *besha* is put on by children as well as adult males. Cost-wise this besha, being very cheap, is preferred by those who are economically not sound. Bagha *besha* is put on by adult males. This *besha* is the costliest among all *beshas* but this is liked most by the Thakurani. Non-*manasika beshas* are of varied nature and these are both entertainment and income-oriented *beshas*.

Offerings

Nadia, kadali, flower, *deepa* and *dhupa* are common items which are offered to the Thakurani when people come to ritually worship her. Sometimes *muan* and *pana-pani* are offered for the peace of the deity. As against their vows, people also offer her metallic eye, tongue and *tilaka* and black *saree.*

Sahi-Bhramana

The *sahi-bhramana* of the goddess during the *yatra* is meant for enabling people of different *sahis* to have a *darsana* of the deities. They also make *puja* to the deities near their houses.

Ratha Exhibition

Thirty to forty years ago, more than twenty *rathas* were exhibited during the Thakurani Yatra but now only five to six *rathas* are installed. All these are meant to increase the beauty of the *yatra*.

LIFE HISTORY NO. 6

Name	:	C.D.
Age	:	66 years
Sex	:	Male
Caste	:	Dalua
Linguistic group	:	Oriya
Education	:	Upper Primary
Sect	:	Vaishnava
Istadevi	:	Tara-Tarini
Profession	:	Business

Family Background

I, Shri Chandramani Dalei, son of Late Shri Nilakantha Dalei and grandson of Late Shri Sania Dalei, belong to Dalua caste, a traditional warrior community of Ganjam. I have only one wife, namely Kanchan who is 55 years old and is also educated upto Upper Primary level. I have five sons, Ramesh, Sudarsana, Niranjana, Babula and Tuna. Among them, only first three sons are married. Apart from that, I have three daughters, Bibi, Basanti and Kakini and out of them, only Bibi is married.

Education

I have read up to Upper Primary level. I was not a good student and because of my poor performance in the examination my father decided to put an end to my education and instead, he took me to train in grocery business.

Profession

During his life time, my father was earning for the family exclusively from grocery business. Later on, I also followed his path and it is the only profession which made me busy day in and day out till the last few years. Now my sons are taking care of our grocery shop and this gives me time to take rest.

Religious Life

Daily Life

Now-a-days most of my time is spent at home. It is, at present, a daily habit with me to take bath, after completing my *nityakarma*, at the pond inside the precinct of the Sakaleswara Mandira in Sankarpur Sahi, Berhampur. After my bath, I make a *darsana* of the deity, Sakaleswara and then, at home, make *puja* to household deities. Then, I take tea and have my breakfast. Before taking my lunch and dinner, everyday, I remember Budhi Santani Thakurani and Tara-Tarini Thakurani.

Deities at Home

At my home I have kept photos of a number of Hindu deities such as Jagannath, Bhairavi, Nrusinhanath, Tara-Tarini, Budhi Santani Thakurani and also of Siva and Parvati. Everyday these deities are worshipped by me or by my wife in the morning as well as at the evening.

Visit

Within Berhampur, I have visited temples of Jagannath, Siva, Budhi Santani, Kali and Nrusinhanath. Outside Berhampur, I have also visited the temples of Tara-Tarini near Purushottampur, Mahuri Kalua near Mahuri Gada and Bhairavi at Mantridi. To the Jagannath temple at Puri, I have gone during the time of Ratha Yatra. Outside Orissa, I, too, have visited the Nrusinhanath temple at Simanchalam to observe the hair sacrifice ceremony of my son.

Role of Thakurani Yatra at Berhampur

From the third day onwards in the Thakurani Yatra, Budhi Santani Thakurani and her sisters are taken out of the Utsav Mandira in the night to visit different *sahis* of Berhampur village. My role was to hold the hands of the 'Thakurani *ghata-dhari*' so as to assist in holding the *ghata*. This is the hereditary role assigned to my family. Now as I have grown old, my duty is performed by my son. During the days of my role in Thakurani Yatra, I was observing certain social restrictions. Thus, I was not taking non-vegetarian food. Before going to my duty in the *yatra*, I was bathing and putting on a washed, white *dhoti* and shirt. Apart from that, I was also keeping a towel on my shoulder. Twenty-five years ago, I was getting three rupees daily from Desabehera against my ritual service.

Supplementary Questions

Mother Goddess

According to sacred literatures all mother goddesses are one but named differently.

Budhi Santani, Kali and Baidhara

As per the tradition, Kali and Baidhara are two deities who are worshipped along with Budhi Santani Thakurani at the Utsav Mandira during the *yatra* but I do not know the relationship among them.

Budhi Santani

As I have seen, at the Thakurani Mandira of Berhampur, only the head of Budhi Santani is propitiated. People say that at Pitala, her trunk and at Boirani, her feet are worshipped, but I have never visited those places. I am also ignorant of the historical background as regards the division of Thakurani into different parts.

The colour of Budhi Santani is red and she possesses a protruding tongue because she normally has such incarnation. Of course, Kali, Laxmi and Saraswati differ from this while Kali looks black, Laxmi and Saraswati have yellow body colour.

Photos of different Deities at Thakurani Mandira

In the darsana-griha of the Thakurani Mandira, photos of deities like Siva, Parvati, Radha, Krishna and Jwalamukhi are found to be hanged on the wall for certain days. These photos are donated by devotees.

Thakurani Yatra

I have heard that Desabehera's house is the paternal house of Budhi Santani Thakurani. In every alternative year, Desabehera invites the goddess to visit her paternal house and paternal village. On the eve of her visit, a *yatra* is celebrated which is named as Thakurani Yatra.

Itamala Flower

Itamala is a flower of *ita* or brick colour. A *phulamanda* specially made of *itamala* flowers is kept on the head of Budhi Santani Thakurani and when a ritual invitation is made on behalf of Desabehera, I have seen the *phulamanda* jumps down from her head implying her willingness to visit her paternal house. This *phulamanda* is brought as her sacred symbol and placed in a *ghata* in the Utsav Mandira during the Thakurani Yatra.

Subhakhunti

Subhakhunti is a bamboo pole of limited size which is ritually made auspicious at the Thakurani temple prior to the beginning of the Thakurani Yatra. It is, then, placed in front of Desabehera's house where the Utsav Mandira is to be constructed. By doing this, it is expected that the *yatra* can be completed without any disturbance.

Dharma Jhanda

At the Utsav Mandira, *pana-pani* and *sankhudi bhoga* are forbidden to be offered and hence, these are offered at the *dharma jhanda*, which is placed a few yards in front of Utsav Mandira.

Participation of various Castes in Thakurani Yatra

In the organization of Thakurani Yatra, a number of services such as supply of flowers, beating drum, blowing of trumpet, performance of daily *puja* and supply of *changudi* are rendered. These being the traditional services performed at the local level by certain castes towards others, certain families of these castes have, therefore, been hereditarily entrusted with such responsibilities.

Ghata Sansthapana

At the Utsav Mandira during Thakurani Yatra, *sansthapana* of nine *ghatas* is made. These *ghatas* are believed to be the abodes of nine goddesses among which one is Budhi Santani Thakurani and rest eight goddesses, whose names I do not know exactly, are said to be her sisters.

On the day when Budhi Santani Thakurani returns to her temple, devotees, irrespective of differences among them in terms of caste, sect, language and occupation, make *sansthapana* of *manasika-ghatas* in the name of Budhi Santani Thakurani. These *ghatas* are, then, carried on head by them to the Thakurani Mandira along with the return procession of the Thakurani.

Besha

During the Thakurani Yatra, as a traditional practice people come to participate in it by attiring themselves with different *beshas*. These *beshas*, which make the *yatra* more attractive, are broadly of two types, *manasika beshas* and non-*manasika* or *sraddhaa beshas. Manasika beshas*, such as *beshas* of Krishna, Radha, Rama, Laxman, Babaji and Bagha are put on by the devotees by following certain rules. The non-*manasika beshas* are of wide variation and these are put on for *sraddhaa* towards Budhi Santani. These *beshas* are meant for pleasure and entertainment and, hence, the rules are not strictly followed.

Offerings

When devotees come to the Utsav Mandira during the Thakurani Yatra for a *puja* to Budhi Santani Thakurani, they bring *kadali, nadia* and *muan* as *bhoga* of the goddess because it is a common practice here at Berhampur to offer these *puja* offerings. Along with these *puja* offerings, *deepa; dhupa* and *puspa* are also offered because these are the *puja* materials as per the sacred literatures. Apart from that, some devotees also make *manasika*-offerings such as black *saree*, metallic tongue and eyes to the goddess.

Sahi-Bhramana

Budhi Santani Thakurani and other deities who are worshipped at the Utsav Mandira are taken for a *sahi-bhramana* from the third day onwards of the *yatra* so as to facilitate people of different *sahis* to have a *darsana* of the deities.

Ratha Exhibition

It is a tradition among the people of different *sahis* of Berhampur village to exhibit *rathas* carrying various Hindu deities. These *rathas*, as a whole, increase the beauty of the *yatra* and devotees after worshipping the Thakurani go round to observe these *rathas*. Earlier, when I was twenty years old, I remember, the *yatra* was continuing for 35 to 40 days and around twenty *rathas* were exhibited. But now-a-days, while the days of observance of *yatra* has been reduced to about 21 days, the number of exhibition of *rathas* has also reduced to only 7 or 8.

LIFE HISTORY NO. 7

Name	:	R.C.D.
Age	:	34 years
Sex	:	Male

Caste	:	Dalua
Linguistic group	:	Oriya
Education	:	Class VI
Sect	:	Vaisnava
Istadevi	:	Tara-Tarini
Profession	:	Grocery Business.

Family Background

I am the eldest among the five sons of my father, Shri Chandramani Dalei. I have three sisters and the eldest among them is now married. I have only one son, Dambaru, who has been named according to his horoscope.

Marriage

At the age of 27, I got married to my wife, Santilata. My marriage was arranged through negotiation by my parents. I had not taken any dowry during marriage although dowry is a permissible custom in our community. For an auspicious occurrence of my marriage by the blessings of Budhi Santani Thakurani, my father had arranged a *puja* at the Thakurani Mandira offering the Thakurani *muan* and *pana* for her *bhoga* on the day before my marriage day. On the marriage day, before the nuptial ceremony I had visited Sakaleswara temple of Sankarapur Sahi, Gramadevi temple of Grama-devi Sahi, Jagannath temple and Raghunath temple of Khaspa Sahi.

Education

During my childhood days, I was very much frickle in my behaviour. Mostly I was passing my time by playing with my friends. Study was a burden to me but I was very much afraid of my father who was interested to educate me. With much trouble, I could read upto sixth class but thereafter, I could not pass the examination. Finding me not interested in study, my father took me out of school and started training in grocery business.

Profession

After a successful training from my father in the line of grocery business, I opted for it as my future profession. With a poor educational background, I had never had a dream to get a service. On the other hand, my father being old enough to take the strain of business, I am now taking care of the grocery business.

Religious Life

Daily Life

Basically I am a late-riser. I get up from my bed at about 7.30 a.m. and immediately finish my *nityakarma*. Then I take bath and visit Kedareswara temple at Desabehera Sahi to have a *darsana* of Lord Siva. After returning home, I take *bhata* moistened with water and vegetable fry and then go to our grocery shop. At 1 p.m. I come to home, take rest upto 3 p.m. after my lunch. In the afternoon, I again go to grocery shop and remain engaged in business upto 10 p.m. After closing the shop at night, everyday, I go to the Thakurani Mandira to have a *darsana* of Budhi Santani. Thereafter at home, normally I take rest after having my dinner. I do not find time to read *puranas* but at times, I listen to the recitation of *puranas* at night by my sisters.

Deities at Home

At home, we have photos of Jagannath, Bhairavi, Budhi Santani, Tara-Tarini and Nrusinhanath. These deities are worshipped daily by my parents.

Visit

From the childhood, I have an interest in visiting temples. During my school days I had visited almost all temples existing at Berhampur. When I grew young, I had a group of friends. All of us had gone in different occasions to the temples of Tara-Tarini, Mahuri Kalua, Narayani, Bhairavi, Bagdevi and Ganesha, present in Ganjam district. Apart from that, I have also visited Ugra-Tara temple near Khurda, Raghunathji temple at Odagaon, Lingaraj temple at Bhubaneswar and Ladubaba temple at Saranakula. My visit to Jagannath temple at Puri was during the occasion of Ratha Yatra. To the Nrusinhanath temple at Simanchalam I had gone along with my father to observe my Balapaka ceremony.

Role of Thakurani Yatra at Berhampur

As my father grew old, I took the responsibility to play the hereditary role of our family in the Thakurani Yatra. I have played my role for the last six *yatras*. During the *yatra*, when the Thakurani goes for a *sahi bhramana*, I remain near the Thakurani *ghata-dhari* holding one of her hands in order to assist in carrying the *ghata*.

Supplementary Questions

Mother Goddess

I have heard from the *pujakas* of Thakurani Mandira that Budhi Santani Thakurani is Parama-Vaishnavi and Mahamayee. All other goddesses have taken their origin from her.

Budhi Santani, Kali and Baidhara

The deity Baidhara is the son of Budhi Santani Thakurani and he finds a place near the Thakurani at the Thakurani Mandira as well as Utsav Mandira. Goddess Kali is supposed to be the daughter-in-law of Budhi Santani. At the Utsav Mandira during the Thakurani she is also worshipped along with the Budhi Santani.

Budhi Santani

Budhi Santani had been sliced and her body parts were thrown into different places as per a myth, which I do not know. Her head fell at Berhampur and is now worshipped at the Thakurani temple. Her body, which fell at Pitala, is worshipped in another temple. Her feet remained at Boirani and people now worship only to her feet at the temple of Budhi Santani at Boirani. Budhi Santani is regarded as a Thakurani and hence, she possesses the usual red body colour and a protruding tongue like all Thakuranis.

Photos of different Deities at Thakurani Mandira

Inside the *darsana-griha* of the Thakurani Mandira photos, donated by devotees, of Siva, Parvati, Vishnu, Laxmi and Durga are sometimes found hanged on the wall.

Thakurani Yatra

During the *yatra*, Budhi Santani comes to her paternal house and visits different *sahis* of her paternal village. She also fulfils the *manasikas* of the villagers.

Itamala Flower

It is the tradition that *itamala* flowers are to be used for the preparation of *phulamanda* which, as the symbol of the Thakurani, is worshipped during the *yatra*.

Subhakhunti

Subhakhunti, as per the local tradition, is placed to mean the auspicious beginning of the Thakurani Yatra.

Dharma Jhanda

Dharma jhanda, being a red flag tied to the top of a very long bamboo pole, enables people to locate the Utsav Mandira from distant places. At the bottom of this pole, devotees offer *pana-pani*.

Ghata Sansthapana

All total, *sansthapana* of nine *ghatas* are made in the Utsav Mandira during the *yatra*. All of these *ghatas* represent the *ghatas* of Budhi Santani Thakurani. Apart from this, *sansthapana* of *manasika ghatas* are also made in the name of Budhi Santani Thakurani on the last day of the *yatra* by numerous devotees.

Participation of Castes in Thakurani Yatra

In the Thakurani Yatra, specific families of different castes play their roles in organizing the *yatra*. These families enjoy a traditional right to play such roles.

Besha

Varieties of *beshas* such as Krishna, Radha, Babaji, Bagha, Rama, Hanumana, Siva, Pilakhai-Dahani, Leprosy patient, Jaina saints, Kandha dancers, school teacher and school mistress are put on by the people at the time of Thakurani Yatra. Among these, some are *manasika beshas* whereas others are non-*manasika beshas*. The latter are put on for *sraddhaa* to the Thakurani.

Offerings

When devotees come for a *darsana* of Budhi Santani during the *yatra*, they offer *nadia, kadali, muan, deepa, dhupa, kala chudi* and *pushpa* as per the traditional practice in this locality. But such materials as black *saree*, metallic tongue, eye and *tilaka* are offered by the devotees on the basis of their *sahanikas*.

Sahi-Bhramana

It is a tradition with Budhi Santani Thakurani to go for *sahi-bhramana* during the Thakurani Yatra. In the *sahis*, she is respected by the people through various offerings.

Ratha Exhibition

During the first phase of *sahi-bhramana*, Budhi Santani Thakurani expresses her desire to the people of certain *sahis* to exhibit their *rathas* during the *yatras*. These *rathas* are, then, exhibited on behalf of different *sahis*.

LIFE HISTORY NO. 8

Name	:	G.C.P.
Age	:	34 years
Sex	:	Male
Caste	:	Dalua
Linguistic Group	:	Oriya
Education	:	Class-II
Sect	:	Vaishnava
Istadevi	:	Tara-Tarini
Profession	:	Business

Family Background

My father, Shri Bhagirathi Patra, son of Late Shri Arakhita Patra, has two sons and two daughters, all of whom are now married. My wife, Bhabani, is now 28 years old and she has passed Class-VII. I have two sons, Bishweswara and Jagannath and a daughter, Lalita.

Marriage

My marriage was an arranged one. It was arranged by my father. I have not married to my maternal uncle's daughter, although our community permits it. On the day before my marriage, a *puja* had been made to Budhi Santani offering her *pana* and *muan* at her temple. On the day of marriage, I had visited Sakaleswara temple of Sankarpur Sahi, Radha-Krishna temple at Raja Sahi, Grama-Devati Mandira at Grama-Devati road, Jagannath temple and Nrusinhanath temple at Khaspa Sahi of Berhampur.

Education

Because of financial crisis at my home, I failed to continue my study beyond class-II.

Profession

After making an end to my educational career, I shifted my interest to business which is my only profession.

Religious Life

Daily Life

Everyday I finish my *nityakarma* before 6 a.m. After a morning bath, I take my breakfast and then, go for my business engagement. Before proceeding towards business engagement, I always remember the deities Tara-Tarini, Budhi Santani and Sakaleswara. I come to home for lunch at 2 p.m. and take rest for an hour. I again go to my work at 3 p.m. After closing my shop, I visit Ganesh temple at the vegetable market for a *darsana* and then, come back to home. Thereafter, normally I take food and go to bed. Occasionally, before dinner, I go to Bada Bazar to listen to the recitation of *Purana*. Seven years ago, I was daily attending to the recitation of *Puranas*.

Deities at Home

At home, photos of deities like Tarini, Budhi Santani, Siva, Ganesha, Laxmi, Durga, Jagannath, Saraswati and Narayana are worshipped by me everyday. In the morning, I offer *dhupa* to these deities while at the evening, my wife performs the *arati* ritual.

Visit

I have visited most of the temples existing in Berhampur. In Ganjam district, I have also visited the temples of Bhairavi, Tara-Tarini, Mahuri

Kalua, Bagdevi, Narayani and Ganesha. Besides that, I have also gone to the Jagannath temple at Puri and Lingaraj temple at Bhubaneswar. In Andhra Pradesh, Nrusinhanath temple at Simanchalam, Kanaka Durga temple at Vijayawada and Satyanarayan temple at Annavaram have been visited by me. I have also visited the world famous Tirupati temple. Among the *yatras*, I have observed the Thakurani Yatra at Berhampur, Boirani and Gosani Nuagaon, Dola Purnami *yatra* at Chatrapur and *Ratha yatra* at Puri.

Role in Thakurani Yatra

My family has been hereditarily entrusted with a role to play in the Thakurani Yatra. On behalf of my family, I attend to my duty. My duty is to hold one of the two hands of the Thakurani *ghata*-carrier during the *sahi-bhramana* of the goddess. Before the commencement of each *yatra*, the Desabehera, who patronizes the *yatra*, sends an invitation to me reminding my role to be played during the *yatra*. Against my ritual service, he gives me a *chhancha*.

Supplementary Questions

Mother Goddess

I believe that all mother goddesses are one but they are named differently at different places.

Budhi Santani, Kali and Baidhara

The deity Baidhara is worshipped as the son of Budhi Santani. Both at the Thakurani Mandira and the Utsav Mandira he is placed near Budhi Santani goddess. Kali is also propitiated along with Budhi Santani in the Utsav Mandira. She is conceived as the sister of Budhi Santani.

Budhi Santani Thakurani

As I mark at the Thakurani Mandira of Berhampur, only the head of Budhi Santani is worshipped by the people. But I have not heard anything about the place where other portions of her body are worshipped.

Thakurani Yatra

Thakurani Yatra is celebrated on the occasion of the visit of Budhi Santani Thakurani to her paternal village.

Subhakhunti

Subhakhunti is placed about 15 days before the commencement of Thakurani Yatra. It is placed for the auspicious beginning of the *yatra*.

Dharma Jhanda

Dharma jhanda is placed a few yards in front of the Utsav Mandira. At the *dharma jhanda* people offer *pana-pani* before entering into the Utsav Mandira for a *darsana* of Budhi Santani Thakurani.

Ghata Sansthapana

Ghata sansthapana occurs at the Utsav Mandira on the third day of the *yatra*. These *ghatas* are all total nine in number. One among them is the *ghata* of Budhi Thakurani whereas other eight *ghatas* are of her eight sisters. Apart from that, on the last day of *yatra* people also make *sansthapana* of *manasika ghatas* in the name of Budhi Santani. These are taken on head by them to the Thakurani Mandira along with the return procession of the Thakurani at the end of the *yatra*.

Participation of Castes in Thakurani Yatra

In the organization of the Thakurani Yatra, people of different castes such as Damla, Raula, Dhoba, Hadi, Medri and Bhandari participate in performing certain ritual services. These services are offered to them in accordance with the traditional services rendered by their own caste in the locality. Participation of these communities in the Thakurani Yatra ultimately generates integration and cohesion among them.

Besha

In the Thakurani Yatra, *beshas* of Krishna, Radha, Rama, Sita and Babaji are popularly put on by the children. It is because these are traditional *beshas* commonly appreciated in connection with the *sahanikas* made by the parents of the children. Non-*Sahanika beshas* are of varied nature and these are put on the express *sraddhaa* to the Thakurani.

Offerings

Among the offerings, *nadia, kadali* and *muan* are commonly offered by the devotees to Budhi Santani during the *yatra*. Along with these, they also offer *pushpa, dhupa* and *deepa* as per the customary practice. But sometimes, black *sarees*, metallic tongue, eye and *tilaka* are also given as *sahanika* offerings.

Sahi-Bhramana

As a customary practice, Budhi Santani and other deities go on a *sahi-bhramana* during the Thakurani Yatra. People worship them at their *sahis* by offering *pana-pani* and *nadia*.

Ratha Exhibition

During the Thakurani Yatra, people of different *sahis* organize themselves to exhibit *rathas* carrying large images of Hindu gods, goddesses and puranic heroes. This is done to make the *yatra* more attractive.

LIFE HISTORY NO. 9

Name	:	S.G.
Age	:	45 years
Sex	:	Male
Caste	:	Hadi
Linguistic group	:	Oriya
Education	:	Class-V
Sect	:	Shakta
Istadevi	:	Budhi Santani Thakurani
Profession	:	Ritual Associate in Budhi Santani Thakurani Mandira and Scavenger in Berhampur Municipality.

Family Background

I am the elder between the two sons of my father, Late Shri Raghu Ghadei. My grandfather is Late Sri Para Ghadei and great grandfather is Late Sri Rama Chandra Ghadei. My mother Shrimati Rami Ghadei is living along with me. She is now 65 years old. I have four sons, Basudeva, Narana, Kailash and Dushmanta and a daughter, namely Jashoda. Naming of all my children have been made as per the analysis of horoscope. I have also performed *balapaka* ceremony for all my children.

Marriage

My marriage took place through parental negotiation. I have married to my paternal aunt's daughter. My wife is very much devoted to me.

Education

I have educated myself only upto Upper Primary level. I could not continue my study since I had to add to the family income by doing private services.

Profession

Primarily I earn for my family by working as a scavenger in the Berhampur Municipality. But at the same time I manage to render my ritual services, hereditarily entrusted to my family, at the Thakurani Mandira.

Religious Life

Daily Life

I wake up by 4.30 a.m. everyday. During the days of my ritual services at the Thakurani Mandira I go to the Mandira after taking bath. My work at the Mandira is concerned with scavenging, which I complete within an hour. Then, I attend to my Municipality duty. At about 11 a.m., I come back to home, get bathed and then take rest after my lunch.

At 3 p.m., I again go to Municipality duty after which I go to the Thakurani Mandira to do my ritual service in the evening. In the night, I remain engaged with household works. Sometimes, I read *Puranas* before going to bed.

Deities Worshipped at Home

In a separate room of my house, photos of Budhi Santani, Brahma, Vishnu, Maheswara, Parvati, Laxmi and Narayana have been kept. Daily worship to these deities is performed either by me or by my wife. At the time of *arati* to these deities, I also worship the goddesses, namely Ujudi, Tarini, Kalua and Durga by remembering them in mind.

Visit

I have visited almost all the temples of Jagannath, Siva and mother goddesses which exist inside Berhampur. Outside Berhampur, I have gone to the temples of Tara-Tarini near Purushottampur, Durga near Chatrapur, Bhairavi at Mantridi, Mahuri Kalua near Mahuri Gada, Jagannath at Puri and Nrusinhanath at Simanchalam in connection with the observance of *balapaka* ceremony of my children. I have also visited the Chandi temple at Cuttack and Lingaraj temple at Bhubaneswar to have a *darsana* of the deities. Apart from the Thakurani Yatra at Berhampur, I have observed the Ratha *yatra* at Puri and the Thakurani Yatra at Chatrapur.

Participation in Thakurani Yatra

In the Thakurani Yatra, I do not perform the work of a scavenger. Instead of, my ritual service is concerned with the beating of drum. Thus, by beating the drum I make various announcement on behalf of the Desabehera in different *sahis*. Beating my drum, I also go at the front of the processions concerned with the invitation, reception, *sahi-bhramana* and return of Budhi Santani Thakurani. Against my ritual service, I get *chhancha* from the Desabehera.

Supplementary Questions

Mother Goddess

There are numerous mother goddesses worshipped at different places but all of them have sprouted from Budhi Santani Thakurani.

Budhi Santani, Kali and Baidhara

Goddess Kali is treated as daughter-in-law of Budhi Santani. Baidhara is a deity worshipped near Budhi Santani at the Thakurani Mandira but I do not know in what way he is related to her.

Budhi Santani

I do not correctly know about the places where different parts of Budhi Santani are worshipped. But I have seen that only her head is worshipped at the Thakurani Mandira of Berhampur.

Photos of Deities inside Thakurani Mandira

Since I am not allowed to enter into the *darsanagriha* of the Thakurani Mandira, therefore, I am unable to speak about photos of which deities are exhibited in the *darsana-griha*.

Thakurani Yatra

Thakurani Yatra is held on the occasion when Budhi Santani Thakurani visits her paternal house. At present, the house of Desabehera, headman of Dera community staying at Desabehera Sahi, is regarded as her paternal house. But I have heard from my father that seven or eight generations ago, the *yatra* was patronized by the Senapati, who is the headman, of Kalinga Kumuti community. The Senapati was inviting the Thakurani and organizing the Thakurani Yatra near his house at Jeora Sahi.

Subhakhunti

Placement of Subhakhunti prior to the Thakurani Yatra makes people confirmed about the commencement of the *yatra*.

Itamala Flower

It is a brick colour flower. It is liked most by the Thakurani and, hence, there is the custom of making the *phulamanda* of only this flower.

Dharma Jhanda

The place of *dharma jhanda* is regarded as the store house of the Thakurani and, hence, people make offerings like *pana-pani* at this place.

Ghata Sansthapana

I am not allowed to enter into the Utsav Mandira and, hence, I have not seen the pattern of *ghata sansthapana*. But I know that all total *sansthapana* of nine *ghatas* are made and among these, one is called as the Thakurani *ghata*.

Participation of Castes in Thakurani Yatra

The Thakurani Yatra is held with the participation of specific families of different castes. These families play certain ritual roles which are hereditarily entrusted to them.

Besha

People visit the Thakurani Yatra by putting on various *beshas* and, thus, make the *yatra* more colourful. All these *beshas* can be classified as *sahanika besha* and *sraddhaa beshas. Sahanika Beshas* are those *beshas* which are put on by people on the basis of a vow made by them. On the other hand, such a vow is not made for putting on a *sraddhaa beshas*. These are put on to express *sraddhaa* to the Budhi Santani.

Offerings

It is a local tradition at Berhampur that devotees offer *nadia, kadali, muan, deepa, dhupa* and *puspa* to Budhi Santani Thakurani during the *yatra*. They offer these in connection with their *puja* to the Thakurani. The *puja* is made for the peace of the goddess. Other offerings like black *saree*, metallic tongue and eye are made because of *sahanika*.

Sahi-Bhramana

It is the tradition to take the Thakurani for *sahi-bhramana* during the *yatra*. People offer *pana-pani* and *bhoga* to her at the time of *sahi-bhramana*.

Ratha Exhibition

Rathas carrying different deities and puranic heroes are exhibited during the *yatra* by people of different *sahis*. This makes the *yatra* more attractive.

LIFE HISTORY NO. 10

Name	:	T.P.
Age	:	19 years
Sex	:	Male
Caste	:	Damla
Linguistic group	:	Oriya
Education	:	Class-V
Sect	:	Shakta
Istadevi	:	Budhi Santani Thakurani
Profession	:	*Pujaka* in Budhi Santani Thakurani Mandira at Pitala.

Family Background

I, Shri Tuna Patra, am the only child of my parents. My father, Late Shri Khali Patra, expired 15 years ago. He was the son of Late Shri Sura Patra and grandson of Late Shri Tarini Patra. After the death of my father, my mother, Shrimati Damayanti Patra, 42 years old, is taking care of me.

Marriage

I am only 19 years old and I have not yet married.

Education

I have passed fifth class. But the sudden demise of my father made me leave school and take up the family profession.

Profession

After my father, I shouldered the responsibility of performing the puja of Budhi Santani Thakurani at her temple in my village, Pitala. My primary source of income is from the *dakshina* offered by the devotees who visit the Thakurani Mandira. Besides that, in the afternoon, I assist in the weaving work of the Deras in my village and thereby make some earning.

Religious Life

Daily Life

Everyday I have made the habit of leaving my bed before 5 a.m. Immediately I complete my *nityakarma* and bathing. Then, I wear a yellow silken *dhoti*, keep a towel on my shoulder and go to the Thakurani Mandira to perform the *mangala arati*. After this, I come home to take boiled rice moistened with water and curry as my breakfast. Again I come to temple where I perform *puja* to the Thakurani on behalf of the devotees who come to visit her. At the temple my mother assists me in cooking food for the Thakurani throughout the day. After the *bhoga* of the deity, we consume our food at the temple. In the afternoon I go to my weaving profession for four hours.

Deities worshipped at Home

At my home, apart from the photo of Budhi Santani Thakurani, photos of Laxmi, Saraswati, Ganesha, Siva, Parvati and Jagannath are worshipped. *Arati* is given to these deities both in the morning and evening.

Visit

In addition to the temples of Jagannath, Siva and Grama Devati existing in our village, I have visited the temples of Mahuri Kalua near Mahuri

Gada and Tara-Tarini near Purushottampur. My father had taken me to the Nrusinhanath temple at Simanchalam to observe my *balapaka* ceremony. Of the *yatras*, I have observed the Thakurani Yatra celebrated at Chatrapur. Besides that, I have played the role of a *pujaka* in the Thakurani Yatras held at Berhampur, Boirani and Bhanjanagar.

Role in the Thakurani Yatra at Berhampur

A few days before the commencement of the Thakurani Yatra at Berhampur, I am invited by the Desabehera, patron of the *yatra*, to play my role as one of the *pujakas* of the Utsav Mandira. Being a *pujaka* from Damla community, I know the tantric way of worshipping the Budhi Santani Thakurani. During the *yatra*, I am entrusted with the responsibility of making the daily *puja*, which is done tantrically, of the goddesses at the Utsav Mandira. The rituals of Thakurani *ghata sansthapana, diga bandhana* and *sansthapana* of *Hajare akhi thiba ghata* are done tantrically by me and other Damla *pujakas*. I also go along with other Damla *pujakas* during the *sahi-bhramana* of the Thakurani to guard the *ghata* carriers against the tantric influence of tantrists who often come to the *yatra* to test their tantric knowledge by experimenting upon these goddesses. During the daily *puja* at the Utsav Mandira, while one among the Damla *pujakas* perform the *puja*, others blow conchshells and assist him in the performance of ritual.

Supplementary Questions

Mother Goddess

Saraswati, Laxmi, Durga, Parvati, Bhairavi, Tara-Tarini, Budhi Santani and Bagdevi are not same but different goddesses. These goddesses are bestowed with different powers.

Budhi Santani, Kali and Baidhara

Goddess Kali is regarded as the daughter-in-law of Budhi Santani and, therefore, when Desabehera invites his daughter Budhi Santani from her parent-in-law house, i.e., the Thakurani Mandira to his house, he goes to the nearby Kali temple to inform the goddess about his desire to take Budhi Santani.

Budhi Santani

According to a myth, Budhi Santani was sliced by a person at Boirani into three parts, head, body and feet. He threw her head which fell at Berhampur village and her feet remained at Boirani. People now worship it keeping inside a temple. Budhi Santani is of red colour and possesses a protruding tongue. This is common with all the Thakuranis.

Thakurani Yatra

I have heard that Desabehera's house is the parental house of Budhi Santani. But Thakurani Yatra is celebrated by people in order to pacify Budhi Santani and other deities by making a number of offerings as a result of which the people can live peacefully without being affected by the harmful activities of these deities.

Itamala Flower

Itamala flower is appreciated most by Budhi Santani Thakurani and, hence, the *phulamanda*, which is worshipped as her symbol, is made of this flower.

Subhakhunti

It is a bamboo pole of about 6 feet height. It is taken after the commencement of public meeting in a procession to the Thakurani Mandira. It is made auspicious by ritual performances made before Budhi Santani and then placed at the place where the Utsav Mandira is to be constructed for the *yatra*.

Dharma Jhanda

Dharma jhanda is the red flag tied to a very long bamboo pole which is placed a few yards ahead of the Utsav Mandira. The place of *dharma jhanda* is regarded as the store house of Budhi Santani and, hence, people offer *pana-pani* there to pacify her.

Ghata Sansthapana

Since the *phulamanda* is forbidden for public observance, from the third day onwards of the *yatra*, therefore, *sansthapana* of *ghata* is done to keep the *phulamanda* inside it. *Phulamanda* is kept in the Thakurani *ghata* but apart from that, *sansthapana* of eight *ghatas* is made of which one belong to goddess Kali and the rest belong to the seven sisters of Budhi Santani.

Participation of Castes in Thakurani Yatra

The Thakurani Yatra of Berhampur takes place with the co-operation of people of different castes. Specific families of these castes have been hereditarily assigned to perform certain ritual services during the *yatra*. Thus, certain families of Damla castes extend their ritual services as *pujakas* of the goddess at the Utsav Mandira. A few families of Odia Medri caste supply *changudi* and play musical instruments. A family of Raula caste gives the *phulamanda* and plays the *kahali*. These families have been assigned with such ritual services which correspond to the traditional occupation of their own castes.

Beshas

Irrespective of differences in caste, occupation, education and linguistic group, parents, for various reasons, make *sahanikas* to take their children putting on *beshas* mostly of Krishna and Babaji, to the Utsav Mandira to have a darsana of Budhi Santani Thakurani. Apart from these *sahanika beshas*, people also put on non-*sahanika beshas* and come to the Utsav Mandira for a *darsana* of the Thakurani.

Offerings

As far as I know, *nadia* and *kadali* are common food items offered by people to gods and goddesses for their *bhoga. Deepa, dhupa* and *pushpa* are offered in order to please the deities. Black *saree*, metallic eye, tongue and *tilakas* are offered as *sahanikas* by the devotees who feel that the Thakurani has helped them at the time of their distress.

Sahi-Bhramana

From the third day onwards during the Thakurani Yatra, the *ghatas* are taken for a *sahi-bhramana*, so that the Thakurani can get *puja* in different *sahis*.

Ratha Exhibition

Rathas are exhibited after 10 days of commencement of the Thakurani Yatra. These carry big images of mythological gods, goddesses and puranic heroes. As a whole, these *rathas* make the *yatra* more colourful and attractive.

APPENDIX-IV

SOCIAL LIFE NO. 1

RAULA

Raulas are popularly known as the priests of Siva temple in south Orissa. This priestly community has no sub-groups and synonyms. The people have not been awarded with any title. They identify themselves at regional level although they do not have any puranic reference and historical account in this regard. Thurston (1975: reprint) provides a brief report on the community but neither this report nor the people are able to speak about the origin and migration of the community. They claim that around seven hundred households are spread in the Ganjam district where they are mainly concentrated in villages, namely Raulapalli, Gangapur, Bikrampur, Tanganapalli, Sukunda, Golanthara, Bhabinipur, Berhampur, Banagalapalli, Kharida, Gudipadar and Chandipadar. Apart from Ganjam, they claim to exist in Koraput, Phulbani, Puri and Bolangir districts of Orissa and Rajpur, Gullpada and Chaligram villages in Andhra Pradesh.

Raulas live in plain areas where the climate is moderate, rainfall is medium, humidity is high and there is no forest and snowfall. Population figure of the community is not available. Oriya is their mother tongue. In Orissa, they converse in Oriya with their kinsmen and with people of other communities. Those who are staying in Andhra Pradesh have also learnt Telugu in order to talk with the Telugu-speaking people. However, Oriya is used as script by them. They do not have any specific style of dress for their women who like other backward communities cover their body with a *saree* and a blouse. The dress pattern and body markings of the Raula men are identifying features of their community. They put on one yellowish silk *dhoti* to cover the lower part of their body. The upper part of their body is covered by one yellow silk or cotton towel. Apart from it, they wear a necklace of Tulsi (*Ocimum sanctum*) beads and smear three parallel lines of sandal paste on forehead. Their caste council also uses an emblem having the photos of Lord Siva and Goddess Parvati which identifies their professional deities. They are not enlisted in the Backward Class list of the State although they deserve to be. Bio-anthropological studies have not been made on this community.

Raulas take vegetarian as well as non-vegetarian foods. Vegetarian foods are moderately consumed and non-vegetarian foods like fish and mutton are taken in the days when they do not have their turn of priestship in the temple. Rice, *urad* or *moong* dal and a curry prepared of groundnut oil are their staple food. They do not consume roots and tubers but everyday they take tea in the morning. None of them drink liquor which is strictly forbidden by the caste council. Fruits are occasionally consumed by them. By and large, they have not changed their food habits.

Social differentiation among the Raulas exists only at social level. The community is divided into certain *gotras* such as Nageswara, Matsyasa, and Kasyapa. These *gotras* being exogamous help in the regulation of marriage alliances. Unlike the Kumutis, Viramushtis and Devangas, the *gotras* among the Raulas, are not further classified into family names. Raula is the only one surname used by the entire community. They recognise *varna* system and claim to be Sudras. They regard the Brahmins, Karanas, Kumutis, Goudas, Devangas, and Daluas as communities having a higher social status whereas the Hadis, Bauris, Dandasis, Jagilis, Nolias and Reddikas are considered to be lower castes in comparison to them.

As like the Damlas, endogamy is practised both at community and surname level among the Raulas. But Raulas, unlike the Damlas, strictly adhere to exogamy at *gotra* level. While selecting a bride, they prefer to the maternal cross-cousins than the paternal cross-cousins. Marriage with the latter was forbidden earlier but at present it is socially permitted. In no case, marital relationship is established with parallel cousins who are treated as consanguines. The community does not allow anybody to marry with more than one person at a time. Only in case of premature death of one's husband or wife, the person is permitted to marry again. In such a situation, junior sororate and junior levirate marriages are not objected. However, senior sororate and senior levirate marriages are strictly forbidden. The earlier practice of child marriage has been abandoned and instead, all marriages, in the present days, take place after puberty. Brides are acquired mostly through negotiation at parental level but in certain occasions, the principle of exchange of sisters is adopted for this purpose. Payment of dowry occurs both in the form of cash and kind. After marriage a woman stays at her husband's parental residence. She smears vermillion on forehead and wears lac bangles of red colour and silver toe rings to identify her marital status.

Divorce is permitted among them due to adultery, incurable diseases or insane behaviour of wife. It takes place rarely but always it needs the approval of caste council. Divorce compensation is given to wife whether the case is initiated by wife or husband. The liability of children is entrusted to either mother or father as per the decision of caste council. Divorce takes place in a ritual ceremony when husband sits under a cart and his wife sits on it. Divorce is materialised as soon as wife breaks her bangles and pour water on her husband. A divorcee, whether male or female, is permitted to marry again.

Raula families are mostly vertically extended type. Mixed extended families are also seen among them. A married woman keeps up an avoidance relationship with her husband's father and maternal uncle and elder brother whereas she is permitted to joke with the younger brother and sister of her husband. Similarly a married man establishes an avoidance relationship with his mother-in-law but pays jokes with younger brother and sister of his wife. In the family the grandparents are also found to have a joking relationship with their grandchildren. Their family life being coherent, conflict hardly occurs among the family members. When it occurs, the reason is mainly due to disobey to the elders. Raulas have patriarchal families where the authority is handed over automatically to the eldest male member after the death of father. Parental property is inherited only by the sons who shares equally among them.

Household activities in the family are done by the women who also bring potable water from the nearby water sources. However, they do not collect fire-wood for the purpose of fuel. At the time of leisure, they prepare garlands of various flowers. During the season of cultivation they assist their husbands in agricultural operations. They have a role in social functions. Certain rituals and religious activities are also performed by them. But in comparison to men, they enjoy a lower social status. As such, they are forbidden to participate in the activities of political institutions. They also do not have any control over family expenditure.

As regards the life cycle rituals, Raulas have much similarity with other communities of Ganjam. Thus, they observe taboos but no rituals before delivery. The first delivery of a woman, as a rule, takes place at her paternal house. Again, post-natal rituals like Panchuati and Athuari are also observed by them on fifth and eighth day respectively after the birth. These rituals are performed by women who always remain present near the child to guard against the possible evil effect of the spirit named as Sathi Budhi. For this purpose they read *puranas* and eat fried pulses not to sleep in the night. Post-natal pollution and social restrictions are observed for eleven days by the kinsmen and for twenty-one days by family members, after which a purgatory ritual is observed and the restrictions are outlifted.

Raulas celebrate the name giving ceremony either on the twenty-first day or one year after birth. They invite an Oriya Brahmin *purohit* who performs the ritual and prepares a horoscope for the baby. He finds out a suitable name according to the horoscope which is then whispered in the ear of the baby by the parents. Raulas perform *mundan* ceremony for their boys and girls but do not observe any ritual for the attainment of adulthood by a boy. When a girl attains her puberty they celebrate a ritual on the seventh day after puberty. During these days the girl observe certain social restrictions. Only female and no males are allowed to visit her. On the day of ritual, she anoints turmeric and oil and embellishes herself after taking bath. Kinsmen and friends are invited on this occasion and treated with a feast. As soon as a bride is selected for marriage, a ritual is performed in commemoration of negotiation at bride's residence. The ritual is held in the presence of the kinsmen and the authority of village level caste council and on the occasion, bride's father as well as bridegroom's father takes an oath of materialising the marriage. Earlier practice of celebrating the nuptial ceremony at bride's residence still continues but recently in certain occasions, the ceremony is found to take place at bridegroom's residence. The feast in marriage is given by the parents in whose residence the nuptial ceremony is held. The Raulas cremate their dead, observe a period of pollution for eleven days. One year after the death, they celebrate the *barsikia sraddha*. Like other Oriya communities, they also ritually worship their ancestors on the day of *Mahalaya*. They have not changed the customs of ritual observances and, hence, rituals have become more expensive for them.

Priesthood is the primary source of income for the Raulas. Apart from it, they sell flower garlands and have their subsidiary income. They also cultivate the temple-lands to make some earnings. Recently, some of them have taken up business or services as their primary source of income. They have a direct link with the daily market and exchange their commodities by cash payment. They are not labourers and do not practise bonded labour as well as child labour.

Raulas have their own caste council, which functions at village level as well as at community level. At village, the headman of the caste council is called as 'Behera' whereas at community level he is called as 'Dalabehera'. The primary function of the caste council is social control. Recently along with the Muni community they have formed an association named as 'Siva Sevaka Muni ba Raula Sangha'. In this association, they have a President, a Vice-President, a Secretary, a Treasurer and ten Advisers. This association mainly functions to preserve as well as reform the social customs. Apart from the caste council, Raulas also take part in the affairs of traditional village council which settles inter-community disputes. In their villages, they have post-Independence statutory panchayat which takes steps for the welfare and development of villages. In the caste council, adultery, disrespect for traditional norms, insult to traditional council and theft are considered to be offences and the offenders in such cases are punished in the form of cash payment or ex-communication. The caste council, however, does not have the provision of giving rewards to the people.

Although Raulas are professional priests of Siva temples, they worship all Hindu gods and goddesses. Certain mother goddesses are revered by them as family deities. A bridegroom, as a rule, visits temples and offers a *puja* to the deities before the nuptial ceremony. Apart from the family deities, they also worship village deities and deities of regional and universal importance. Some of them have gone on pilgrimage to different sacred centres. They celebrate all the major Hindu festivals, however, the festivals related to Lord Siva are more ceremoniously celebrated. During festivals, they make vows before the deities and sometimes, invite their kinsmen for a visit. They have not changed any of their religious practices. They have also not involved themselves in socio-religious movements.

Raulas do not practise any other craft except making flower-garlands of various designs. They have not professionalized any art, however, their women make artistic floor painting during festive occasions. They have oral traditions, folk tales, folklore and folk songs as common to other Oriya-speaking communities. They do not practise dance but play on wind instruments. Except Brahmins and Goudas, they have the social restriction that is not to accept water and cooked food from other communities. However, with the impact of modernization, this restriction is losing its strength. In the present days, they do not have any taboo in accepting or exchanging kachcha food with other communities. Inter-community marriage and putative kinship are not practised by them. They share crematorium, but not wells and water sources, with lower communities. They visit shrines and participate in festivals along with other communities. They have specific roles in festivals. They render services during the observance of rituals by other communities and with some of them they have a cultivator-labourer relationship.

Raulas are economically and educationally backward but they are not included in the State list of Backward Classes. They favour to impart formal education to their children. The caste council has also provisions to extend financial help for higher studies to boys and girls of poor families. But the need to step into paternal profession mostly restrain the boys to continue their studies beyond matriculation. The girls, however, drop out mostly at secondary level due to social as well as economic reasons. At the time of illness, Raulas use both modern and traditional medicare. They realise the benefits of family planning and prefer to sterilise after three children. They do not have any special preference for sterilization, for men or women.

Drinking water is available by the Raulas from dug wells or tube-wells. Their habitations are electrified and their lands are chiefly irrigated by rain water. Their settlements have road communication but no railway connection. Post office is not far off from their localities. They listen to radio and occasionally visit cinema but they are poor enough to purchase television. They mostly depend on firewood as fuel resources. Some of them also use cowdung cakes for this purpose. They have not modernised their cultivation with the use of modern implements, chemical fertilizers, insecticides and high-yielding-variety seeds. Cowdung is mainly used as manure for their cultivation. Nutritional programmes are not introduced for the Raulas, who, of course, avail the facility of food distribution through fair-price shop. They do not like to be dependent on money-lenders and shopkeepers and generally they have the habit of saving for future. They regret that they are unable to get the benefits of the rural employment and development programmes of the government since they are not treated as a backward community. They aspire to be self-employed with assistance from financial institutions. The community does not have any restriction if self-employment programmes like agriculture, animal husbandry, small-scale business and transport may be introduced for them.

REFERENCE

Thurston, E. (1975). *Castes and Tribes of Southern India*, Reprint, Vol. VI, New Delhi: Cosmo Publications, pp. 243-47.

SOCIAL LIFE NO. 2

DAMLA

A small community is found to have existed in the Ganjam district of Orissa, who traditionally serve as the priests in the temple of village goddesses. To them Thurston (1909) has referred as Dammula but, at present, they are being called as Damlas. The community has no sub-groups and the people have not been awarded with any type of title. They now identify themselves only at local level. The Damlas who do not have any synonyms, speak that they are ignorant of the history with regard to the origin of their own community. Moreover, no information could be collected about the history of the community either from any *puranas*, ethnographic accounts or historical studies. It has been recognised by them that they were earlier the inhabitants of Andhra Pradesh and have migrated to Ganjam since long back. But there is no historical account as regards their migration to the present habitat. The people also fail to recall it.

The Damlas are thinly distributed in villages like Ambapua, Pitala, Seragada, Bhabinarayanpur, Kirtapur, Bhaliajala, Pata Paulia, Narendrapur, Jarada, Berhampur, Aska and Parlakhemundi in Ganjam district. Household-wise their distribution ranges within one to twenty in these villages. An exact population figure of the community is not available from any sources but they speak that their population may be around one thousand. The Damla settlements are linearly arranged and exist in the plains where the climate is moderate, humidity is high and rainfall is medium. Their habitats are devoid of forest and snowfall. The houses consist of two to five rooms which are arranged in a line. Each house has a frontyard which is common feature with the people of Ganjam.

Although the Damlas recognise their earlier affiliation with the Telugu culture, the entire community in the present days, has adopted Oriya as the only spoken language and script for communication with persons both within and outside the family and kin group. The community cannot be identified with any features except the traditional style of male dress used during their service at temples. They put on a yellowish or reddish silk *dhoti* to cover the lower part of their body. A yellowish or reddish silk towel is kept usually on the right shoulder whereas a conch-shell is kept hanging on the left shoulder. So far, no bio-anthropological study has been done on this community.

Damla men and women take both vegetarian and non-vegetarian foods. Among the non-vegetarian foods, they consume only fish, egg, mutton and chicken. The usual items of their food are *bhata, moong* or *urad dal* and a vegetable curry prepared by groundnut oil. Owing to poverty, vegetables are moderately consumed. They do not eat roots and tubers but occasionally take fruits and non-vegetarian food. The soaring price-rise of the commodities and the economic backwardness of the community have caused them to consume less vegetables, pulses and fruits. Damlas are habitual tea-takers both in the morning and evening. They drink milk only at the time of illness. Sometimes their men are socially permitted to take alcoholic drinks which are purchased from the local market. This privilege is, however, not enjoyed by the women.

All the Damlas of Ganjam belong to only one *gotra*, namely Nageswara. The community, instead, is divided into a number of family-names such as Uditandri, Udu, Ipili and Durgasi. This social division helps in the regulation of marriage alliances and in the indication of ancestry. Unlike other communities of Ganjam, the Damlas have only one surname, i.e. Patra. Although they have family-names like Telugu-speaking communities, they do not use these while referring their names in the present days. They affiliate themselves to the Sudra *varna* and perceive their social status at the middle in the regional context.

Since the Damlas have only one *gotra* for the entire community, endogamy is practised among them at the level of community as well as *gotra*. Exogamy exists at the level of family-names. They treat their parallel-cousins as blood relatives whereas the same attitude is not extended to the cross-cousins. The latter are, therefore, chosen for marriage but among them the maternal cross-cousins are mostly preferred. A marriage between maternal uncle and niece is considered to be illegal although they are not regarded as consanguines. In case of the death of one's wife or husband at the young age, the person is socially permitted to marry again. In these contexts, junior sororate and junior levirate marriages are not objected but rarely practised among them. The earlier child marriage custom has become obsolete and all marriages now take place only after the attainment of adulthood. For the purpose of marriage, they still maintain the tradition of acquiring mates by negotiation at the level of parents. One husband can keep only one wife at a time as per the existing rule of marriage. At the time of marriage, they demand dowry which is given both in cash and kind. The caste council has taken no steps in curbing this social practice. After the marriage, as a rule, the bride stays at her husband's paternal house. She identifies her marital status by smearing vermillion on forehead and by wearing a *mangalsutra* and toe rings. Among the Damlas, husband and wife are found to lead a family life tinged with peace and mutual co-operation and hence a breach of their marital life culminating in divorce is rarely seen. However, only in the context of adultery, either husband or wife can move for a divorce which has to be approved by the caste council. In such cases, divorce compensation may be given to wife but it is done only as per the decision taken by the caste council. The caste council also gives decision whether the mother or the father has to take the liability of the children in divorce cases. After the divorce both male and female are not socially restricted for re-marriage.

Damla families are mostly vertically extended type. A few mixed extended families also exist among them. In their family life, a married woman maintains an avoidance relationship with her husband's elder brother, father and maternal uncle whereas she keeps a joking relationship with the younger brother and sister of her husband. A married man is permitted to cut jokes with the younger brother and sister of his wife but not his mother-in-law with whom he has an avoidance relationship. Among the Damlas, a joking relationship is also found between grand-parents and grandchildren. The Damlas normally do not indulge in any conflict but confrontations arise occasionally owing to a challenge to the authority of elders. In the family only the sons have a right over the paternal property which is inherited by them with equal sharing. Normally, a father is treated as the headman of the family but after his death, the eldest male member, *suo motu*, becomes the headman.

Damla men are primarily engaged in various economic activities and thereby earn for the family. Their women do not contribute to family income but they do not sit idle. All the household activities are done by them. Apart from it, they bring potable water from the nearby water sources to meet the requirements of the family. They also collect wood for the purpose of fuel and during the season of cultivation they assist their men in different agricultural operations. They have a role in social functions and religious performances. Certain rituals at the family are performed by them. However, they are not allowed to participate in political activities and in the mechanism of social control beyond the family level. They also do not control the family expenditure which is done by men. As such, women are given a lower social status in comparison to men in their society.

Like other communities of Ganjam, Damla perform certain rituals and observe taboos in relation to the major stages in life. Thus, when a married woman becomes pregnant, she is forbidden to take any food outside her family till the seventh month of pregnancy. After that a ritual is performed to propitiate the goddess Sathi. The propitiation ritual is performed by a woman belonging to Damla community who offers a hen during the ritual. As a rule, since the first delivery of a woman has to take place at her paternal house, her father comes on this day to take her for this purpose. Apart from the celebration of rituals, certain pre-delivery as well as post-natal restrictions are observed upto fifth day by the mother and till seventh day by the family. After the birth of a child, Damlas also perform Panchuati and Athuari rituals on the fifth day and eighth day respectively. On the twenty-first day, *ekoisia* or naming ceremony is held when a name is given to the child. A Brahmin *purohita* is invited who prepares a horoscope for the baby and finds out a name according to the horoscope which is then whispered in the ear of the baby by its parents. At the end of the ritual, sweets are distributed among the children of the locality.

It is a common practice among the Damlas to celebrate the *balapaka* ceremony for their son and daughter at the temple of their family deities after one year of age. Some of them repeatedly observe this ceremony at Nrusinhanath temple of Simanchalam and Jagannath temple of Puri in accordance with certain vows made by them. They, however, do not perform the circumcision and *annaprashan* ritual.

After the attainment of adulthood, a ritual is observed only for females. As a custom, a girl for seven days after puberty is kept confined to her house and men, not women, are prohibited to visit her. On the seventh day, she anoints herself with turmeric and oil and then, takes bath early in the morning. After that, in the company of females, she visits the temple of Lord Siva for worship. In the evening a ritual is performed by female relatives, after which a feast is offered to the kinsmen who are invited for this ceremony.

As soon as a bride is selected for marriage, a ritual is held at bride's residence where the parents and kinsmen of both bride and bridegroom negotiate among themselves with regard to the date of nuptial ceremony and payment of dowry. The nuptial ceremony takes place at bride-groom's residence. The rituals are performed by a Brahmin, as per the Oriya customs. The ceremony is celebrated in the night and before it the bridegroom visits the village shrines for worship. For the occasion of this ceremony, kinsmen, villagers and friends are invited and offered with a feast. The bride remains at her groom's house for ten days and thereafter, she goes back to her parental residence to stay for two or three months.

In case of a death, the Damlas burn the dead and observe a period of pollution for eleven days. Certain taboos are practised owing to this pollution till the observance of a purgatory ritual on the eleventh day. On this day kinsmen and friends are invited and treated with a feast having non-vegetarian food items. No change in the ritual observances is marked among them and these rituals are becoming more expensive because of the price rise of ritual commodities.

The traditional occupation of priesthood still remains as the main source of income for most of the Damlas. Apart from it, they also earn by cultivating the temple-land. Sometimes, they are invited to blow conch-shell during marriage ceremony for which they are also paid. In the present days, some of them have taken up either business or government as well as private services as their primary occupation. Those engaged in business and services somehow manage to perform their traditional role as a priest and conch-shell blower to make subsidiary income, both in cash and kind, during the Thakurani Yatras of different localities. The Damlas have a direct contact with the daily local market and exchange their commodities through cash payment. The practice of bonded labour and child labour is not seen among them.

Like other communities of Ganjam, the Damlas, also have their traditional caste council. Their caste council exists at two levels—village and community. At the village level, the headman of the caste council is called as Behera and at the community level, he is called as Dalabehera. The caste council, where the posts are hereditarily acquired, functions to settle intra-community disputes. The Damlas stay in multi-ethnic villages and participate in the affairs of traditional village council where inter-community disputes are solved. In their villages, post-Independence statutory panchayat also exists and it primarily makes plans for the development and welfare of the villagers. It also takes steps to implement these plans. In these political institutions rewards are not given but when any offence occurs in the form of adultery, dispute over land and water, violation of traditional norms and theft, the offender is punished to pay cash fine or is excommunicated.

Although the Damlas serve as the priests in the goddess temples, they like other Hindus, worship all Hindu gods and goddesses at home everyday. They visit the temples of their family deities as well as the deities having regional and universal importance. They also observe different festivals of these deities. These festivals bear a socio-religious significance for them. They make various vows before the gods and goddesses and also invite their kinsmen for a visit to these festivals. Till present, the Damlas, have neither changed their religion nor have involved in any socio-religious movements.

The Damlas have not specialised any art or craft except the floor painting which is done by their women during festive occasions. They have oral traditions, folk songs, folk tales and folklores as common to the Oriyas. They do neither play any musical instrument nor practise any dances. They accept water and food only from the higher castes but do not exchange with them. Putative kinship does not exist among them. They share the crematorium, visit the shrines and participate in religious festivals along with other communities but do not bring water from places used by the untouchables.

The Damlas desire to educate their boys and girls but due to economic reasons and the need to take up hereditary professions, they cannot pursue them to study beyond matriculation. When they suffer from illness, they make use of both modern and traditional medicare. They have a favourable attitude towards family planning and prefer to sterilise after three children. They do not have any special preference for men or women for sterilization which is done by modern methods.

Damla settlements are furnished with electricity, tubewells, dug-wells, ponds, post office and road communication. They listen to radio but poverty restrains them to visit cinema and purchase television. Their lands are irrigated only by rain water and except organic manure they are incapable to use chemical fertilizer, insecticides and high-yielding-variety seeds to increase the agricultural output. As such, the Damlas have not been benefited out of any nutrition and employment programmes sponsored by the government. This makes them to remain as an economically backward community. Due to poverty they heavily depend upon the food distribution system through fair-price shops. They do not like to be dependent on money-lenders. They have a favourable attitude towards savings and aspire to take up business with assistance from financial institutions.

REFERENCE

Thurston, E. (1975). *Castes and Tribes of India*, Reprint, Vol. II, New Delhi: Cosmo Publications, p. 106.

SOCIAL LIFE NO. 3

TULABHINA

Tulabhinas are referred by Thurston (1975: 204) as Tulabhinas, who derive their name from tula, the beam of a balance, and bina (or vina) a stringed musical instrument which resembles the apparatus used by them in cleaning cloth. This nomenclatural explanation is not accepted by the community who bespeak that their name is so because they are the professional Tulabhinalis or cotton carders. There are two sub-groups of this community such as Tulabhinas and Kuli Tulabhinas. The latter enjoy a lower social status because unlike the former, they drink liquor and practise poultry and inter-caste marriage with Tantis, Bhulias and Ranganis. There is neither any scriptural reference nor any oral tradition as regards the history and migration of the community. The Tulabhinas, who identify themselves at regional level, are scattered over the districts of Puri, Cuttack, Dhenkanal, Phulbani and Ganjam in Orissa. Although an exact figure of their population is not available, they claim that the figure may be within 5,000 to 10,000.

Tulabhinas reside in plain areas where the climate is moderate, humidity is high, rainfall is medium and there is no forest as well as snowfall. Their habitations have a linear settlement pattern. Their houses consist of three to four rooms, which are also arranged linearly. Each house has a frontyard which faces the village street. Oriya is used by them as script and spoken language during interaction with kinsmen and others. The community has no features of identification. Till present, no bio-anthropological studies have been done among them.

They consume both vegetarian and non-vegetarian food. *Bhata, urad* or *moong dal* and a curry prepared of groundnut oil are their staple food. They consume fruits as well as vegetables moderately but non-vegetarian food items prepared by fish, egg, mutton or chicken are occasionally taken by both men and women. However, roots and tubers are not devoured by them. During the recent past, they have been increasingly eating non-vegetarian food and have developed a habit of taking tea. The entire community disapproves the habit of taking liquor.

Tulabhinas claim to be Sudras and consider the Brahmins, Daluas, Goudas and Telis to be higher castes whereas they treat the Tantis, Ranganis, Deras, Malis, Kalinjis, Bhandaris as lower castes. Surnames like Prusti, Das, Nahaka, Behera, Hati and Sahu are popularly used among them. Earlier, a marriage between the two sub-groups of the community was objected but at present, the restriction is not strictly practised. Each sub-group is further divided into certain *gotras*. Marriages within a *gotra* or a village are permitted. Marital relationships are established only when the names of the couple are found to match each other. A marriage with one's parallel cousins, paternal cross-cousins, maternal uncle or a niece does not get a social recognition. Maternal cross-cousin marriage, which was rarely seen earlier, is now a general phenomenon among them. Only except junior sororate, levirate and senior sororate marriages are socially not sanctioned. For the last forty years, Tulabhinas have been practising adult marriage in replacement of child marriage. At the time of marriage, brides are acquired mostly by negotiation at parental level and occasionally through exchange of sisters. Till present, they have adhered to the principle of monogamy. Payment of dowry, both in cash and kind, takes place during marriage. After marriage a bride stays at her husband's paternal residence. In order to identify her marital status, she smears vermillion on forehead and wears toe rings. Although divorce is permissible, it rarely occurs. Both husband and wife can initiate a case of divorce which needs an approval by the caste council. Divorce is approved only when the reason is adultery, maladjustment, chronic sickness, cruelty or involvement in the practice of witch-craft and sorcery. After the approval of a divorce, compensation is given to wife and the children become the liability of father. A divorcee, either male or female, is, however, permitted to get re-married.

Tulabhinas lead a vertically or a mixed extended type of family life. In a family, a married woman has a joking relationship with her husband's younger brothers and sisters whereas she maintains an avoidance relationship with the father, maternal uncle, paternal uncle and elder brothers of her husband. Similarly, a married man is allowed to joke with the younger brothers and sisters of her wife but he keeps up an avoidance relationship with his mother-in-law. Apart from this, a joking relationship also persists in between the grandparents and grandchildren. The Tulabhinas enjoy a coherent family life where confrontations occasionally occur due to a challenge to the authority of elders. The sons, and not the daughters, have a right over parental property which is inherited on the principle of male equigeniture. The father is treated as the authority in a family and after his demise, the eldest male member, *suo motu*, succeeds him as the family headman.

In the family, the household works are mostly done by women who also bring potable water and collect fuel for the home. At the time of leisure, they assist their men in carding the cotton. They also participate in agricultural operations and play a role in social functions and religious rituals. However, they are not allowed to be involved in the affairs of the caste council. While they contribute to family income, they do not control the family expenditure. In fact, they enjoy a lower social status than their men.

Like other Oriya communities, Tulabhina women also observe certain pre-delivery taboos and rituals and post-natal restrictions. Thus, a pregnant woman is prevented to visit a crematorium. Further, she is disallowed to consume white gourd, coconut, bean and groundnut. During the seventh month of her pregnancy, her father and elder brother come to take her to their home for the purpose of delivery. Before her departure, a ritual is performed when the seven varieties of cakes brought by her father are offered to the family deity of her husband. After the delivery, birth pollution is observed for twenty-one days by parents and for twelve days by kinsmen.

During these days non-vegetarian foods are restricted to be eaten and religious rituals are not celebrated. On the fifth and eighth day after delivery, rituals are performed by their women to ward off a spirit called *Sathi* who is apprehended to cause harm to the baby.

Ekoisia or the naming ceremony is held among them on the twenty-first day after delivery. They do not make any horoscope for the baby but a ritual is performed at their family deity. At the end, a name is given to the baby by the headman of the family and then, a feast is offered to the kinsmen. The parents also celebrate the *mundan* ceremony both for their sons and daughters when hairs are sacrificed at the temple of their family deity. Among the Tulabhinas, a ritual is held on the seventh day after the attainment of puberty by girl. The girl observes certain restrictions till the end of this ritual. After the performance of the ritual, kinsmen are offered with a feast. As a rule, negotiation ritual as well as nuptial ceremony takes place at bride's residence. However, the marital feast is given by the parents of bride and bridegroom separately. The nuptial ceremony occurs on an altar and it is officiated by a Brahmin *purohita*. Prior to the ceremony, the bridegroom visits the shrines of his own locality. In case of a death, the Tulabhinas cremate the corpse and observe the death rituals for twelve days. During these days certain restrictions are followed. Brahmins are invited on the third, fifth and seventh day and offered with specific food items such as *palua* (a soup prepared of Indian arrowroot) and *ukhuda* (fried paddy seasoned with sugar or molasses). The purgatory ritual is performed by a Brahmin *purohita* on the tenth day whereas on the eleventh day and twelfth day feasts are offered to kinsmen and others respectively.

Tulabhinas are traditional cotton-carders who also prepare and sell beds, pillows and *rejais*. They make wicks which are purchased by the local temple servants for the use of ritual worship to the deities. In some places, they officiate as priests of mother goddesses. Tulabhina is a landless community but those who work as priests cultivate the temple-lands whose ownership lies in the name of the temple-deity. For the sale of their production, they depend on the daily market where they have a direct link with their consumers. They adopt only cash form of exchange. But the local market is not fully regulated by them. They do not practise either bonded labour or child labour. In the present days, many of them are found to have opted for government services as their primary occupations.

The Tulabhinas have their own caste council which is not so organised as that of the Kumutis and Daluas. Their caste council exists primarily at taluka (a revenue division) level where it consists of a Behera as the headman and two Bhalabhais. The main function of the Behera is to take steps with respect to social control within the community. As such, the Tulabhinas do not have a caste headman at the community level although they had launched a caste meeting in 1958 at Puri where the Behera of Puri taluka had presided over the meeting. As per the custom, the Behera is always invited by the parents of the bride as well as the bridegroom at the time of marriage. Tulabhinas reside in multi-ethnic villages and they take part in the affairs of the traditional village panchayat whose primary function is to solve inter-ethnic disputes and to organize village level festivals. Their villages come under the jurisdiction of post-Independence statutory panchayat which mainly implements the welfare and developmental activities. Although rape, theft, elopement and dispute over land and water are considered to be crimes by them, they inform the police to handle these cases. However, at the caste council level, adultery, disrespect to traditional norms and disobedience to the order of caste council are regarded as offences and the offenders are dealt with punishments in the form of cash fine or ex-communication. Neither the caste council nor the village panchayat has any provision to reward a person who makes significant achievements.

Tulabhinas are Hindus and they celebrate all major religious festivals of Vaishnava, Saiva and Shakti cults. However, Durga Puja is regarded as the most important festival by them. On this day, they do not card any cotton and instead, clean the carding implements and keep them near goddess Durga. A book of *Bhagabat Geeta*, China rose flowers and bael leaves are also kept near the deity. The deity is ritually worshipped and at the end, vermillion is brought from her forehead and anointed on the carding implements. By and large, the festivals bear a socio-religious significance for them. Each Tulabhina family has its own family deity who is worshipped everyday. But apart from it, they also refer the village goddesses and the deities of regional as well as national importance. The Tulabhinas have not involved themselves all the customary practices of religious observances.

Except preparation of wicks, beds, pillows and quilts, the Tulabhinas professionalise no other craft. Similarly, they do not practise any art as a profession. But their women make artistic floor paintings during the celebration or religious festivals. They share the folklores, folk songs, folk tales and oral traditions, which are common among the Oriya-speaking communities. They do neither use any musical instruments nor practice any dances. As per the earlier custom, Tulabhinas do not exchange water and food with any other communities. However, now they accept water and food only from the higher castes but not from the castes having lower social status than them. They strictly reject inter-community marriage and do not share well and water sources with lower communities. Under the impact of urbanization, these restrictions in social intercourse do not become much effective, at present, among them. As regards establishing a putative kinship and sharing a crematorium, they do not have such social restrictions. They visit the same religious shrine and participate in traditional festivals along with other communities. They have specific roles in certain festivals. Thus, during the Thakurani Yatra at Berhampur one of their castemen carries the *subhakhunti*. Moreover, another casteman, who functions as the priest of the temple of goddess Ellamma, conducts the Jhamu *yatra* as the chief sacred specialist. In the present days, many of their community work as teachers or hold various white-collar jobs.

Among the Tulabhinas the parents desire to impart formal education towards their sons and daughters but mostly due to poverty, they fail to educate them beyond the secondary level. At the time of illness, they make use of both indigenous traditional and modern medicare. They do not have an unfavourable attitude towards family planning and for this purpose they use both indigenous and modern methods. At present, they mostly prefer to get sterilized after three children and for sterilization they do not have any special preference either for men or women. Drinking water is available to them within their localities and the sources are mainly the dug wells and tube wells. Their habitations are provided with electricity. Post office is not far off their localities. Their villages have road, and not railway communication. They have electrified their houses but for the purpose of fuel they depend on firewood. They listen to radio and sometimes visit cinema but poverty has restrained them to purchase television. Their lands are irrigated only by rain water and depending on it they manage to make a single crop production. They are interested to modernize their cultivation by the use of modern agricultural implements, pesticides, chemical fertilizer and high-yielding-variety seeds but due to economic reasons they are discouraged.

The Tulabhinas have an inherent attitude of saving for future. They avoid to be extravagant and regulate their expenditure according to the income of the family. They do not depend on money-lenders and shop-keepers for financial assistance. In their localities, the State Government has opened fair-price shops through which they avail the facility of ration distribution. Nutritional programmes sponsored by the government are yet to be implemented in their villages. They regret that although most of them are educationally and economically backward, they do not get the help from the employment programmes of the government. They claim to be included in the Backward Class list of the State so that they can avail the benefit of various welfare and developmental programmes introduced by the government. They desire to participate in the self-employment programmes of the government which are related to agriculture, animal husbandry, transport, general merchandise and small-scale industry.

REFERENCE

Thurston, E. (1975). *Castes and Tribes of Southern India*, Reprint, Vol. VII, New Delhi: Cosmo Publications, p. 204.

SOCIAL LIFE NO. 4

DALUA

Dalua is a traditional warrior caste, but most of them are agriculturists at present. They were professional armsmen in the army of the local kings during the feudal regime. The original name of their caste was Dalapati meaning as chief of a group of soldiers. There is no puranic description and myth regarding the origin of the caste. They were original inhabitants of Cuttack and Puri districts of Orissa. As armsmen of the Gajapati king, Purushottamadev, of Puri, they had participated in the historical Kanchi war in the second half of 15th century. On their return journey after victory, they were attracted to the fertile tracts of land at Vijayawada, Vijayanagaram and Ganjam. Since then, they have settled there with the permission of the king.

At present, around thirty thousand Daluas reside in different villages and towns of Ganjam. Apart from it, a few families have settled at Athagada in Cuttack district and at Patia village near Bhubaneswar. Daluas of Ganjam do not have any ethnic contact with these families and also with those staying at Vijayawada and Vijayanagaram in Andhra Pradesh.

During the feudal regime, Dalua leaders were popular as dedicated and brave soldiers. Many of them had been awarded by the local kings with titles such as Ranasinha, Baliarsinha, Ranasandha, Jagatasinha, Ranabaja, Bairiganjana, Ranahandola, Bahubalendra, Sandhisardar, Uttarakabata, Dakshinakabata and Bharimalla. Apart from the titles, Daluas use surnames like Samal, Kothia, Jena, Patra, Bishoyi, Rauta, Sahani, Dalai, Nahaka and Parida. In the past, the community had no other identifying features except these titles and surnames. But at present, they have an emblem, a flag and a flag-hoisting song to represent the entire community.

The settlements of Daluas are found in plain areas of Ganjam where the temperature is moderate, rainfall is medium and the land is fertile. Their houses consist of three to five rooms which are arranged in a linear fashion. Each house has a front yard and in villages, *khanis* (underground storages for paddy) are made in front of the houses. The houses are either mud-walled or brick walled and exhibit a linear settlement pattern. The roofs are mostly thatched in villages and tiled or cemented in urban areas.

There is no customary style of dress among Daluas. Earlier, *dhoti* and shirt were commonly used by men and *sarees* by women. At present, this practice is restricted to older generation in rural areas. Youngsters now prefer to wear modern garments. Women are found to have embellished with bangles, earrings and necklace which are made of gold.

Daluas consume both vegetarian and non-vegetarian food items. Rice, *dal* of *moong* or *urad* and a curry or a fry are common items in a meal. During festive days special dishes like cake, fried rice, sweetened rice and *khir* are prepared at home. Non-vegetarian items such as egg, fish or mutton curries are invariably cooked when they invite any guest for a dinner. They are habitual tea-takers at the time of breakfast. However, they dislike drinking liquor.

Daluas are classified, at the socio-economic level, into Rabas and Lenkas. Social life of the latter is marked with poverty and uncleanness and their women work as unskilled labourers. At the kinship level, they are further divided into a number of *gotras* such as Nagasa, Bharadwaja and Surya. The *gotra* classification is utilized for marital negotiation and *gotra* exogamy is accepted as an established principle. Inter-caste marriage is normally not seen and not approved by the caste council.

The practice of maternal cross-cousin marriage is widely prevalent. Paternal cross-cousins were earlier objected for nuptial relationship but not at present. Marriage in between mother's brother and sister's daughter is considered by them to be a taboo. Junior sororate and junior levirate are, however, socially permitted under exigencies. Polygamy is strictly disapproved and the caste council has decided to ostracise the person violating this principle. The earlier practice of child marriage is not seen today. All marriages are post-pubertal and men and women usually marry at the age of twenty-five and twenty respectively. Women smear vermillion on forehead and wear toe-rings and *manglasutra* to identify their marital status. There is wide prevalence of the demand of dowry at the time of marriage but to curb this practice, the caste council has also initiated a campaign against it. Like other Oriya communities, Dalua women after marriage resides at her husband's parental house.

In villages, Daluas are found to have formed mostly extended families whereas in urban localities they have preferred to stay in nuclear families. In the family, a married woman maintains avoidance relationship with her father-in-law and her husband's elder brother. She also behaves in the similar manner with her husband's paternal and maternal uncles. However, she is entitled to have a joking relationship with her husband's younger brother and younger sister. In an extended family grandparents and grandchildren also cut jokes with each other. Conflict among the family members is occasionally seen and in most cases it is due to disobedience towards elders. Dalua families are patriarchal where the authority in the family is inherited on the principle of male primogeniture. But at the time of distribution of parental property Daluas adopt the principle of male equigeniture.

As per the custom, a Dalua woman, does not visit burial ground during pregnancy. She is also forbidden to move across a river. Like the Kumutis and Devangas, the first delivery of a Dalua woman takes place at her parental house. Her parents, therefore, come with a packet of sweets and cakes to take her during the seventh month of pregnancy. Before her departure, she takes bath, embellishes herself and offers a *puja* to the family deity. This practice is, however, not strictly followed during further deliveries.

Pollution owing to birth is observed for twelve days by the parents as well as the kinsmen. Religious festivals are, therefore, not celebrated during these days. On the fiftieth day, Panchuati ritual is performed. In the morning, both mother and child take bath after anointing their body with turmeric and oil. The child is decorated and then kept on a bed under which a piece of leather and a book of *Bhagabat Geeta* are placed. It is believed that a spirit named as Sathi Budhi is likely to come through the wall and cause harm to the baby. Therefore, care is taken to see that the bed does not touch the wall and, hence, the spirit cannot come to bed. To prevent the arrival of the spirit, elderly females remain present near the baby throughout the day and night. To avoid dozing in the night, they eat fried pulses and read out puranic books. This ritual is repeated on the eighth day when it is called as *Athuari*. On the 12th day a purgatory ritual is observed when the house is cleaned with water, old utensils made of clay are replaced with new ones and metallic utensils are cleansed.

Name-giving ceremony or the *Ekoisia* is celebrated on the twenty-first day among Daluas. The ritual is performed by a Brahmin *purohita* who prepares a horoscope for the baby. He selects a name as per the horoscope and the name is, then, whispered in the ear of the baby by the parents. Kinsmen visit the baby with presentations and at the end, sweets are distributed among the children of the locality.

It is a common practice among Daluas to celebrate the *mundan* ceremony for their children at the nearby temple of their family deity. In addition to it, some of them again perform the ceremony at the Nrusinhanath temple of Simanchalam in Andhra Pradesh. Like the Kumutis and Devangas, puberty ritual is also observed among Daluas. The ritual is performed on the seventh day after puberty. During these days she is kept isolated from males and only female relatives and friends give her company. On the seventh day the girl takes bath after anointing her body with turmeric and oil, puts on new dress and decorates herself with ornaments. On the same day, kinsmen and friends are invited and treated with a feast at night.

Among Daluas, negotiation ceremony takes place at bride's residence. Negotiation is formalised when bridegroom's parents offer sweets and gold ornaments to the bride. Recently, as per the decision taken by the caste council, the authority of the village level caste council is invited to the negotiation ceremony to approve it. Nuptial ceremony takes place in accordance with the Oriya customs at bride's residence. The groom along with his parents, kinsmen and friends comes in a procession to bride's house for this purpose but before that, he offers a *puja* to his household deity and nearby shrines of his locality.

Daluas usually burn their dead but a child below the age of five is cremated. The dead is carried to the burial ground on a bamboo frame by adult males. The female kinsmen of the dead carry food along with them. In the midway, the dead body is placed on the road where the food is offered ritually to the spirit of the dead. The females, thereafter, come back to home. On their way to the burial ground, coins and *lia* (fried paddy) are thrown on the road by the kinsmen. Death rituals are observed upto the eleventh day. On the tenth day, *suddhi-kriya* (purgatory ritual) is performed and next day a feast is served to the family relatives and invited guests. Like other Oriya communities, Daluas also celebrate the annual death ritual and the ancestral worship. A Brahmin *purohita* is always invited to perform these death rituals.

During the feudal regime, Daluas were professional armsmen in the militia of the local kings, who, in turn, had allocated them with patches of land for cultivation. Some of them were appointed as *karji* (adviser), by the local *zamindars*. At present, for most of them cultivation is the major source of income but a large section has also professionally resorted to business and government as well as private services. Dalua women work as house-wives. Apart from the household activities, they bring potable water from nearby water sources. They ar not restricted to observe the religious rituals and are allowed to be members in the caste council.

Daluas are Vaishnavites. Earlier, they were wearing a rosary of *Tulsi* beads but this practice has become obsolete among the younger generation in urban localities. Shri Krishna Janmastami, Gurubara Osha, Shamba-Dasami, Ganesh Chaturthi, Saraswati Puja, Durga Puja, Thakurani Yatra and Deepavali are the major religious festivals which are celebrated by Daluas. Among all these festivals, Durga Puja bears a special significance to them. During this festival, they bring out their ancestral weapons which are cleaned and smeared with oil. These are, then, placed near the goddess Durga on the day of Dasahara. The goddess is ritually worshipped and vermillion from her head is brought and smeared on the weapons. Thereafter, a hen or a green gourd is chopped with the help of a sword so as to maintain the traditional function of the weapon which is kept near the household deity for the whole year. Apart from Durga Puja, they celebrate the Gurubara Osha in reverence of goddess Laxmi. On this occasion, they decorate the front yard and walls of their house by artistic paintings. Special food items like cakes and *khir* are prepared and ritually offered to the goddess and then consumed by the family members. Like other communities of Ganjam, Daluas also celebrate the Thakurani Yatra by offering various sacred sacrifices to the deity. They also invite their kinsmen for a visit to the festival.

The ordinary caste council system, with a hereditary headman, was absent among the Daluas and the affairs of the caste were settled by leading members thereof (Thurston, 1909). In June 1984, Daluas have formally set up a Dalapati Mahasabha which acts as the caste council at community level. The Mahasabha functions democratically and accepts members of both men and women above the age of eighteen. The Mahasabha has a working committee comprising of the Presidents of all *anchalika* (regional) committees as members. Among them a President, a Vice-President, a General Secretary, a Joint Secretary and a Treasurer are elected who work for a period of three years. The committee makes organisational decisions at its annual meeting with respect to educational development, socio-economic progress, social control, intra-community cohesion and cultural reformation.

Daluas are territorially grouped into a number of *anchalas* (regions) where each *anchala* consists of three to twenty *gramas* (villages). At *anchala* level, they have an *anchalika* committee which structurally includes a President, a Vice-President, a Secretary-cum-Treasurer and maximum twelve members. The anchalika committee conducts its meeting quarterly in a year. At *grama* level, a *grama* committee exists in a *grama* where at least ten Dalua families have settled. The *grama* committee consists of a President, a Vice-President, a Secretary-cum-Treasurer and four to eight members. *Anchalika* committee as well as the *grama* committee takes steps to implement the organizational decisions undertaken at *Mahasabha* level. The *Mahasabha* has formulated an *acharana bidhi* (rules of behaviour) for the castemen. It has decided to excommunicate those who will violate the *acharana bidhi*. On the other hand, *Mahasabha* has also prescribed rewards in the form of cash, certificate and title to the students, artists, sportsmen, cultivators and craftsmen among them for outstanding achievements.

Apart from the caste council, Daluas also participate in the affairs of traditional village council in multi-ethnic villages and co-operate the authority in solving inter-community disputes and in organizing village-level festivals. They have actively involved themselves in the national politics both before and after the Independence. Some of them have played roles in the planning and implementation of welfare and development programmes through the post-Independence statutory bodies such as Panchayat, Municipality, Legislative Assembly of the State and Parliament.

Daluas like other communities of Ganjam maintain certain restrictions regarding traditional inter-community relationships. They accept water and *kachcha* food from Brahmins, Karanas and Goudas but not from Viramushtis, Kumutis, Devangas, Kalingis, Raulas, Tulabhinas, Pandaras, Damlas and the untouchables. However, they share water sources and crematorium, participate in festivals, and visit religious shrines along with these communities. A number of Daluas have emerged as businessmen, teachers, doctors, administrators, engineers and political leaders who have established modern inter-community linkages.

By and large, Daluas encourage their children towards formal education. The caste council also provides financial assistance for higher education to the children of poor families. Mostly, boys and girls continue their studies upto college and thereafter, they search for employment. Daluas resort to modern medicare for the treatment of health. They have realised the importance of family planning and prefer to have three children. Generally women get sterilized in order to have a birth control.

Dalua habitations are facilitated with water sources, electricity, irrigation, post offices and road communications. Most of them listen to radio and those who stay in urban localities also watch the television. In villages, Daluas have adopted modern means of production to increase the agricultural output. They avail the facilities from banks and public distribution system but nutritional programmes like mid-day meal scheme and ICDS are not provided to them. Many of them are able to earn their livelihood through IRDP and self-employment programmes sponsored by the State government.

REFERENCES

Patra, G.C. (1986). *Ganjam Dalapati Mahasabha Upabidhi*, Berhampur, Orissa: Sujata Press.

Samal, S.B. (1984). *Ganjam Dalapati Mahasabha*, Berhampur, Orissa: Sujata Press.

Thurston, E. (1909). *Caste and Tribes of Southern India*, Vol. II, Madras: Government Press, pp. 171-73.

SOCIAL LIFE NO. 5

ODIA MEDRI

Odia Medris are traditional basket-makers who are ethnically different from other basket-making communities including the Telugu Medris. The community has neither any sub-groups nor any synonyms. As regards the history and migration of the community, there exists no scriptural references and oral tradition. They identify themselves at regional level. Although an exact population figure of the community is not available, they claim that around fifteen hundred households are scattered over Ganjam, Koraput, Puri, Cuttack and Kalahandi districts of Orissa and Srikakulam, Vizagapatanam and Vijayanagaram districts of Andhra Pradesh. In Orissa, most of them are distributed in various places of Ganjam, namely Berhampur, Aska, Bhanja Nagar, Saroda, Badagada, Boirani, Hinjilikatu, Purusottampur, Belaguntha, Dharakote, Upuluda and Parlakhemundi.

Odia Medris prefer to reside in plain areas having a moderate climate, high humidity and medium rainfall. Their habitations lack forests and snowfall. They have a linear pattern of settlement where the houses are mostly mud-walled and thatched. Each house has a front yard where their men and women make baskets. Sometimes they do this on the road of their *sahi*. Unlike the Telugu Medris, whose mother tongue is Telugu, Odia Medris use Oriya as their script and spoken language at the time of their interaction with kinsmen and others. In Andhra Pradesh, they, however, converse in Telugu with the Telugu-speaking communities. They do not have any identification markers for the entire community. But in comparison to the Telugu Medris, their women have a different style of dress. Thus, the latter put on *sarees* without having *kunchi* (crimped folds) which is present in case of the formers. They do not have constitutional status like scheduled caste and as regards the bio-anthropological information of the community, nothing is available.

Odia Medris are consumers of both vegetarian and non-vegetarian foods. Non-vegetarian foods prepared from egg, fish, mutton or chicken are, however, occasionally taken. Their women are not prevented to eat non-vegetarian dishes. *Bhata* (boiled rice), *muga dali* (soup made of *moong*) and a vegetable curry prepared of groundnut oil, are usual items of their food. Previously, they had the habit of taking *torani* (cold rice gruel) early in the morning but at present, instead of *torani*, they are taking tea. While their women are restricted to consume liquor, most of their elderly men take it during the night. Among the fruits, mangoes and banana are mostly consumed but they do not have the practice of consuming roots and tubers.

The Odia Medri community is differentiated by social level into *gotras* and family names. Generally, family names like Munjati, Paleka, Rakam, Mantri, Kota, Nageswara and Ganta are popular among them. Both *gotras* and family names are exogamous and they help in the regulation of marriage alliances. They do not use surnames. They claim to be Sudras and perceive the Brahmins, Daluas, Kumutis and Devangas to be communities with a higher social status. They treat the Dandasis, Hadis, Bauris, Mochis and Panos as castes with a lower social status in comparison to them. By and large, other communities of the region keep a low perception towards them.

As a rule, marriage is monogamous among the Odia Medris. Both maternal and paternal cross-cousin marriages are prevalent. Brides are mostly acquired through parental negotiation but occasionally the principle of exchange of sisters is adopted. The earlier practice of child marriage has become obsolete and for the last fifty years, marriages have become post-pubertal. Junior sororate and junior levirate are not socially objected but practically do not occur at present. At the time of marriage, dowry is accepted both in cash and kind. As per the custom, a woman, after marriage, resides at her husband's paternal house. She smears vermillion on forehead, and wears lac bangles, *mangalasutra* and toe rings to identify her marital status. Divorce is permissible only after a social approval but practically, the Odia Medris do not go for a divorce. If at all, a divorce initiated by either husband or wife, is materialised, the dowry payments are returned to wife's parents. However, the children remain as liability of father in divorce cases. A divorcee, male or female, is later on permitted for a remarriage. The Odia Medris, in no case, establish a marital relationship with the Telugu Medris and other communities.

The families among the Odia Medris are mostly of vertically extended type. In certain cases, mixed extended as well as nuclear families also occur. Like the Oriya-speaking communities, a married woman in the family has a joking relationship with the younger brothers and sisters of her husband but preserves an avoidance relationship with the latter's father and elder brothers. Similarly, a married man keeps an avoidance relationship with his wife's mother and elder sisters but he is socially permitted to play jokes with the younger brothers and sisters of his wife. Odia Medris normally lead a coherent family life. Confrontations among the family members occasionally come to surface especially when there is a challenge to the authority of elders. Father acts as the authority in a house but when he dies, the eldest male member of the house, *suo motu*, holds the authority. Only the sons have a right over the paternal property which is inherited on the principle of male equigeniture.

The women among the Odia Medris primarily do the household works but they do not sit idle at the time of their leisure. They bring potable water for the use of the family. They also prepare various baskets made of bamboos. While they have a role in social functions and religious rituals, they have also a place in the mechanism of social control. They are permitted to take part in the affairs of their caste council as *badalokas* (elderly persons). In addition to their contribution to the family income, they control the expenditure of the family. However, in the social life, the women enjoy a lower social status than the men.

As regards the lifecycle rituals and taboos, Odia Medris exhibit much similarity with the Oriya speaking communities. Thus, soon after conception, a woman is forbidden to eat coconut and potato till delivery. She is also objected either to sleep or to cut anything during eclipses. The first delivery takes place at her parental residence and for this purpose, she is ritually invited by her parents after the completion of six months of pregnancy. Pollution due to birth is observed for twelve days by the kinsmen as well as the family members. During these days non-vegetarian food is not taken and religious rituals are not celebrated. Post-delivery rituals such as *panchuati* and *athuari* are observed on the fifth and eighth day respectively so as to prevent a spirit, namely *sathi* from causing harm to the baby. On the day of ritual, elderly women remain present near the baby and perform the rites. Throughout the night they read out *Puranas* and do not sleep to keep attention to the baby.

Ekoisia or naming ceremony is held on the twenty-first day after delivery. The baby is bathed, dressed and kept sleeping on a cradle on this day. An Oriya Brahmin *purohita* is invited to perform the ritual. He makes a horoscope for the baby and in accordance with the horoscope he selects a name which is then whispered in the ear of the baby by his parents. At the end, sweets are offered to the children of the locality and the family members enjoy a feast. When the baby becomes one year old, they celebrate *mundan* ceremony at the temple of their household deities. But after the attainment of adulthood, they perform rituals only for girls and not boys. A girl is kept isolated from the company of male members for seven days after puberty. She is forbidden to take non-vegetarian food and visit any temple. Only females are permitted to see her. On the seventh day, she takes her bath early in the morning, wears a yellow *saree* and then visits a temple of Lord Siva for a ritual worship in the company of females. Kinsmen and friends are invited on this occasion and treated with a feast in the evening. Marriage rituals are performed both at bride's and bridegroom's residence. However, the nuptial ceremony, like the negotiation ritual, is held at bride's residence. On the occasion of the nuptial ceremony, a feast is given to the guests by bride's parents. The marriage rituals are performed by an Oriya Brahmin *purohita* who does it as per the Oriya customary practices. When a person dies, the corpse is cremated and death rites are observed for twelve days by the family members as well as kinsmen. The corpse is taken to the crematorium on a bamboo frame only by their male relatives. Female relatives accompany the dead but on the mid-way they ritually offer food to the soul of the dead and thereafter, come back to their home. After one year of death, *barsikia sraddha* is celebrated. Apart from it, every year, on the day of Mahalaya festival, they perform ancestral worship when oblations are offered to the deceased ancestors. This ancestral worship is done by the Telugu Medris during the Pongal festival. In the celebration of the life cycle rituals, the Odia Medris still follow the earlier customs but for them, these rituals are becoming more expensive due to a rapid price-rise of different commodities related to these rituals.

Basketry is the traditional source of income of the Odia Medris. Both men and women prepare a number of products, namely *dala* (shallow tray), *quli* (rice container), *kundi* (potato or mango container), *patia* (mat), *tati* (screen made of bamboo laths), *changudi* (wicker basket) and *kula* (winnowing fan). Apart from it, their men have learnt playing modern musical instruments as a professional practice. They play music making band parties especially during marriage ceremonies of different communities. In the present days, some of them have taken up government services as their primary occupation. They are a landless community and bonded labour does not exist among them. The children, after the age of twelve, learn from their elders, the techniques of basket making and the art of playing musical instruments. They have a direct link with the market. The local daily market is fully regulated by them.

The Odia Medris have their own caste council, which functions at two levels, i.e. *Sahi* and *Zilla*. In every *sahi* of their own community, the caste council constitutes a headman named as Behera and a messenger called as *Prusti*. At the level of a *Zilla* the caste council consists of a Sabhapati, an Upa-Sabhapati, and the Behera and two *badalokas* of each *sahi*. While the caste council solves the intra-community disputes, for the solution of inter-community conflicts in their locality, they have formed traditional village councils. The latter also take steps to co-ordinate people of different communities in villages for the celebration of village-level festivals. Disrespect to traditional norms, insult to traditional council and theft are considered to be offences among them and in such cases, punishment is given in the form of cash fine or excommunication. Physical punishment, which is now obsolete, was given in the past.

Odia Medris celebrate the festivals of Hindu religion. They worship the Hindu gods and goddesses. Some of them are reverred as household deities whereas others are venerated as deities of regional or national importance. During the festive days, they decorate the frontyard of their houses with artistic floor designs. They make various cakes and *khiri* (gruel prepared with milk) to consume on these occasions. At the time of celebration of important festivals in their localities, they invite their kinsmen for a visit. The community has neither changed the religious practices nor involved in any socio-religious.

Odia Medris do not professionalize any craft other than basketry. Although their women are adept in floor painting, they do not practise it as a source of income. They have oral traditions, folklores, folk songs and folk tales. No traditional dance is performed among them. However, their men are skilled in playing various wind and percussion musical instruments. Odia Medris do not have any restrictions as regards the acceptance of non-cooked food from any community. However, cooked food and water are not received by them from the Dhoba, Panos, Adivasis and Telugu Medris. They also do not share wells and water sources with these communities. As a practice, exchange of water and food and establishment of putative kinship with other communities is prohibited. But they do not have any restriction to share crematorium, to visit same religious shrines and to participate in traditional festivals along with them. For example, at Berhampur some of them have a hereditary role of playing musical instruments and supplying wicker basket during the celebration of Thakurani Yatra. Illiteracy and acute poverty have restrained their people to turn up as scholars, administrators, engineers, doctors, teachers or political leaders. In fact, they have a very limited modern inter-community linkages through some of them who hold white-collar jobs.

By and large, they do not favour to impart formal education to their boys and girls beyond secondary level. The reasons for their dropout are poverty and need to earn for the family. Drinking water is available within their localities and the sources of drinking water are usually tube-wells, dug wells or ponds. While their habitations are electrified, only some of them are able to have electric communication to their houses. Their settlements have road but not railway communication and post office is not far off their locality. They listen to film songs through radios and learn how to play these songs with their musical instruments. They visit cinema but are unable to purchase television. At the time of illness, they use both traditional and modern medicare. They have realised the importance of family planning and express a favourable attitude towards it. They now prefer to be sterilized after three children. Generally women among them get sterilized and for this purpose they use modern methods. Fire wood is used by them as fuel resources. They avail the facility of ration distribution through fair-price shops. They have a favourable attitude towards savings but because of poverty they depend on money lenders and shop-keepers.

Odia Medris have their own grievances against the development and welfare programmes sponsored by the government. Thus, they say that nutritional programmes are not introduced for their children. Moreover, the present employment schemes such as E.R.R.P., I.R.D.P. and TRYSEM introduced by the government practically do not provide them any help for the improvement of their traditional profession. Therefore, they claim to be included in the Backward Class list of the State.

SOCIAL LIFE NO. 6

HADI

Hadis form a low class community among the Oriyas. They are treated as untouchables by the higher communities who feel polluted if touched by them. The Hadi community has sub-groups like, Hadi proper, Relli Hadi and Chachadi Hadi, which are endogamous divisions. While the Hadi proper has synonyms like Sudha Hadi and Godomalia Hadi, the Rellis are often called as Bhatta or Karuva Hadis. The Hadis are named so in Orissa because their members collect and sell hadas (bones) of various animals as a means of living. The Hadis proper claim Orissa to be their original homeland but the Rellis, who have settled mostly in Ganjam district, reveal their migration from Garribidi now a village in Srikakulam district of Andhra Pradesh, almost two hundred years ago.

Hadis prefer to settle in villages and towns of plain areas. In a traditional village or a town they are found to reside at the outskirt of the locality. The Hadis proper use Oriya as their mother tongue whereas the Rellis, who have now adopted Oriya as a script as well as kinsmen and others, were Telugus prior to their migration to Ganjam. The Hadis do not have any community identification markets with regard to dress pattern, ornaments or body markings. In Orissa they are treated as a Scheduled Caste. So far, no bio-anthropological studies have been made on the Hadis who claim their population to be around 20,000 scattered all over Orissa.

Hadis consume both vegetarian and non-vegetarian foods. Non-vegetarian foods, which are occasionally taken, are devoured by men as well as women. They do not eat roots and tubers but consume fruits like mango, jackfruit and banana during festive days. *Bhata, dali* and a vegetable curry are their staple food. Country liquor is a common drink among their men who also smoke *bidi* and cigarette.

As regards their dress pattern and ornaments, an impact of modernisation is visibly marked especially among the younger generation. the old persons mostly tick to traditional dress pattern. While the old males wear *dhoti*, the old females put on low priced *sarees*. Males of younger generation preferably clothe pant and shirt of low price whereas the females of the same generation attire a little more costly *sarees*, blouses and other under-garments. Boys are found to put on pants and shirts and the girls dress frocks and *sarees*. Small children most of the time remain naked. Use of gold ornaments is mostly absent among the females. Nose rings, earrings, necklaces of low cost glittering metals and bangles are ornaments which are popularly used by women to embellish themselves. However, the widowers are forbidden to wear ornaments. A few among the men are found to wear rings and wrist watches.

The ground plan of their houses is squarish. Almost all houses are thatched by straw. Each house has a verandah and two rooms. Front room is used for sleeping whereas the other one is used as kitchen. Verandah is mostly used for sitting and during summer season it is often used for sleeping. The walls are mostly made of mud and smeared with cowdung. However, some of them, who are economically better off, have their houses with cemented floors and walls and asbestos or concrete roof. The settlement of their locality exhibits a linear pattern of house arrangement.

Hadis are aware of *varna* system of classification of Hindu society and recognize their place among the *Sudras*. The community's self-perception as well as its perception by other community is low at regional level. They consider the Jagili and the Dandasi to be communities having lower social status than them. They do neither accept nor exchange food and water from these two communities.

Hadi community is classified, like other Oriya communities, into certain exogamous *gotras*, which are used for regulation of marriage alliances and also for identification of ancestral relationship. They have surnames like Behera, Ghadei, Nayaka and Parichha but these surnames have nothing to do with the regulation of marital relationship.

The Hadis observe endogamy at community level. Any violation of this custom is met with punishment in the form of cash fine or excommunication as decided by the caste council. They regard their parallel cousins as consanguines and, hence, a marriage with them is thought to be incestuous. Unlike the usual Oriya custom, the practice of *menarikam* (marriage with maternal uncle's daughter) is prevalent. However, a marriage between the maternal uncle and niece is strictly objected. Among the Hadis, the popular way of acquiring one's mate is by parental negotiation. But occasional cases of acquiring a mate by exchange, elopement, or court registration are also found. While child marriage is not practised among them, a girl is considered for marriage only after her puberty. Junior sororate and junior levirate are permitted among them but such practices are rarely seen. A girl after marriage smears vermillion on her forehead and wears *mangalsutra* and toe ring to identify her marital status. Payment of dowry, both in the form of cash and kind, takes place at the time of marriage. After marriage a bride stays at her husband's paternal residence. Dissolution of marriage is not an easy task among the Hadis and, therefore, its occurrence is infrequent. Neither the spouse nor the parents of the spouse have the freedom to materialise a divorce at their own will. Divorce, if at all initiated by either husband or wife, takes place only after the approval of the caste council. Behera, the headman of the *kula panchayat* (caste council), adjudicates the case in a *kula sabha* (caste meeting). Before giving his verdict, he thoroughly scrutinizes the grievances and evidences put forward by the aggrieved parties. The decision of Behera is acknowledged to be final and abiding and if any aggrieved party violates it, he or she is then, ostracised. In case the parents have a child, the liability of rearing the child, after divorce is vested upon either father or mother as per the decision taken by the Behera. Remarriage of a divorcee, male or female, takes place but only after the permission obtained from the caste council.

Hadi families are mostly linear extended type. A few cases of nuclear and mixed extended families are also seen. As like the Oriyas, their family members are bound with joking as well as avoidance, relationships. Thus, a married woman is seen to have a joking relationship with her *nananda* (husband's younger sister) and *diara* (husband's younger brother) and an avoidance relationship with her *swasura* (father-in-law), *malasura* (husband's maternal uncle) and *dedhasura* (husband's elder brother). On the other hand, a married man is socially permitted to keep a joking relationship with his *sala* (wife's younger brother) and *sali* (wife's younger sister) but with his *sasu* (mother-in-law) and *dedha sasu* (wife's elder sister) he preserves an avoidance relationship. Apart from this, grandparents and grandchildren have the social sanction of cutting jokes with each other. In a Hadi family, father is treated as the head and after his death the eldest male member, *suo motu*, succeeds him. Parental property, as among other Oriya speaking communities, is inherited only by sons. At the time of inheritance of property, apart from the *jyesthansa* given to the eldest son, all sons get equal share.

Household activities are mostly done by the women among the Hadis. Besides, they also bring potable water from the nearby water resources to their homes. Amidst their daily engagement in household activities, they find out time to sell fishes. In fact, many of them have got services in the Municipality and hospital as scavengers or sweepers. Thus, they have their personal earnings to contribute to family income. Along with their husbands, they also control family expenditure. They have a role in the performance of life cycle rituals and religious festivals at home. But they are not allowed to take part in the affairs of the caste council. By and large, they enjoy a lower status in social life in comparison to their men.

Hadis follow the Oriya custom and traditions during the observance of their life cycle rituals. They also observe certain social restrictions in connection to these rituals. As per the custom, a mother observes both pre-delivery and post-natal social restrictions. For example, she does not visit a crematorium and also does not eat dry fishes prior to delivery. After delivery she is also forbidden to cook till the end of *Ekoisia* ritual. Since post-delivery observation of pollution exists among them, religious festivals are forbidden to be celebrated for eleven days among kinsmen and for twenty-one days among the family members of a new-born baby. Post-natal rituals like *panchuati* and *athuari* are performed among them to prevent the baby from the possible evil impact of a spirit, namely Sathi Budhi on the fifth and eighth days after delivery respectively. On the twenty-first day, the *Ekoisia* ritual is held when an Oriya Brhamin *purohita* is invited to perform the ritual. After the usual *puja*, the *purohita* prepares a horoscope for the baby and according to the horoscope he finds out a suitable name for the baby. This name is called as *jataka nama* (name as per the horoscope). Apart from the *jataka nama*, the parents often give another name to the baby. As a practice, Hadis prefer to give the names of gods, goddesses and puranic heroes. On the day of *Ekoisia*, both paternal and maternal grandparents visit the baby and offer presentations of gold ornaments. At the end, kinsmen and others, who are invited for the ritual, are treated with a feast.

On the day of completion of one year to the baby, a ritual, namely *barsapurami*, is held among the Hadis. This ritual is, of course, not observed as strictly as the naming ceremony. Those, who observe it, call for an Oriya Brahmin *purohita* for the performance of the ritual. Special dishes like *kanika* (sweetened rice with spices), *pitha* (cakes) and *khiri* are prepared for this occasion. These are first offered to the tutelary deities during the ritual observance and thereafter, served to the kinsmen and family members. *Balapaka* or *mundan* ceremony is popularly observed among them. As soon as the baby becomes two or three years old, this ceremony is celebrated at the sacred centre of the tutelary deity of the concerned family. This ceremony is often repeatedly held on the basis of a specific vow made by parents at sacred centres of other deities like Budhi Santani Thakurani at Berhampur, Bairavi Thakurani at Mantridi, Lord Jagannath at Puri and Nrusinhanath at Simanchalam. Rituals related to first feeding of cereals ceremony, thread wearing ceremony and circumcision are not observed among them.

The attainment of puberty in case of a girl is commemorated ceremoniously by the Hadis. Soon after puberty she is kept in seclusion for seven days. Males are not allowed to see her whereas she is only accompanied by female friends and elderly women of her family during these days. Till the seventh day, she does not take bath and instead, keeps her body anointed with turmeric paste and oil. On the seventh day she takes bath early in the morning and visits a Siva temple for a *darsana*, along with girl friends and female relatives. She, then, attires herself with a new dress and embellishes with ornaments. Kinsmen, who are invited on this occasion, usually come with presentations like new clothes, banana and cocoanut. Till the seventh day, she is treated as polluted and, hence, not allowed to enter into the place where family deities are kept. She is also restricted to cook during this period.

Marriage negotiation is usually initiated by the parents of the groom either directly or with the help of a *madhyasthi* (arbitrator). However, the negotiation is ritually confirmed on an auspicious day when *nirbandha* (betrothal) ceremony is commemorated in presence of the Behera, headman of the village level caste council. Apart from this, seven days prior to nuptial ceremony, seven married female relatives of the bride perform the *badi-paka* (preparation of cakes of pasted pulse) ritual as well as the *mugajai ragada* (grinding of *moong*) ritual. These two rituals are also performed at bridegroom's house by seven married female relatives of the groom. Nuptial ceremony, which involves a series of rituals, is celebrated at bride's residence. For this purpose, the groom comes to bride's residence along with a procession including kinsmen and friends. But prior to it, he visits the sacred centres of his locality for a ritual worship to the deities. The rituals during the nuptial ceremony are officiated by an Oriya Brahmin *purohita* and during the commemoration of nuptial ceremony, a feast is given by bride's parents to kinsmen and the invited guests. After the nuptial ceremony, bride comes to bridegroom's house where post-nuptial rituals like *chaturthi* or *chauthi* and *sata-mangala* are performed. On the occasion of *chaturthi* ceremony, kinsmen and others are invited by groom's parents, who treat them by offering a feast. On the tenth day after the nuptial ceremony, a *kothamelani* ritual is performed at bride's residence. On this occasion, bride as well as bridegroom are invited by bride's parents and are offered with new dresses. Apart from this, Hadis also celebrate the *barsapurami* ritual (ritual commemorating the first marriage anniversary). On this day, the tutelary deity is ritually worshipped and at the end, the basket containing the *karpura mala* (camphor garland), *mukutas* (crowns) of bride as well as bridegroom and the *ganghuala luga* (cloth used to tie both bride and bridegroom) which were used during nuptial ceremony, is thrown in a pond.

The Hadis normally bury their dead but those who are economically sound cremate. In observing the death rituals they follow the Oriya customs. Death rituals are performed for twelve days but death pollution is observed till the eleventh day when the purgatory ritual is held. For example, non-vegetarian food and clarified butter are forbidden for consumption. Besides, paring of nails, shaving of face and trimming of head-hair are also tabooed during these days. On the eleventh day, sons and grandsons shave their faces and become bald. They also pare their nails, take bath and put on new clothes. Kinsmen and others are invited on this day and offered with a feast. Next day, *bara-patra* ritual is observed. On this occasion twelve male members of their caste are invited and offered with special dishes like *khiri* (gruel prepared with milk) and *chakuli pitha* (a kind of cake prepared from rice and pulse). The Hadis also celebrate a ritual called *barsikia* (first death anniversary) when the bones of the dead are disposed in water. Like the Oriyas, Hadis observe the ancestral worship on the day of *Mahalaya* festival, i.e. the new moon day of the month of *Aswina*.

Collection and trade of bones, beating of drums during marriage and religious festivals, scavenging and sweeping are the traditional occupations of the Hadis of Orissa. But for the Relli Hadis of Ganjam, who have migrated from Andhra Pradesh, collection and sale of sea fishes in local market is also a traditional occupation. In the present days, many of the Hadis have opted for government services. They are now mostly serving as scavengers or sweepers in Municipality, as attainders in hospitals and as *khalasi* (labourer) in Railway Department. A few among them domesticate pigs as well as hens. Hadis are landless and mainly depend on labour as a means of earning for their livelihood. However, the practice of either bonded labour or child labour is not seen among them. Those who work as labourer usually get their payment in cash.

Hadis have their own traditional caste council which is named as *Jati Sabha*. In course of time, their *Jati Sabha* has shown structural changes. Thus, earlier the *Jati Sabha* was constituted of two caste officers entitled Behera and Nayak. In addition to them there were in some places, other officials called *Adhikari* or *Chowdhury* or *Badaparichha* and *Bhalabhai*. While Behera was acting as the headman of *Jati Sabha*, Nayak was playing the role as his assistant. At present, Behera functions as the headman but his assistant role is played by *Chowdhury* and not by *Nayak*, a post which does not exist in the *Jati Sabha*. The present day *Jati Sabha* has a third post, namely Dakua which functions as a messenger. Previously these posts were hereditary but now-a-days an election takes place for these posts among the married male members of the community. Apart from acting as a dispute-settler, Behera, in the past was officiating as *purohita* in the nuptial ceremony but today, Behera no more plays the role of a *purohita*. In addition to his role in connection with social control, he takes part in the marriage negotiation of the castemen.

Like all other castes, Hadis share the common beliefs and rituals endowed in the Hindu religion. Festivals like Gundicha Jatra, Kartika Purnima, Janhi Osha, Saraswati Puja, Ganesh Puja are celebrated among them with pomp and ceremony. Among all these festivals, they give prime importance to Gundicha Jatra. Except the Hadis, all other Oriya communities observe it as the festival of Lord Jagannath, the State deity of Orissa. Hadis, instead, commemorate it as the festival of a mother goddess, namely Budhi Maa Thakurani. Like the festival of Lord Jagannath, who is placed in a chariot and pulled by the devotees, Hadis keep the Thakurani in a chariot and pull it on the same day. Apart from the Budhi Maa Thakurani, other deities, namely Kalimukhi, Tara-Tarini, Sata Bhaunia and Baidhara are also worshipped by them as tutelary deities.

Hadis do not professionalize any art or craft. However, their women decorate their houses by making artistic floor designs during festive days. The community does not nourish any traditional dance but they are the traditional users of percussion musical instruments. As per the tradition, Hadis accept but do not exchange both water and cooked food from higher communities. They do not share wells and drinking water sources with other communities. They participate in traditional festivals but do not share the crematorium with other communities. They render services to other communities. In the post-Independence period, some of them have become political leaders and may hold white-collar jobs. These people have established modern inter-community linkages with other communities. Although the stigma of untouchability has not wiped out of their mind and behaviour, its rigidity has lost its strength sharply.

Literacy rate among the Hadis is much below in comparison to the average literacy rate of the State. However, it is increasing with the growing interest among the parents to educate their children. Their children largely drop out at secondary level since they have to earn to support their family. The attitude of the Hadis to modern medicare and family planning is favourable. There is no special preference among them for sterilization for men and women. They obtain drinking water from tubewell and the dug-well which are present within their localities. They listen to radio and sometimes visit cinema. Road communication exist to their localities which are also furnished with electricity. They mostly use fire-wood as fuel. They also avail the benefit of food distribution through fair-price shops.

SOCIAL LIFE NO. 7

KUMUTI

The Kumutis or Komatis are distributed all over the South India and everywhere they have got used to the local cultures. Their passion for adjustment with the local cultures accounts for the formation of a varied number of sub-divisions within the community. Thurston (1909: 311) writes, "these sub-divisions are either territorial, occupational or religious in character. Thus there are Penukonda and Veginadu Komatis of whom the former belong to the town of Penukonda in the Godavari district and the latter to the Kistna district in Andhra Pradesh. Again, there are Siva, Vaishnava and Madhava Komatis. Of occupational sub-divisions, the following may be noted: *Nune* (oil), *Nethi* (ghi), *Dudi* (cotton), *Uppu* (salt), *Gone* (gunny-bag) and *Gantha* (torn cloth)." But broadly two major sub-divisions of Kumutis, called as Gaura or Gavara and Kalinga, are present. A section of Kumutis maintained the *gauravan* or social prestige of the community by sacrificing themselves in the fire-pits along with the goddess, Kanyakamma and, hence, they are called as Gaura Kumutis. Kalinga Kumutis claim that they were originally the Gaura Kumutis of Penukonda. It is noted, in the Kalinga Vaishya Mahasabha Niyamabali, 1977 that they had paid a royal honour to the Gajpati King, Purushottamadeva, of Kalinga kingdom after his victory in the legendary Kanchi war. Some of them had come along with him as royal guests, to Puri for pilgrimage. At Puri, they were served with non-vegetarian *bhoga* of the goddess, Vimala which they failed to recognise and consumed. As a result, they were ostracized by their castemen who were staunch vegetarians. After the excommunication, they migrated to Kalinga to initiate their business and, henceforth, they were named as the Kalinga Kumutis. The Kumutis, at present, claim to be Vaishyas and accordingly, they also refer themselves as Gaura Vaishyas and Kalinga Vaishyas.

The Kumutis are mostly concentrated in Andhra Pradesh. But they are also found in Tamil Nadu, Karnataka, Maharashtra and Madhya Pradesh. In Orissa, they are largely present in the Ganjam district. Besides, some of them are scattered over the districts of Phulbani, Koraput and Puri. In Ganjam, they are widely distributed with a population concentration of around forty thousand. An exact population figure of the community is, however, not available from any sources.

As regards the naming of the community the various opinions noted by Thurston (1909: 306-307) are presented here. By some, the name Komati is said to be derived from Ko-mati, meaning fox-minded; others say that it is from go-mati, meaning the possessor of cows. But according to a legend from the *Kanyaka Purana* the sacred book of the Komatis, it is derived from go-mati meaning sprung from the cow.

Kumuti habitations are more prevalent in plain areas having a high humidity, medium rainfall and a moderate climate. But some of them have also stayed along with the tribals in hilly areas. Their houses are mostly found to be arranged in a lincar fashion. In most cases, they make use of the front room of their houses as a shop. Kumutis generally speak Telugu. However, in different regions, they have also learnt the regional languages. In Ganjam, the Kalinga Kumutis converse in Oriya among the family members and kinsmen but many of them often talk in Telugu with other communities. They are mostly fond of vegetarian food items which are of south Indian style. However, the Kalinga Kumutis occasionally consume non-vegetarian curries, prepared of ground-nut oil, along with rice and *urad dal*. It is a common practice among them to take a cup of tea or coffee for refreshment in the morning. However, the entire community disapproves both men and women to take alcoholic drinks.

The sub-divisions of the community are further split up into *gotras* and family names. Each family name represents a group of consanguineal families. This social classification helps in the regulation of marriage alliances and identification of ancestral relationship. The sub-divisions are also classified into certain territorial units for the organization of the caste council. Thus, among the Kalinga Kumutis, the entire community is divided into a number of *anchalas* and the latter are further divided into certain *penthas*, which are the smallest territorial units comprising of a group of families.

The Kumutis have preserved till today, many of their old customs with regard to marriage. Thus, they adhere strictly to monogamous marriage. Again, in accordance with the custom of *menarikam*, they still claim their maternal uncle's daughter for marriage. The paternal uncle's daughter, on the other hand, are treated as blood relatives. The earlier practice of acquiring a bride through negotiation is also followed today. Sometimes, marriages are settled through the exchange of sisters. A woman, after marriage, smears vermillion on forehead, and wears toe-rings and a *mangalsutra* to identify her marital status. She also stays at her husband's paternal residence after marriage. During the last fifty years, a major change has taken place with respect to the age at marriage. Thus, when, previously, child marriage was the practice, at present, all marriages are post-pubertal.

By and large, Kumutis do not object to the payment of dowry which is given both in cash and kind. Divorces rarely occur among them and when they occur the reasons are either adultery or cruelty. A divorce case, whether initiated by either husband or wife, always needs the approval of the caste council as well as the court. Widow and widower may remarry among them.

In the present days, Kumutis still prefer to stay in mixed as well as vertically extended families. However, the cases of nuclear family have also been noted among them. In the family, a woman as a rule, maintains an avoidance relationship with the elder brother of her husband but with his younger brother and sister, she keeps up a joking relationship. On the other hand, a man can behave jokingly with his wife's younger brother and sister but not with her elder sister. The eldest male member is treated as the head of a family and after his death the next seniormost male, *ipso facto*, becomes the head. Only the sons have a right over the property of their father. All the sons, however, have equal shares in it.

Kumuti women do not sit idle. While their men are engaged in business, they manage the family. They bring potable water from the nearby water sources and perform the religious rituals at home. At the time of leisure, they prepare leaf-plates, paper containers, curry-powder papad, mixture and pickles. Occasionally, they also manage the shop in the absence of their husbands. However, they enjoy a lower status in comparison to men. They do not have decision-making powers and are forbidden to participate in the affairs of the caste council as well as the village panchayat.

Stoppage of menstruation continuously for two months is considered to be a sign of pregnancy among the Kumutis. Before the delivery, they do not perform any ritual in relation to pregnancy but certain behavioural restrictions are followed by a pregnant woman. Thus, she is forbidden to go near a burial ground. She is also restricted to observe any function connected with eclipses.

Soon after the birth, care is taken to protect the child from the impact of evil spirits. Day and night, the mother or any other elderly woman remains present near the child. On the fifth and eighth day, rituals called as *panchuati* and *athuari* respectively are performed by the women to guard the child against the possible attack of an evil spirit named as Sathi Budhi. It is believed that Sathi Budhi comes through the wall and, hence, the bed of the child is always kept away from the wall. In the night, elderly women, who stay along with the mother and the child in the same room, do not sleep. In order to remain awakened they read out *Puranas* and eat fried grams. They have the faith that by doing so, Sathi Budhi will not come to that room to harm the child.

Owing to birth, family members and kinsmen are treated as polluted and are forbidden to perform any religious ritual. This restriction, however, is nullified after the observance of a purgatory ritual on the twelfth day. On the twenty-first day, a Brahmin astrologer is invited, who after the performance of a ritual, prepares a horoscope for the child. Then, on the basis of the horoscope, he finds out a name which is whispered in the ear of the child by its parents. At the end, sweets are distributed among the children of the locality.

As soon as a child becomes one year old, the parents celebrate the *mundan* ceremony at the temple of their family deity. Some of them repeatedly observe this ceremony, in which the hairs of the head are sacrificed at the Nrusinhanath temple of Simanchalam in Andhra Pradesh.

When a girl attains her puberty, she remains at home being isolated from the males for seven days. On the seventh day, puberty rites are observed and kinsmen, who are invited on this occasion, are treated with a feast in the evening. Among the Kumuti, negotiation is ritually held at bride's residence. At present the Kalinga Kumutis perform the negotiation in the presence of the *Pentha-Prusti* of bride's locality. The ritual is officiated by a Brahmin *purohita*. After the ritual bride's father makes a detail declaration of the dowry to be given, which is noted by the Prusti in his file. At the end, sandal paste is distributed to everybody. Nuptial ceremony also takes place at bride's residence. The rituals are performed by a Brahmin *purohita* in accordance with the Hindu customs.

When a person departs, the family members and relatives mourn and observe a period of pollution for twelve days. During these days, they do not celebrate any religious rituals. Non-vegetarian foods are also not consumed. The Kumutis cremate their dead, but the corpse of a child or a Lingadhari is buried. Before taking to the crematorium, they wash the corpse with cold water and cover it with a new white cotton cloth. After that, it is kept on a bamboo frame and taken to the funeral ground by the adult male relatives. Death rituals are performed by a Brahmin *purohita* as per the Hindu customs. On the twelfth day, the purgatory ritual is observed. Kinsmen and friends are invited on this day and treated with a feast. Just one year after the death, they perform the *barsikia* ritual.

Business is the traditional occupation of the Kumutis. They are popular as merchants, grocers and money-lenders. By shrewd business tactics they regulate the local market. But with the impact of modern education, recently, many of them are found to be interested towards government as well as private services. Some of those, who are engaged in services also carry on grocery business at the time of leisure. The children learn the techniques of business while they assist their parents in the shop.

The caste council of the Kumutis is highly organised at present. The earlier pattern of authority structure in the caste council has changed. Thus among the Kalinga Kumutis of Ganjam the caste council now operates at the level of entire community whereas earlier there was one caste headman called Senapati, in a village and another called Vaishya-raju who was the headman of a group of villages. At the level of a *Pentha*, they form the caste council called as *Pentha Sabha* in which the headman is called as 'Prusti'. He is assisted, in matter of organization, by a 'Secretary', a 'Treasurer' and eight members. All of them are democratically elected in a general meeting of the community to work for a period of one year. Primarily, they are concerned with the solution of intra-community disputes, and the implementation of welfare and developmental measures for the community. But, they, simultaneously, take steps to rehabilitate the disabled men and women to construct religious institution in the *Pentha* and to extend financial assistance to poor students. Sometimes, intra-community disputes are not solved by them. In such cases, the caste council at the level of Anchala called as the *Anchala Sabha* is consulted. The *Anchala Sabha* may have maximum twenty-five members who are representatives from the *Pentha Sabha*. Among these members, one is elected as the President and another as the Secretary. The caste council at the highest level is called as the *Kalinga Vaishya Mahasabha*. It has its jurisdiction over the entire community. Representatives from the *Pentha Sabha* are treated as the members of the *Mahasabha* and from among them, one President, one Vice-President and General Secretary are elected. In the meeting of the *Mahasabha*, which takes place biennially, decisions are taken regarding the intra-community integration, the moral, economic and educational progress of the community and the reformation of the society. The caste council considers them to be offenders who violate the traditional norms, possess an attitude of non-cooperation towards the caste council or indulge in adultery, elopement and inter-caste marriage. Punishment is given to these offenders in the form of cash fine and excommunication. The traditional village council which is present in their locality primarily solves the inter-community disputes and organises village-level festivals whereas the post-Independence statutory panchayat and Municipality implement various welfare and development programmes which benefit the Kumuti as well as other communities.

Kumutis are broadly classified as Vaishnavas and Saivas. Among them, the Kalinga Kumutis are Vaishnavas. In spite of the sectarian division, the Kumutis venerate all Hindu gods and goddesses. Everyday early in the morning, they take bath and make a *puja* (ritual worship) to their household deities. After that, they visit the nearby temples for a *darsana* of the deities. Their women clean and wash the front yard of their houses daily and make artistic floor designs to welcome goddess Laxmi. Every Kumuti has kept photo of different deities in their shops. These deities are also worshipped with an offer of *dhupa* in the morning as well as evening. They celebrate the religious festivals by decorating their houses with various floor designs and by consuming specially prepared food items. Among all the festivals, the Thakurani Yatra has a special significance to them in Ganjam. They make several vows before the goddess which are fulfilled at the time of *yatra*. They also invite their kinsmen from distant places to come for a visit to the *yatra*. Goddess Kanyaka Parameswari is worshipped by them as their caste deity. At places they have erected temples for the deity.

Previously Kumutis were not accepting water and *kachcha* food from the *Sudras* but such restriction in social intercourse is not strictly followed by the youngsters at present who have putative kins among the *Sudras*. They share water sources and crematorium and participate in the religious festivals along with other communities. Further, many of them have come out as doctors, teachers, engineers or government servants and they have established relationship with other communities.

Modern civilization has its inevitable impact on the social life of the Kumutis. The Kumuti parents are now taking all possible measures to educate their children. They are preferring to modern medicare for the treatment of illness. Both, men and women, realise the benefits of family planning and do not hesitate to sterilise themselves after two or three issues. The advent of radio, television and cinema, have changed their outlook. The recent facilities of bank, transport, communication and electricity have developed their enterprising quality.

REFERENCES

Senapati, T.N. (1977). *Kalinga Vaishya Mahasabha Niyamabali*, Vol. II, Berhampur: Orissa Printing Works.

Thurston, E. (1909). *Castes and Tribes of Southern India*, Vol. III, Madras, Government Press, pp. 306-48.

SOCIAL LIFE NO. 8

BHANDARI

The barber community in Orissa is named as Barika or Bhandari. In the past, apart from their traditional profession of shaving, some of them were appointed as *Upadestas* (advisers) by the local kings in the Central and North Orissa. Since these *Upadestas* were admonishing the kings after a thoughtful selection, they were called as Barikas.* In South Orissa, the barbers were appointed by the local kings as store-keepers.

* As per Oriya language, Barika means Bari kare je se which can be interpreted in English as he who makes a thoughtful selection.

In Oriya language a store-keeper is called as *bhandara-rakshaka*, and hence, the barbers in South Orissa were called as *bhandari*, a corrupted term of *bhandara-rakashaka*. The Bhandaris are said to have four social divisions, namely Gadia Bhandari, Odia Bhandari, Beja Bhandari and Kampa Bhandari. The Gadia Bhandaris who serve the royal community draw the highest social status among them whereas the Kampa Bhandaris, who serve the local tribes, derive the lowest social status. An exact population figure of the community is not available. However, they claim that they comprise more than five lakhs in Orissa and in the Ganjam district around one lakh of their population are distributed.

The Bhandaris prefer to settle in the plains. In Ganjam district they are distributed in places where the climate is moderate, rainfall is medium, humidity is high and there is neither any forest nor any snowfall. They are vegetarians as well as non-vegetarians. Non-vegetarian foods are occasionally consumed. Consumption of liquor is limited to the illiterate males. *Bhata, dali* and a vegetable curry are their staple food.

The Bhandaris claim to be *Sudras*. The community is divided into certain exogamous *gotras* such as Nagesa, Kasyapa and Kausaka. Marriages among them are strictly monogamous and brides are acquired primarily through parental negotiation but sometimes, the principle of exchange of sisters is adopted for this purpose. Earlier practice of child marriage is not seen today. As a rule, all marriages, at present, are post-pubertal. After the marriage, a bride stays at her husband's paternal residence. She smears vermillion on forehead like all Hindu married women to identify her marital status. For the same cause, she also wears toe-rings. Payment of dowry is still prevalent among them although their caste council has already launched a campaign against it. Both maternal and paternal cross-cousins are acquired as brides. Under exigencies, junior sororate and junior levirate marriages are permitted but these rarely occur. In case of adultery, cruelty or maladjustment a person is allowed to seek divorce. However, after divorce, the children become the liability of father.

Bhandari woman neither visits a crematorium nor eats dried fish till delivery. After delivery, birth pollution is observed for eleven days by the kinsmen and twenty-one days by the family members. During these days religious festivals are not celebrated. Like the Oriyas, post-delivery rituals such as *panchuati* and *athuari* are held among them. On the twenty-first day, they observe the name-giving ceremony. A Brahmin *purohita* is called for, who performs the ritual. At the end, he prepares a horoscope for the baby. As per the horoscope he finds out a suitable name which is whispered in the ear of the baby by the parents. On this occasion, *bala bhoga* (food offering to children) prepared of sweetened fried paddy are offered to the children of the locality. When a baby becomes one year old, *mundan* or hair-sacrifice ceremony is commemorated at the sacred centre of their tutelary deities. *Mundan* ceremony is repeatedly performed by some of them at sacred centres of other deities. While *mundan* ceremony is celebrated for both boys and girls, adolescence rites are observed only in case of girls. For seven days after the attainment of puberty, a girl is kept isolated from the males. She is treated as polluted for these days and hence observe certain social restrictions. On the seventh day, she visits a Siva temple after bath early in the morning. She, then, embellishes herself with ornaments and new dress. In the evening, a feast is offered to the kinsmen and others who are invited for this purpose. Negotiation ritual as well as the nuptial ceremony are held at bride's residence following the Oriya customs. On the day of nuptial ceremony, a feast is offered by the bride's parents to kinsmen and relatives. In case of death, the corpse is cremated. However, if the dead is a child, less than one year in age, the corpse is buried. When somebody dies out of small-pox, they simply lay the dead body on the ground. The corpse is taken on a bamboo frame only by men. Female relatives of the dead go along with the funeral procession but on the midway, they perform a ritual and come back to their homes. Death pollution is observed for eleven days by kinsmen as well as family members. On the eleventh day, a purgatory ritual is performed when kinsmen and others are invited and treated with a feast. Annual death ritual and ancestral ceremony are also held among the Bhandaris. The latter is performed on the day of Mahalaya like the Oriyas.

In the present days, the Bhandaris primarily depend upon their traditional occupation as source of income, whereas some of them have taken resort to new occupations. The traditional occupations of the Bhandaris are barbery and ritual associates to the Brahmin *purohitas* during the celebration of lifecycle rituals. In certain villages, they live on priesthood in the sacred centres of mother goddess. These priests also make some earnings by cultivating the temple lands. Recently, they preferred to business or services as sources of income.

The Bhandaris have their own caste council, which primarily takes step with regard to social control within the community. The caste council, prior to 1935, was functioning at two levels, *Mutha* (cluster of villages) and *Taluka*, now operates at three levels—*Mandala, Zilla* and *Pradesh*. The caste council at each level structurally constitutes a

Sabhapati, an *Upa-Sabhapati*, a *Sampadaka* (Secretary), one or two *Saha-Sampadaka* (Assistant Secretary), a *Kosadhaksha* and one or more *Upadesta*. In addition to this, at *Mandala* and *Pradesh* level, the caste council has one or more *Sangathanika Sampadaka* (Organising Secretary). The caste council at the State level is known as *Nikhila Utkala Barika Samiti* and this *Samiti* has taken its shape in 1935. Apart from solving disputes within the community the caste council extends financial assistance to poor persons with regard to higher education and performance of marriage or funeral ceremony. The caste council is based on a democratic set-up and hence the post-bearers are elected from among the members. Bhandaris reside in multi-ethnic villages and they also take part in the affairs of the traditional village panchayat whose main function is to solve inter-community disputes and to organize village level festivals. Welfare and developmental programmes sponsored by the government are, however, implemented not by the caste council or traditional village council but by the post-Independence statutory Panchayat and Municipality. Bhandaris consider them to be offenders who are involved in adultery, elopement, theft, inter-caste marriage, violation of traditional norms and non-cooperation to the caste council. These offenders are punished by the caste council in the form of cash fine or excommunication.

Although in certain sacred centres of mother goddesses Bhandaris officiate as priest, they worship all Hindu gods and goddesses. They rever mother goddesses of regional importance, namely Narayani, Budhi Santani Thakurani, Tara-Tarini and Bhairavi as their *ishtadevis*. At their home, in addition to the photos of their tutelary deity, they keep the photos of other Hindu deities like Ganesh, Siva, Parvati, Laxmi, Vishnu, Jagannath, Kali, Durga and Nrusinhanath. These deities are worshipped everyday in the morning as well as evening by them. They celebrate all major Hindu festivals but the Thakurani Yatra (Mother goddess festival) bears most significance for them. During the celebration of Thakurani Yatra in different villages of Ganjam, they participate as sacred specialists or sacred associates. As sacred specialist, they have a *jajman* relationship with the pilgrims.

In general, Bhandaris do not professionalize any art or craft. However, a few among them, who serve as temple priests prepare model images of mother goddesses like Kali, Durga, Chandi and Sapa-Sapuani which are hired by people to exhibit during festivals and rituals as a part of their vows. Their women have the knowledge of making artistic floor designs but such designs are made to decorate their own houses only during certain festive days. Dance and music are not nourished by them either for amusement or as a source of income. As per the earlier tradition, Bhandaris were accepting cooked food and water only from Brahmins, Kshatriyas and Karanas. At present, under the impact of secularisation, urbanisation and modernisation, this restriction in social intercourse is losing its identity. Many Bhandari youths are found to exchange food and water with communities like Kumutis, Devangas, Raulas and Tulabhinas. In the present days, many of them prefer to take tiffins in hotels where the food is not supplied by a Brahmin, Kshatriya or Karan boy. In villages, where they have jajmani relationship with regard to their traditional occupation of barbery, they do not extend services to the untouchable castemen. But, where instead of *jajmani* relationship they have set up saloons, they extend services to the untouchables also. However, they do not have any social restriction in sharing crematorium and participating in religious festivals along with other communities.

Most of the Bhandaris desire to educate their boys who can opt for government services but the need to earn to support their family by stepping into the hereditary occupation still causes a large scale dropout among the boys. On the other hand, apart from those who are educated and working as government servants, others do not favour to educate their daughters beyond primary level on social reasons. They realise the importance of family planning but only a few are seen to opt for sterilization. At the time of illness, they, at present, prefer to modern medicare. Bhandaris have been modernising their outlook. Those who do not pursuit priestly profession, are not found to put on modern dresses. They do not maintain the traditional priestly style of life. Apart from the days of services at the temple, they spend their leisure by listening film songs from radio or tape-recorder. Some of them have purchased television and keep themselves aware of the national issues by observing television. Bhandaris settlement has a linear pattern of arrangement of houses. They have electrified their houses and use drinking water from tubewells.

SOCIAL LIFE NO. 9

DEVANGA

The Devangas of Ganjam district are professional textile weavers. They are popularly called as 'Deras' by the Oriya-speaking communities whereas the Telugu-speaking communities call them as 'Devangulus'. Thurston narrates two myths regarding their origin. As per the first-one, once the Devas (gods) and men prayed Brahma to solve the problem of their nudity. Brahma took them to Siva, who at once, created a lustrous spirit and called him Devalan. Siva asked Devalan to weave clothes for Devas and men. His descendants are in consequence called Devangas. The second myth speaks about Narada to have prayed Parameshwara to devise clothes for the naked gods, demons and human beings. Parameshwara created a man from his body and named him Deva Angam (Body of god) in allusion to the manner of his birth. He, then, sent Deva Angam to Shri Maha Vishnu, who ordered him to weave cloth for the inhabitants of the universe. For this purpose Deva Angam created ten thousand weavers whose descendants are now called as the Devangas. A third myth is given in the *Uttara Khanda* of *Brahmanda Purana* and as per it, Siva with the request of Narada to solve the problem of nakedness of the inhabits of earth, threw a small bunch of his matted hair to create Devanga *rishi*. Siva asked him to weave clothes for the human race. Devanga *rishi* is claimed to be the ancestor by the Devanga of Ganjam.

The original homeland of the Devangas was Rajmahendry of Andhra Pradesh. They recall on oral tradition of their migration to Ganjam. Once the king of Mohuri estate had gone to Rajmahendry of the then Vijayanagaram kingdom on a royal visit to see the Thakurani Yatra. He was very much impressed by the organization of the *yatra* and highly appreciated the workmanship of a silk cloth presented to him by the local Devangas. The king invited the Devanga, who, then, migrated to settle and initiate the weaving business at Berhampur of his estate. At present, they are distributed at places of commercial importance, namely Berhampur, Pitala, Boirani and Bhanjanagar in Ganjam. As such, there is no record of their population in census but they claim to be around thirty thousand in the district. They are plain-dwellers and their places of habitat have a moderate temperature, high humidity, medium rainfall and do lack forest and snowfall. They are a Telugu-speaking community but are able to write and talk freely in Oriya.

The traditional dress of Devanga men usually consists of a white handloom cloth measuring 8 feet by 3 feet as the lower garment and a full-shirt. Currently men of younger generation prefer to wear pants and shirts. Women's dress consists of cotton *saree* and blouse. Silk *sarees* are worn only on festive occasions. Earlier there was a practice of wearing 'Lingam' (phallus symbol of Lord Siva) and anointing sandal paste on forehead among men. This tradition, at present, is not followed by the young men. The Devangas are a general caste people and affiliate themselves with the *Sudra varna*. Bio-anthropological studies have not been made so far on the community.

Vegetarian dishes like rice, *dal*, vegetable curry, *charu* and *chalha* and non-vegetarian food items of chicken, fish, egg and mutton are consumed by them. The Linga-dharis are, however, strictly vegetarians. Devangas do prepare their food by mustard oil. Fruits are taken on festive days. A change from vegetarian to non-vegetarian food habit is marked corresponding with a reduction in the practice of wearing *lingas*. At religious level, Devangas are differentiated as Lingadharis and non-Lingadharis. They are also occupationally categorised as cotton-weavers and silk-weavers. Apart from it, the community is divided into *gotras* for regulation of marriage alliances and each *gotra* is again subdivided into family names for indication of ancestry.

Endogamy at community level and exogamy at *gotra* level are practices among the Devangas. Marriages are monogamous and arranged by parents in cognizance of the caste council. Parallel cousins are treated as consanguines but nuptial relationship is established with cross-cousins. Maternal cross-cousins marriage is of common occurrence and paternal cross-cousins marriage is held only on the principle of exchange. Junior sororate and junior levirate are permitted but rarely practised. Earlier practice of child marriage had become obsolete. At present, post-pubertal marriage takes place. Boys of twenty-four years and girls of nineteen years are considered to be at average age of marriage. Vermillion, bangles, finger-ring, and toe-ring are symbols of married women. Dowry is accepted both in cash and kind. Patri-locality is the strict rule of residence after marriage. Divorce is permissible through social as well judicial approval. However, divorce rarely occurs and the reasons are adultery and extreme case of cruelty. Divorce compensation is given to wife; and children are liability of either father or mother. Previously widow remarriage was not permitted but at present both widow and widower are allowed for re-marriage. Male as well as female divorcees are not prohibited for re-marriage. In the post-Independence period, an increase in age at marriage, and a growing demand of dowry have been observed.

Devanga families are mostly mixed or vertically extended types. Recently migrated families are only found to be nuclear. Avoidance relationship exists in liberal manner between mother-in-law and son-in-law, daughter-in-law and father-in-law and younger brother's wife and husband's elder brother. Elder brother's wife and husband's younger brother, elder sister's husband and wife's younger brother and younger sister, and grandparents and grandchildren are permitted to establish joking relationship. Cordiality prevails over confrontation within the family but at times, conflict emerges due to dispute over property and disobedience to elders. Inheritance of parental property is decided on the principle of male equigeniture. Succession of authority in family takes place by eldest son. The Devangas have so far preserved all the traditional rules of family life.

Devanga women are primarily house-wives but at the time of leisure they assist in weaving. They bring potable water from the nearby water resources. They have a special role during the Thakurani Yatra. The Thakurani *ghatas* are carried on head by them at the time of Thakurani's visit to different localities. However, they are not permitted to play a role in the political bodies. By and large, they enjoy a lower status in relation to men.

Pre-delivery taboos are prescribed for the women. They are forbidden to enter into any place of worship and are not allowed to perform any ritual after seven months of pregnancy till the twenty-first day of delivery. Delivery takes place in hospital or at home in presence of *chakali*, an old woman of washerman caste. *Chakali* cuts the umbilical cord and also performs the *pretinue dinemo* (birth ritual), *wayaluloveyutta* (name giving ceremony) takes place on the seventh day, or the twenty-first day. Both mother and child anoint sandal paste on body, take bath and then wear new dresses. A Brahmin astrologer is invited who prepares a horoscope for the baby. In accordance with it he suggests suitable names and one among these is selected by the elderly kinsmen. The kinsmen, then, bless the baby and enjoy a feast offered to them. The earlier practice of selecting an ancestral name is not practised these days and instead modern names are preferred.

Initiation ceremony for the girls is observed on the eighth day after puberty. Till then she is tabooed to come out of house. On the day, she being escorted by her mother and female relatives, bathes in the nearest tank, embellishes herself with new dress and smears sandal paste on forehead. Sweets are then distributed among the kinsmen and villagers. Previously, an ear-perforation ritual was observed for the initiation of the boys after the age of eighteen. But this practice has now become obsolete.

Negotiation is held at bride's residence, in the presence of Sahi Senapati and Desabehera. A few days after negotiation, *Tambulam* ritual is performed by offering a *tambulam* (betel-leaf) along with an unbroken *gua* (betel-nut) to the eldest male kinsman as a token of invitation.

Marriage ceremony, is celebrated at bride's residence. Firstly, the 'nail-cutting' ritual is performed by the elderly women who cut down bride's nail. Then, 'the bathing ritual' follows and the bride is bathed with turmeric water by seven women. Marital solemnization takes place on an altar in assistance of a Brahmin *purohita*. *Jeera-karabelam* ritual is first performed on the altar. It involves smearing of a paste of *jeerakara* (cumin seeds) and *belam* (molasses) by bride and bridegroom on each other's forehead. In the *mangalasutram* ritual the bridegroom ties the *mangalasutram* (auspicious marital thread) around bride's neck. Thereafter, in *chakrapadulu* ritual the bride lifts groom's feet kept on a brass plate. In the *talambralu* ritual both bride and bridegroom exchange each other's crown and camphor necklace. During this ritual, dowry-items are offered and the bride's kinsmen bless the couple and give presentations. Soon after it, *chuka chustandi arundhati* ritual is observed to show the bridal pair the Arundhati star in the sky who is regarded to be one of the witnesses of their sacred union. For this custom, marriage is organized in night and is continued till early morning when Arundhati star appears in the sky. *Ungaralu dewadam* ritual is then performed which involves a search for a gold-ring in a water-filled pot by the couple. At the end, the couple seek blessings from the village goddess, Lord Ganesh, and all elderly kinsmen.

The Devangas bury the dead in sitting posture. The burial work is initiated by the dead's eldest son but it is completed by a washerman. Death ritual is observed on the eleventh day. In case of a death due to small-pox, diarrhoea or an accident, the body is thrown outside and burial rites are not observed. For a period of three days, kinsmen do not take non-vegetarian foods. Thereafter, the death rituals are performed with the assistance of a *brahmin purohita*. An annual observance of ancestor worship is practised among them. No change in ritual performances is marked and due to accretion of modern decorative items, rituals are gradually becoming more expensive.

Devangas are landless and sustain their life primarily by weaving cotton clothes of superfine quality. At Berhampur, some of them weave silk cloths and a few have adopted to wholesale business of grocery items or vegetables. All members of a family above the age of ten participate in weaving. A clear-cut division of labour on the basis of age and sex is marked. Weaving at the loom and gumming the thread are generally done by men. Children assist them at loom while women dye the yarn and spin the thread. Poverty drags them to be exploited by depending on middlemen for supply of raw-material and sale of their products. Acharya and Mohanti (1986) reveal that processes of modernisation such as State patronization, market promotion, cooperativization, institutional financing etc. have encouraged them in retaining their craft.

Devangas have a well-organised caste council which is composed of a Desabehera, Sahi Senapatis and a Messenger. Desabehera is the head among the Sahi Senapatis. A Sahi Senapati is the caste headman of one Sahi. All these posts are hereditary. While the Messenger works as a messenger Desabehera and the Sahi Senapatis solve the intra-community disputes, organize Thakurani Yatra and participate in marriage alliances. In multi-ethnic villages Devangas also participate in the village council. The village council functions in solving inter-community conflicts. In the caste council as well as village council, punishments are given in the form of cash fine or excommunication. Adultery, deviation from traditional norms, theft and rape are regarded as offences. Adjudication is made for the first two cases at the level of caste council and for the latter two cases they inform the police to take action. Some of them have participated in the modern statutory council and demanded for implementation of welfare programmes.

Devangas are basically Lingayats. They observe all the Hindu festivals but those related to Siva and Shakti cults are celebrated with much rejoice. Many of them have the habit of visiting Siva and Shakti temples everyday for offering a *puja*. Goddess Choudheswari is respected as the caste-deity. Everyday before weaving they offer worship first to Ganesh, establish on a small platform at a corner near the loom in every house and then to Choudheswari to get blessings for success in weaving. Apart from it, they also worship other Hindu deities in their families. In Ganjam they have a special reverence to Budhi Santani Thakurani who is mythically regarded as the married daughter of Desabehera. Desabehera patronizes a festival for the goddess, named as Thakurani Yatra, in which the Devangas co-operate with him and participate in the *yatra*. They depend on sacred specialists of other communities like Barber, Damla, Reddika, Raula, Washerman and Brahmin for performances of various rituals. Festivals bear a socio-religious significance for them. They are able to invite kinsmen especially for a visit to Thakurani Yatra. They also make various vows to their deities to get supernatural blessings.

The Devangas consider Viramushtis to be their traditional preceptors, and from them they take precepts before wearing *lingam*. They practise commensal relationship as common to *sudras*. They share the crematorium and visit the same religious shrines along with other communities but they do not share the well with the untouchables.

Modern inter-community linkages are established by some of them through wholesale business and political leadership at village council and modern statutory council. Most of them are illiterates. They desire to educate their children but poverty and necessity of assistance in weaving have forced for a dropout at primary level. They make use of both indigenous traditional and modern medicare at the time of illness. They do not have a favourable attitude towards family planning since they consider children to be economic assets in weaving profession. They avail the facility of electricity to work at night. They make use of coal and fire-wood as fuel resources. Drinking water is available to them from dug-wells and tube-wells. They listen to radio for entertainment. On the festive days, when they stop weaving, they visit cinema. Poverty has restrained many of them to purchase television. They avail the facility of food distribution through fair-price shops.

Devangas have the obvious attitude of entrepreneurship. They aspire for an increase in the efficiency of production. For this purpose, help is extended to them both from government and bank through programmes like IRDP, TRYSEM and ERRP. But they express their resentment against the faulty implementational procedures which incur them a loss in their craft. Acharya, Das and Dash (1986) have suggested that if government will take steps regarding timely payment of subsidy and rebate money, supply of dyed and twisted yarns, national and international advertisement of the products, extensive introduction of tassar and sericulture in the nearby locality and supply of qualitative implements; then the weaving craft can be improved through co-operative movement among the Devangas.

REFERENCES

Acharya, P.K.; Das, P.K. and Dash, B.K. (1986). *Co-operatives and the Weaker Section: A Case Study on Silk-Weaver's Co-operative Society of Berhampur City (Orissa)*, (Unpublished) paper submitted to National Colloquium on Population, Development and Culture, Bhubaneswar, Orissa, Feb. 27, 1986.

Acharya, P.K. and Mohanti, K.K. (1986). *Pata-Weavers of Berhampur City: An Ethno-technological Study*, National Conference on Natural Heritage Conservation, Berhampur, Orissa, June 4, 1986 (Abstracts): 57-58.

Thurston, E. (1909). *Castes and Tribes of Southern India*, Vol. II, Madras: Government Press, pp. 154-66.

APPENDIX-V

LIST OF RITUAL MATERIALS USED IN CHANGUDI PUJA

Item No.	*Items as locally called*	*English meaning*
1.	*Gamuchha*	Towel
2.	*Gota haladi*	Unbroken turmeric
3.	*Gota gua*	Unbroken betel nut
4.	*Chaula*	Rice
5.	*Pania*	Comb
6.	*Darpana (Chhota)*	Mirror (Small)
7.	*Kalakacha*	Black bangle
8.	*Sindur*	Vermillion
9.	*Chaku*	Knife
10.	*Chandana Katha*	Sandal wood
11.	*Dhupakathi*	Incense stick
12.	*Barakoli patra*	Jujube leaf
13.	*Kadali*	Banana
14.	*Nadia*	Cocoanut
15.	*Harida*	Pegion pea
16.	*Akhanda deepa*	Unbroken lamp

BIBLIOGRAPHY

Acharya, P.K.; Dash, B.K. and Das, P.K. (1986). *Co-operatives and the Weaker Section: A Case Study on the Silk-Weaver's Co-operative Society of Berhampur City (Orissa)*, Paper presented at the National Colloquium on Population, Development and Culture, Bhubaneswar.

Acharya, P.K. and Mohanti, K.K. (1986). *Pata-Weavers of Berhampur City: An Ethno-technological Study*, Paper presented at the National Conference on Natural Heritage Conservation, Berhampur.

Acharya, S. (1983). *Puri: A Centre of Pilgrimage*, Unpublished M.Phil. dissertation submitted to Utkal University, Bhubaneswar.

Ashby, P.H. (1974). *Modern Trends in Hinduism*, New York: Columbia University Press.

Babb, L. (1975). *The Divine Hierarchy*, New York: Columbia University Press.

Bang, B.G. (1973). "Current Concepts of the Small-pox Goddess Sitala in Parts of West Bengal", *Man in India*, 53, p. 79-104.

Bharadwaj, S.M. (1973). *Hindu Places of Pilgrimage*, California: Berkeley University Press.

Bharati, A. (1963). "Pilgrimage in the Indian Tradition", in *History of Religious*, 3: No. 1.

——— (1970). "Pilgrimage Sites and Indian Civilization", *Indian Civilization*, Vol. I.

Bhattacharya, N.N. (1974). *History of Sakta Religion*, New Delhi: Munshiram Manoharlal Publishers Private Limited.

Bhowmick, P.K. (1960). "Four Temples in Midnapur", *Man in India*, 40: 81-108.

Bose, N.K. (1959). *Comparative Study of Civilizations*.

——— (1967). *Culture and Society in India*, Kolkata: Asia Publishing House.

Bose, P.N. (1978). *A History of Hindu Civilization during British Rule*, Reprint, Vols. I and II, New Delhi: Asia Publication Services.

Chakrabarti, P. (1974). "Some Observations on the Pilgrims and Their Pilgrimage: A Case Study at Tarakeshwar", Ranchi: *Journal of Social Research*, Vol. XVII-I, pp. 104-15.

Chakravarti, C. (1972). *Tantras: Studies in Their Religion and Literature*, Kolkata: Punthi Pustak.

Chattopadhyaya, S. (1970). *Evolution of Hindu Sects*, New Delhi: Oriental Press.

Chaudhury, B. (1974). *The Bakreswar Temple: A Study on Sacred Complex*, Unpublished P.R.S. Thesis, Calcutta University.

———— (1981). *The Bakreswar Temple: A Study on Continuity and Change*, New Delhi: Inter-India Publications.

Cohn, B.S. and Marriott, M. (1958). "Networks and Centres in the Integration of Indian Civilization", *Journal of Social Research*, Vol. I, No. 1.

Danielou, A. (1964). *Hindu Polytheism*, London: Routledge and Kegan Paul.

Das, M.N. (1977). *Side Lights of Orissa History and Culture*, Cuttack: Vidyapuri.

Dash, M.P. (1965). *A Descriptive Catalogue of Sanskrit Manuscripts of Orissa*, Vol. V.

Diamond, N. (1970). "Fieldwork in a Complex Society" in George Spindler (ed.), *Being An Anthropologist*, New York: Holt, Rinehart and Winston.

Eschmann, A. *et al.* (1978). *The Cult of Jagannath and the Regional Tradition of Orissa*, New Delhi: Manohar Publications.

Forum, O.C. (1980). *Odissara Sakta Sanskruti*, Cuttack: Grantha Mandira.

Freed, R.S. and Freed, S.A. (1982). "Two Mother-Goddess (Durga) Ceremonies of Delhi State in the Great and Little Traditions", *South West J. Anthrop.*, Vol. XVIII-3, pp. 246-77.

Freeman, J.M. (1971). "Occupational Changes among Hindu Temple Servants", *Indian Anthropologists*, 1: 1-13.

———— (1975). "Religious Change in a Hindu Pilgrimage Centre", *Review of Religious Research*, Vol. XVI, pp. 124-33.

Goswami, B.B. and Morab, S.G. (1970). "Occupational Changes in a Priestly Caste of Mysore", *Man in India*, 50: 96-102.

———— (1970). "Castes and Temples" in Surajit Sinha (ed.), *Research Programmes in Cultural Anthropology and Other Related Disciplines*, Kolkata: Anthropological Survey of India.

———— (1974). "Temple as a Civilizational Centre: A Case Study of Chamundesvari Temple in Mysore", Ranchi: *Journal of Social Research*, Vol. XVII-1, pp. 116-23.

———— (1975). *Chamundesvari Temple in Mysore*, Kolkata: Anthropological Survey of India.

Jha, M.N. (1974). "Sacred Performances at Kashi, Ranchi", *Journal of Social Research*, XVII-1, pp. 23-28.

Jha, M. (1971). *The Sacred Complex of Janakpur*, Allahabad: The United Publishers.

———— (1972). "Aspects of Hindu Traditions in Nepal", Ranchi: *Research Journal of Ranchi University*, pp. 137-42.

———— (1973). "Ratanpur: Some Aspects of a Sacred City in Chhatisgarh", Ranchi: *Journal of Social Research*, XVI-1, pp. 49-58.

———— (1974). "Pilgrims and Centres of Pilgrimage in Chhatisgarh", Ranchi: *Journal of Social Research*, XVII-1, pp. 96-103.

———— (1978). *Aspects of a Great Traditional City in Nepal*, Varanasi: Kishor Vidya Niketan.

———— (1979). *The Dimensions of Indian Civilization*, New Delhi: Classical Publications.

———— (1981). *Civilization and Complex Societies in South Asia*, Varanasi: Kishor Vidya Niketan.

———— (1982). *Indian Civilization: Approaches and Methods*, Ambala: The Indian Publications.

———— (1982). *Civilizational Regions of Mithila and Mahakoshal*, Delhi: Capital Publishing House.

———— (ed.), (1985). *Dimensions of Pilgrimage*, New Delhi: Inter-India Publications.

Jindel, R. (1976). *Culture of a Sacred Town*, Mumbai: Popular Prakashan.

Kumar, D. (1987). *The Sacred Complex of Badrinath: An Approach to Study the Himalayan Pilgrimage as Dimension of Indian Civilization*, Unpublished Ph.D. Thesis, Ranchi University, Ranchi.

Mahapatra, L.K. (1973). *Gods, Kings and The Caste System in India*, IX International Congress of Anthropological and Ethnological Sciences, Chicago.

Mahapatra, M. (1974). "The Sacred Geography of Gupta Kashi", Ranchi: *Journal of Social Research*, XVII-1, pp. 75-87.

———— (1981). *Traditional Structure and Change in An Orissan Temple*, Kolkata: Punthi Pustak.

Malik, S.C. (1975). *Understanding Indian Civilization: A Framework of Enquiry*, Simla: Institute of Advanced Study.

Maltby, T.J. (1918). *The Ganjam District Manual*, Reprint, Chennai: Government Press.

Mishra, B. (1934). "Utkalare Matruka Puja", in *Naba Bharata*, Vol. I-5.

Narayan, S. (1974). "Pilgrimage to Kashi", Ranchi: *Journal of Social Research*, XVII-1, pp. 20-22.

Narayan, S. (1983). *Sacred Complexes of Deoghar and Rajgir*, New Delhi: Concept Publishing Company.

Patra, G.C. (1986). *Ganjam Dalapati Mahasabha Upabidhi*, Berhampur: Sujata Press.

Patra, T.C. (1984). *Shree Mahamayee Purana*.

Preston, J.J. (1980). *Cult of the Goddess: Social and Religious Change in a Hindu Temple*, New Delhi: Vikas Publishing House.

———— (1987). *Sacred Centres: Development of a Classificatory Scheme*, Bhubaneswar: Mayur Publications.

Rajaure, D.P. (1988). *The Sacred Complex of Swayambhunath in Kathmandu: A Study in Buddhism-Hinduism Continuum*, Unpublished Ph.D. Thesis, Ranchi University, Ranchi.

Redfield, R. (1956). *Peasant Society and Culture: An Anthropological Approach to Civilization*, Chicago: The University of Chicago Press.

Sahay, B.N. (1974). "The Sacred Geography in Kashi", Ranchi: *Journal of Social Research*, XVII-1, pp. 14-19.

Sahay, K.N. (1974). "The Sacred Geography of Rameswaram and Tirupati", Ranchi: *Journal of Social Research*, XVII-1, pp. 49-51.

Sahu, N. (1987). *The Sacred Complex of Rajrappa*, Unpublished Ph.D. Thesis, Ranchi University, Ranchi.

Sahu, S.C. (1971). "Ganjam Aitihya: Berhampurar Thakurani Parba", *Anupama*, Issue No. 27, pp. 3 and 5.

Samal, S.B. (1984). *Ganjam Dalapati Mahasabha*, Berhampur: Sujata Press.

Saraswati, B.N. (1962). "The Holy Circuit of Nimsar", Kolkata: *Bulletin of Anthropological Survey of India*, VI.3.4, pp. 211-16.

———— (1963). "Temple Organization in Goa", Ranchi: *Man in India*, 42: 131-40.

———— (1967). *Cultivation of Excellence in Religious Organisation*.

———— (1972). "Sacred Complexes in Indian Cultural Traditions", in B.C. Agrawal (ed.), *Anthropological Approaches to the Study of a Complex Society*, New Delhi: Indian Academy of social Sciences.

———— (1974). "Studying Sacred Complex in Kashi", Ranchi: *Journal of Social Research*, XVII-1, pp. 6-13.

———— (1984). "The Sacred Complex: A Trans-anthropological Perspective", in M.K. Gautam and A.K. Singh (ed.) *L.P. Vidyarthi: Contribution to the Development of Anthropology*, New Delhi: Concept Publishing Company.

———— (1985). "An Approach to the Study of Indian Civilization", in L.P. Vidyarthi and A.K. Haldar (ed.), *Research Methodology in*

Social Science in India, New Delhi: Today and Tomorrow Printers and Publishers.

Sarkar, D.C. (1948). "Saktapithas", *Journal of Royal Asiatic Society of Bengal*, p. 11 ff.

Senapati, T.N. (1977). *Kalinga Vaishya Mahasabha Niyamabali*, Vol. II, Berhampur: Orissa Printing Works.

Sharma, J. (1934). *Brahampura Thakurani Yatra*, Berhampur: Ganesh Bhandar.

Singer, M. (1955). "The Cultural Pattern of Indian Civilization", *The Far Eastern Quarterly (Journal of Asian Studies)*, Vol. XV-1.

——— (1972). *When a Great Tradition Modernizes: An Anthropological Approach to Indian Civilization*, New Delhi: Praeger Publishers.

Sinha, A.K. (1974). "Specialists in Sacred Performances at Kashi", Ranchi: *Journal of Social Research*, XVII-1, pp. 29-34.

Sinha, S. (1967). "Complex Religious Institutions and the Study of Indian Civilization: Preliminary Statement", Paper read at the Seminar on Research Programmes in Cultural Anthropology and Related Disciplines, Kolkata: Anthropological Survey of India.

Superintendent (1905). *Madras District Gazetteers (Ganjam)*, Vol. II, Chennai: Government Press.

——— (1934). *Ganjam District: Guide to the Records from 1774 to 1835*, Chennai: Government Press.

Thurston, E. (1909). *Castes and Tribes of Southern India*, Vol. III, Chennai: Government Press, pp. 306-48.

——— (1975). *Castes and Tribes of Southern India*, Reprint, Vol. II, New Delhi: Cosmo Publications, pp. 106, 154-66 and 171-73.

——— (1975). *Castes and Tribes of Southern India*, Reprint, Vol. VI, New Delhi: Cosmo Publications, pp. 245-47.

Upadhyaya, B. (1974). "Some Bibliographical Notes on Sacred Kashi", Ranchi: *Journal of Social Research*, XVII-1, pp. 42-48.

Upadhyaya, V.S. (1974). "The Sacred Geography of Dwaraka", Ranchi: *Journal of Social Research*, XVII-1, pp. 52-74.

Vidyarthi, L.P. (1960). "Thinking about a Sacred City", *Eastern Anthropologists*, XIII-4.

——— (1960). "City and Civilization: A Case of Sacred Complex", Mumbai: *Proceedings of the 47th Session of All India Science Congress*, Part-III (Abstract).

——— (1961). *Sacred Complex in Hindu Gaya*, New Delhi: Concept Publishing Company.

Vidyarthi, L.P. (1965). "The Changing Life of an Indian Priestly Caste: A Case of Desanskritisation", *Indian Sociological Bulletin*, II-4.

——— (1970). "Cultural Personality of a Priestly Community of India", Ranchi: *Journal of Social Research*, XIII-2.

——— (1974). "Sacred Complex as a Dimension of Indian Civilization", Ranchi: *Journal of Social Research*, XVII-1, pp. 1-5.

Vidyarthi, L.P.; Jha, M.; and Saraswati, B.N. (1979). *The Sacred Complex of Kashi: A Microcosm of Indian Civilization*, New Delhi: Concept Publishing Company.

Williams, M. (1951). *Hinduism*, Reprint, Kolkata: Susil Gupta (India) Ltd.

Woodroffe, J. (1929). *Shakti and Shakta*, Chennai: Ganesh and Company.

INDEX